RADIO CONTROL AIRPLANE

How To's

FROM THE PUBLISHERS OF

MODEL AIRPLANE NEWS

Contents

INTRODUCTION

THIS BOOK is a collection of over 50 of the best "how-to" feature articles that have been published in *Model Airplane News*. No longer will you have to flip through past issues, searching for an article that has suddenly become pertinent. A wealth of information that can help you to design, build, fly and maintain your models can now be found all in one place.

Need to improve your landing technique? Then turn to page 117. Looking for tips on how to adjust your carburetor? Flip to page 132. Interested in sheeting or glassing wings? Turn to pages 90 and 93. Need a cable linkage system on your sport plane? See page 46. This book will help you with everything from handling your engine or designing a high-performance electric to plotting airfoils or routing smoke through your model's wings.

Written by modelers for modelers, this volume isn't a mere beginner's manual. It's packed with practical techniques designed to help you meet contemporary modeling challenges. The techniques are explained in clear, succinct, understandable terms, and each article is full of photos and easy-to-follow illustrations. With so much insightful information, this book will surely become a valuable part of your reference bookshelf.

RADIO CONTROL AIRPLANE
How To's

Group Publisher
Louis DeFrancesco Jr.

Publication Director
Edward P. Schenk

Publication Manager
Laura M. Kidder

Editor-in-Chief
Tom Atwood

Senior Editor
Chris Chianelli

Associate Editor
Gerry Yarrish

Editorial Assistant
Julie Soriano

Copy Director
Lynne Sewell

Copy Editors
Katherine Tolliver, Deborah S. Carroll, Karen Jeffcoat

Cover Design
Alan J. Palermo

Cover Illustrations
Jonathan T. Klein

Artists
Mary Lou Ramos, Betty K. Nero, Matthew J. Longley, Stephanie L. Warzecha, Allyson Nickowitz, Robin Demougeot

Photographers
Walter Sidas, Lisa Knorra

Systems Coordinator
Jeff Wasilko

Production Manager
Mary Reid McElwee

Marketing Director
Gary Dolzall

Marketing Manager
Pauline A. Gerry

Published by Air Age, Inc.
251 Danbury Rd.
Wilton, CT 06897

PRINTED IN THE USA

1
CANOPIES

The Model Airplane News "Airwaves" column has received a number of inquiries on how to model a canopy for a scratch-built plane or a favorite kit that's being brought back to life after a long period in the hangar. Two of the basic techniques—stretch-forming and vacu-forming—are discussed in this section. If you're among the expanding group of giant-scale fans and want tips on how to install a canopy that you've created, Jerry Nelson's article on functional giant-scale canopies is for you.

HOW TO

Vacu-Form Your Own Canopies

Custom-form canopies, cowls, wheel pants and more

by CLARKE SMILEY

WHEN I DRAW up a set of plans for a new design, I try to identify the most difficult parts to build at the outset. I like to solve these problems before I dive into the rest of the project.

Recently, I've been working on a scale model of the Fairey Gannet, a British anti-submarine aircraft from the '50s. The first major challenge was the canopy. It contains globe-shaped sections. The best way to create this shape is by vacu-forming. This article summarizes the technique I use when vacu-forming canopies and other parts, such as cowls and wheel pants. The photos and captions outline the process, but be sure to look at the general tips noted below as well.

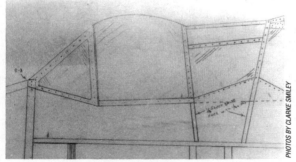

PHOTOS BY CLARKE SMILEY

1 This is my side-view drawing of the forward cockpit section of the Fairey Gannet. Although the front of the cockpit is like any three-piece, flat-plate wind screen, the center section is globe-shaped. This is the "hard" part.

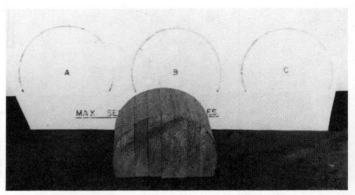

2 To the rear of my rough-cut plug you can see the maximum diameters of the canopy sections to be formed. To make the plug core, I cut out several pieces of balsa sheet and laminated them with Hot Stuff*. I then drew the circular section with a compass. I carved the plug with a razor saw and coarse sandpaper.

3 Here, I have marked a center line. Avoid cutting into the line as you carve the front and rear portions of the section canopy.

4 The rear section of the front canopy has been marked out. The X's mark wood that should be removed.

5 This picture shows the front profile. Note the "A-frame" shape. You can see the mid-section line is still visible. Almost all of the wood has been removed by carving, and the plug is ready for final sanding and an epoxy finish. I finish the plug with epoxy resin and one layer of 2-ounce cloth. After the first coat of resin has cured, remove any hills and valleys by sanding. Try not to sand into the cloth. Apply a second coat of resin.

After this coat has cured, wet-sand the plug with 400-grit wet-or-dry paper. (A drop of dishwashing liquid in the water keeps the paper from clogging.) At this point, you should be able to hold the plug up to the light and check for any shiny spots. These are "valleys," and if they're deep enough, you may have to coat the plug a third time with resin. Hold the plug up to the light—if it appears to be "frosted" or dull, it's almost ready for use. At this point, a light wet-sanding with 600-grit wet-or-dry will give a perfect finish.

6 This is a view of the underside of my 7x6-inch vacuum table. To make a vacuum table, you'll need a small piece of pegboard; a small piece of Masonite or pine board; and pine strips roughly 5/8x5/8 inch in cross section. Cut a piece of pegboard and a piece of Masonite of the same size. The pegboard will be the top of the table, and the Masonite the bottom surface. Cut out a hole in the Masonite for the vacuum source. Glue the pine strips to the Masonite as shown, and glue the pegboard to the top. Now you're ready to make a canopy.

HEATING THE PLASTIC

I leave the shop vac running while heating the material to be formed. Although some modelers will hold the framed plastic, with gloved hands, about a foot above an electric oven burner to heat it (gas burners should not be used), this technique isn't recommended because the plastic is flammable. A better approach is to construct an oven that uses a modeling heat gun as a heating element. This is fairly easy to do. (See "How to Form Giant-Scale Canopies," by Jerry Nelson, on pages 10 and 11 of this book.)

I think that heating the butyrate sheet is probably the most difficult part of this whole process. As it's heated, the sheet will first appear to loosen in the frame, then it will appear to tighten. After this, it will begin to sag. This is what you're looking for. Quickly move the frame over the vacuum table and push downward. As the frame reaches the table's edge, the vacuum will draw the sheet around the plug faster than you'd believe.

Three cautions: don't overheat the butyrate sheet, it will bubble; butyrate sheet is flammable, so have a good fire extinguisher handy; and wear leather gloves and eye protection.

OPTIONAL RELEASE AGENT

Don't use polyester resin when you build the plug, because this will tend to make the formed plastic adhere to the plug during the vacuforming process. Although a release agent isn't required when using epoxy, some modelers do use one, e.g., baby powder, to ensure easy release of the canopy. However, some of the baby powder will become embedded in the inside surface of the canopy during the forming process and will have to be removed by polishing that surface.

7 The epoxy-finished plug is mounted on small rails of scrap balsa on top of the table. This keeps the holes in the pegboard under the plug open. The scrap balsa frame around the vacuum table is used to hold the butyrate sheet for heating. Glue the butyrate to this frame before heating and forming.

8 A sheet of butyrate has been heated and been pulled down around the canopy form until the four sides contact the table. When this happens the vacuum created by the shop vac does all the rest. I use K&S 0.030-inch-thick butyrate sheet for a part this size (0.030 to 0.040 thicknesses are typically used). You'll find that the forming material will be stretched and thinned in places during the forming process. If larger parts are needed, use thicker materials.

9 Note how evenly the butyrate has been formed over the plug—it has also been drawn slightly underneath the plug.

10 The completed canopy has been cut free of the plug. In these views, the globe shape is quite clear. Think of all the lightweight model parts that can be formed for free flight and small rubber models!

FOR CLEARER CANOPIES

If you want to minimize the minor distortions that can result from using a wooden plug, you can polish the inside of the formed canopy with automotive polishing compound. The most distortion-free, clear canopies are formed over professionally cast plugs made of special, industrial-grade tooling epoxy. If you're looking for a canopy of that quality, Lanier R/C* will do custom work on a one-off basis. It will cost a little more, and you'll miss out on the fun of making your own.

SOURCES

The plastics commonly used for vacu-forming are butyrate, acetate, ABS and polystyrene (vinyl). These materials can be purchased from such companies as Lanier RC, Sig Mfg.*, NH Plastics* (polystyrene), K&S Engineering* and Aircraft Spruce and Specialty Company*, which distributes a wide variety of heat-formable materials, including one of my favorites, 0.030-inch-thick acetate in 20x50-inch sheets.

The technique shown can be used to make a wide variety of cowls, wheel pants and other molded parts. Give it a try! If I can help you out with a problem, feel free to contact me at 23 River Bend, Newmarket, NH 03857; (603) 659-3380.

*Here are the addresses of the companies mentioned in this article:
Hot Stuff; distributed by Satellite City, P.O. Box 836, Simi Valley, CA 93026.
Lanier R/C, P.O. Box 458, 4460 Oakwood Rd., Oakwood, GA 30566; (404) 532-6401.
Sig Mfg. Co., 401 S. Front St., Montezuma, IA 50171; (515) 623-5154.
NH Plastics Inc., 315 Bouchard St., Manchester, NH 03103; (603) 669-8523.
K&S Engineering, 6917 W. 59th St., Chicago, IL 60638.
Aircraft Spruce and Specialty Co., P.O. Box 424, Fullerton, CA 92632. ∎

Form Giant-Scale Canopies

It's easier than you think

by JERRY NELSON

There's more than one way to make a plastic canopy for a giant-scale model. The methods include vacu-forming with a male or female mold, free-forming with pressure or a vacuum, and stretch-forming. Vacu-forming and free-forming require tools that most modelers wouldn't have. To stretch-form a canopy, plastic, usually butyrate or vinyl, is heated in an oven, usually at a temperature of about 300 degrees Fahrenheit. (The temperature will vary depending on the type and thickness of plastic you use.) When it's hot enough, it's removed from the oven and stretched over a mold.

Most canopies that are supplied in model kits are vacu-formed over a male mold. From the manufacturer's point of view, this is the best method because it's inexpensive and it saves time, but it does have a drawback: as the mold sets, the material becomes thinner at the base of the canopy. The top will be about as thick as the plastic, but the base can be less than 25 percent of that thickness. A thin base can be a problem when it's time to attach the canopy to the fuselage or the canopy frame, so thicker material must to be used to provide the necessary minimum thickness. Stretch-forming can result in the opposite problem (normal base, thin on top), but that's better for model use.

If you want to make a canopy for a single model, stretch-forming is the simplest. The quality of your canopy will depend on the condition and rigidity of the mold and the cleanliness of the plastic sheet before you melt it.

The canopy shown in this article is one for my $1/3$-scale, prototype, all-aluminum AL-1. For your reference, the AL-1 has a fuselage length of 72 inches, a span of 97 inches and an empty weight of 28 pounds.

MATERIAL

Butyrate sheet, which is often used for model canopies, isn't usually available in the size and thickness that's required for large canopies. It's also quite expensive, especially if the canopy you plan to build is a high, narrow "deep-draw" canopy, for which .062-inch-thick material is sometimes required. A .062-inch-thick, 24x24-inch butyrate sheet can cost $20.

You can also use Plexiglas, but it's expensive, too, and you can't obtain it thinner than $1/16$ inch. It's very strong, but it's somewhat brittle and difficult to cut properly.

Vinyl is readily available (just check your Yellow Pages under plastics), much less expensive and it forms at a lower temperature. It's easy to cut, and it's available in several thicknesses. Its disadvantages are that it isn't as strong as butyrate and, if you plan to glue the canopy to something, there may be an adhesion problem. I used .040-inch-thick vinyl for the AL-1 canopy, with excellent results.

The size of the material you use will obviously be determined by the size of the canopy. You'll need about 4 inches of extra material to attach the plastic to the forming blocks and to allow for trimming. The AL-1 canopy material measured 24x22 inches.

CANOPY MOLD

You can use many materials to make your mold. Hard materials are more durable, but if you only plan to make a few canopies, then softer materials are OK.

Balsa wood is fine, but it's expensive. Pine is good if you have a large band saw

A hobby or modeling heat gun is used to heat the oven box.

The plastic sheet is supported by $3/16$-inch-diameter aluminum tubes that are located near the top of the box.

The simple oven box is built of 1-inch-thick, foil-covered, insulation board. It's held together by 3-inch nails and fiberglass strapping tape.

Giant-Scale Canopies

and a belt or disk sander. I used 2-inch-thick blue Styrofoam insulation material that I bought at a local hardware store. A big sheet costs about $10. Glue the 2-inch sheets together with spray-on contact cement to make a block of a size that suits your needs.

"Rough" the canopy into shape using a carpenter's saw, and then make smaller cuts with a hacksaw. Contour the mold into its final shape using 40-grit sandpaper.

The accuracy of the canopy outline isn't critical because it doesn't usually have to match a particular bulkhead or former exactly. You can stretch the canopy a little to fit the bulkhead.

One problem I encountered when I made the canopy mold for the AL-1 was making the front of the canopy fit the front canopy support bow. The mold was cut to fit exactly behind the support bow, and I shaped the top contour to fit the contour of the front canopy exactly. I traced the support bow outline onto the front of the Styrofoam mold with an ink marker to use as a guide when I formed the canopy.

The front of the AL-1 canopy is also made from .040-inch-thick vinyl. It's wrapped around using flat sheet, so no mold is necessary. It's better to have the front portion separate from the main part of the canopy. The forming process is much easier, since there's only a little stretching required to form to the top outline contour. The AL-1 canopy opens anyway so that I can access the electronics and join the wing to the fuselage.

I added foam blocks to the front and bottom of the mold to allow for easier forming of the plastic. Sand the Styrofoam mold to shape, and outline the intersections of the added blocks with an ink marker. (This outline will help when you have to trim the canopy later.)

After you've sanded the mold, add a 2-inch foam block that's about 1/2-inch narrower than the bottom of the mold to the bottom of the mold. This will help in the stretching process.

Now cover the mold with fiberglass cloth and epoxy resin. (You must use epoxy resin, because polyester resin will dissolve the Styrofoam.) Which weight of fiberglass you use isn't too critical. I used about three layers of .008-inch-thick (medium-weight) material in the AL-1 mold. Add enough epoxy to allow you to sand the mold without sanding into the fiberglass. You may have to add more epoxy later to obtain a smooth surface. The canopy outlines you made with the ink marker will show through the fiberglass cloth. Take as much time as you need to produce a very smooth mold. Irregularities that you leave in the mold may show up in the finished canopy.

OVEN CONSTRUCTION

A kitchen oven wasn't big enough, so I built a simple oven box out of 1-inch-thick, aluminum-foil-backed, insulation foam. You can obtain the foam at any building supply center.

Make the oven about 2 inches bigger than the flat canopy dimensions and about 12 inches deep. Use a carpenter's saw to cut the insulation foam, and pin the pieces of the box into position with 3-inch nails. Reinforce the nails with fiberglass strapping tape. Make sure that the top of the box is removable.

Place two 3/16-inch to 3/8-inch-diameter metal tubes or rods near the top of the box to hold the plastic sheet in position as it heats.

Use a heat gun (for heat-shrinking model-covering material) as the heat source. Cut a hole in a side of the oven box near the bottom, and press-fit the heat gun into place.

FORMING SUPPORTS

From 1-inch-thick pine, cut two 2-inch-wide, 22-inch-long forming supports to the top shape of the canopy. The sides of the AL-1 canopy are parallel to the front of the fuselage turtle deck, and they taper to the rear of the fuselage. I duplicated this shape when I made the pine forming supports. When the plastic is stretched over the mold, it's easier to form the plastic around the mold with the forming supports. The mating edges of the forming supports have a generous radius to prevent the plastic from being cut during the stretching process.

Screw the plastic sheet to the forming supports with several no. 8 or no. 10 wood

(Continued on page 134)

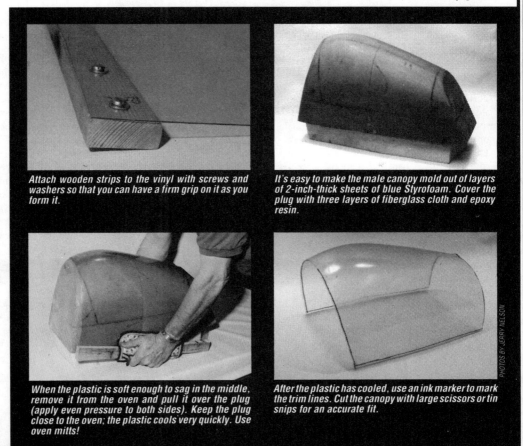

Attach wooden strips to the vinyl with screws and washers so that you can have a firm grip on it as you form it.

It's easy to make the male canopy mold out of layers of 2-inch-thick sheets of blue Styrofoam. Cover the plug with three layers of fiberglass cloth and epoxy resin.

When the plastic is soft enough to sag in the middle, remove it from the oven and pull it over the plug (apply even pressure to both sides). Keep the plug close to the oven; the plastic cools very quickly. Use oven mitts!

After the plastic has cooled, use an ink marker to mark the trim lines. Cut the canopy with large scissors or tin snips for an accurate fit.

PHOTOS BY JERRY NELSON

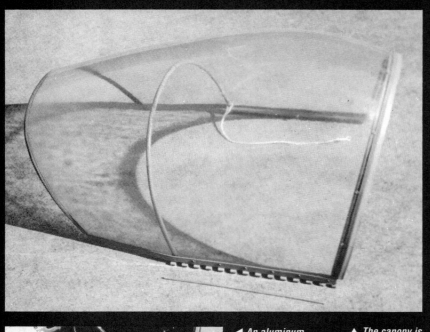

◀ An aluminum piano hinge allows the canopy to be removed from the fuselage.

▲ The canopy is attached to the aluminum tube canopy frame with no. 1 sheet-metal screws. Note the cockpit molding seal at the front and rear of the canopy.

PHOTOS BY JERRY NELSON

Build a Functional Giant-Scale Canopy

by JERRY NELSON

A REALISTIC opening canopy for a medium- to large-scale model can easily be fabricated using a frame made of aluminum tube and an aluminum piano hinge. Described is the canopy frame design used on my AL-1 aircraft. For your reference, the AL-1 has a 97-inch wingspan and a fuselage length of 72 inches.

The AL-1 canopy design is found on many full-scale aircraft. The front, permanently affixed portion is flat sheet plastic (.040-inch-thick vinyl) simply bent as required. The rear, movable portion is shaped over a mold. (Information on how to form a canopy is covered in the article on pages 10 and 11 of this book.)

FRONT WINDSHIELD

The front windshield assembly is made first. Assuming the canopy is formed, the first step of the fabrication process for the front windshield is to make a pattern for the windshield using thin cardboard or stiff paper card stock (old file folders work fine). By trial and error, arrive at the shape desired. You can tape the paper pattern to the fuselage and to the formed canopy to see if it looks right. The height of the front windshield is critical; it must properly match the front bow of the movable section.

Cut out the actual windshield from .040-inch-thick clear plastic. I recommend vinyl because it's inexpensive and readily available.

With the plastic windshield taped in the correct position, fabricate the $3/16$-inch-diameter aluminum-tube windshield bow. The material used is 2024 T-3 aluminum ($3/16$-inch-diameter x .049-inch-thick wall). This aluminum will be used for the rest of the frame.

Make a pattern of $1/4$-inch-thick plywood. Transfer the shape of the windshield onto the plywood and cut and sand the plywood as necessary. Cut a length of tube longer than necessary. By hand, bend the tube to match the plywood template. You have to bend it more than the template requires, because the tube will spring back a little. The hard part is to make both sides of the bow the same. The bow should match the pattern closely because, later, the canopy bow on the movable part

Tips on fabricating metal hinges, fairings and latches

▲ The finished canopy in the closed position.

.040" canopy

$^1/_{32}$" aluminum trim strip

#1 sheet-metal screw

1" piano hinge cut to $^3/_4$"

$^3/_{16}$" aluminum rear canopy bow

$^1/_{32}$" aluminum trim strip

$^3/_{16}$" aluminum side frames

#1 flathead sheet-metal screw

Fuselage

#1 sheet-metal screw

of the canopy will have to fit the same template.

Trim the ends of the windshield bow so that they just touch the fuselage cockpit area and the top of the windshield. In each end of the bow, cut a $^1/_{32}$-inch-wide x $^1/_4$-inch-deep slot parallel with the fuselage. The slot will be used to attach the windshield bow to the fuselage by way of a 90-degree bent metal tab that's approximately as wide as the adjacent canopy bows. The correctly formed aluminum bow is now taped to the windshield and to the fuselage. Fabricate a suitable angle tab of $^1/_{32}$-inch 2024 T-3 aluminum or $^1/_{32}$-inch 4130 steel. It will be screwed with no. 1 sheet-metal screws to a hardwood support that's attached to the inside wall of the fuselage. Drill a hole (about $^3/_{32}$-inch from each end of the bow) that goes through the bow and into the $^1/_{32}$-inch metal angle tab. The drill-bit size should be correct for a no. 0 or no. 1 screw, or for a $^1/_{16}$-inch-diameter aluminum rivet. The bow is attached to the fuselage at these single pivot points. The bow can be moved fore and aft quite easily and seems somewhat insecure at the moment, but as soon as you attach the windshield to the bow, everything becomes very sturdy.

Next, attach the windshield to the frame with no. 0x$^1/_8$-inch or $^3/_{16}$-inch-long flat or round-head sheet-metal screws. Use masking tape to attach the windshield in the correct position to the bow and fuselage. Let the windshield protrude aft of the bow about $^3/_{16}$ inch. This allows for some trimming and provides a place for the cockpit fairing strip to rest.

After the windshield has been attached with tape, mark the locations for the sheet-metal screws. Position the screws about 1 inch apart. Make certain that the hole spacing is symmetrical on each side of the frame. If using flat-head screws, countersink the windshield by hand, with a suitable drill bit that's about $^3/_{16}$ inch in diameter. Install the screws.

FAIRING STRIP

A fiberglass- and-resin fairing strip is fabricated next. The fairing

will be molded directly onto the windshield and fuselage. No pattern or mold is necessary. To keep the resin from sticking to the fuselage and windshield, coat the area of the fuselage around the windshield and the bottom of the windshield with wax. Use a release wax found at fiberglass/resin suppliers. Put several coats on the fuselage and the windshield.

Run a piece of fiberglass strapping tape from the top of the windshield canopy frame forward to the firewall. Don't use masking tape, because it will stretch and break easily. The tape will pull the windshield down onto the fuselage and still allow room for you to work around the joint of the windshield to the fuselage.

Fabricate the fiberglass fairing strip with a piece of 1-inch-wide fiberglass tape cut about 1 inch longer than necessary. Mix up some polyester surfacing resin and hardener, and saturate the fiberglass tape prior to putting it in place. A piece of glass plate works well for applying the resin. Lay the fiberglass tape on the glass, and then saturate the fiberglass with resin. The resin will come off the glass easily later.

Place the freshly saturated (not cured) fiberglass strip around the joint of the windshield and fuselage. Half the glass will be on the fuselage and the other half on the windshield. Don't worry if it isn't exactly in position, because the fiberglass tape will be trimmed to a narrower width later. The tape will stay in place (it will stick to the wax surface). After the resin has set (several hours for a full cure), sand the tape with some 60-grit sandpaper. Be careful not to sand into the fuselage or windshield. If you accidently scratch the windshield, don't worry. (You can make another windshield using the scratched one as a pattern.) A layer of medium-weight 2-ounce fiberglass cloth cut about 1$^1/_2$ inches wide is coated with resin over the 1-inch-wide fiberglass tape. The

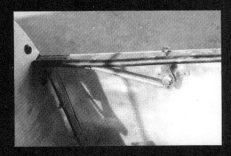

▶ The canopy is held open with a thin nylon cord. Note the locking pin in front of the canopy bow.

◀ Detail of the locking mechanism as seen on the inside of the fuselage. Note the spring that keeps the lock closed.

additional fiberglass cloth's main purpose is to provide a smooth finish over the 1 inch fiberglass tape.

After the resin has fully cured, sand the fairing smooth. Insert a thin spatula between the fairing and windshield/fuselage junction. The fiberglass will pop loose quite easily. Now the fairing can be correctly trimmed to a width of $5/16$ to $3/8$ inch on each side. Tin snips work quite well for the trimming operation. The fairing will be reasonably strong, but be careful during the cutting and sanding operations. After sanding, go over the fairing with another coat of resin.

▲ The canopy locking system in the closed position. Note the locking mechanism in the upper part of the photo.

▲ The 90-degree angle tab anchors the canopy bows. ▼ Detail of fiberglass fairing strip attaching the windshield to the fuselage.

▲ Here, you can see how the aluminum-tube front canopy bow is attached to the main frame tube with a 4-40 screw. Note how the fiberglass fairing strip is used to hold the windshield in place.

ATTACHING THE CANOPY

Attach the front windshield and the fairing to the fuselage with no. $1 \times 1/4$-inch-long round or flat-head sheet-metal screws. These go through the fiberglass fairing into the windshield or through the fairing and the fuselage. Carefully position the screws so that they're about 1 inch apart and are spaced symmetrically on each side of the canopy. Countersink the holes if flat-head screws are used. Countersunk screws aren't necessary, but they certainly look better.

Reinforce the fuselage from underneath with fiberglass cloth or hardwood inserts to support the fairing screws. The screws can be tightened without stripping the windshield and fuselage if some reinforcement is provided. Experiment with different size drill-bits for the screws. Make the smallest hole that will still accept the screw.

The entire canopy, bow, and fairing strip can be disassembled later for painting.

MOVABLE PART OF CANOPY

The frame is constructed of the same aluminum as the front windshield bow.

Form the front bow portion of the canopy over the same pattern used with the front windshield. Leave it longer than necessary for now. It should match the front bow as closely as possible.

Next, form the rear bow. No pattern is necessary because it doesn't have to match anything. The shape of the rear bow on the AL-1 is determined by the fuselage turtle deck. The rear bow could be eliminated on some designs, and you would just have a straight piece going from each side.

Cut to the proper length two $3/16$-inch diameter parallel portions of the frame that run along the base of the canopy. Allow space for the two $3/16$-inch-diameter bows. Each end of the paral-

lel portions are tapped with a 4-40 tap about $3/8$ to $1/2$ inch deep. The inside diameter of the tube is the right size for the 4-40 tap. With a small, round, rat-tail file, file $1/2$-inch round grooves vertically in this tube to accept the canopy bows.

The canopy bows are now attached with 4-40 screws about $3/8$ inch long. Drill no. 33 holes in the ends of the bows at the right spot so that the 4-40 screws will hold the bows in the correct position. The front canopy bow will have to be slightly higher than the windshield canopy bow owing to the curvature of the canopy. Minor adjustments can be made by bending the bows or screws. The ends of the bows are cut and filed flush with the bottom of the parallel frame tubes.

The canopy frame should sit on the fuselage and fit properly without forcing it to the correct shape.

HINGING

Cut the $1 1/16$-inch aluminum piano hinge to length. Trim the width to $3/8$ inch on each side. Steel and aluminum $3/4$-inch piano hinges are available from some specialty suppliers, but can be difficult to obtain. The cut-down $1 1/16$-inch size works satisfactorily. The hinge is attached with no. 1 flat head screws to the fuselage as shown in the cross-section drawing.

The trimmed canopy is now placed in position onto the frame. Final fitting of the canopy is required, especially where it touches the front windshield. The canopy doesn't have to fit perfectly, but do the best you can. The molding strips will take care of minor errors in the fit. The canopy should overlap the canopy frame about $3/32$ to $1/8$ inch. This is to allow for the canopy molding. Tape the canopy in position on the sides to

(Continued on page 134)

2
ELECTRICS

Would you like to know the key to designing a high-performance electric-powered airplane? See "Electric Twins" by master electric modeler Keith Shaw. (This article is also full of insights that apply to "single-engine" electrics.) If you're interested in miniature electrics, Tom Davis's article reveals his secrets for success. Finally, Joe Beshar offers a design for an electric test stand that will prove highly useful if you wish to experiment in this exciting, growing area of aeromodeling.

ELECTRIC Twins

by KEITH SHAW

"Sunshine glints on the most graceful twin ever designed— the deHavilland Comet." Keith's 1/6-scale version was modeled after Amy and Jim Mollison's "Black Magic," which competed in the 1934 England-to-Australia MacRobertson Race.

TWINS! There probably isn't a modeler alive who hasn't dreamed of building and flying a twin. The classy lines, unique appearance and sound are but a few of the attractions. But the reality of cramming two engines, two mufflers, two fuel tanks and some creative throttle linkage into the nacelles is a bit challenging. Of course, the wing spar must be much stronger and more torsionally rigid to support all that extra weight and vibration. Then there's the fun of trying to tune two engines and getting the throttle responses to match, along with all those weird resonances. Finally, there's the worry of the one-engine-flameout-on-takeoff nightmare. With all these concerns, most modelers just think "maybe next year."

Fortunately, electric power provides an almost total solution to the twin dilemma. Since both motors are powered by a single battery pack, worries about asymmetric thrust or single-engine failures are non-existent. Even as the battery runs down, the motors stay in sync. Installation is almost trivial, as the only thing in the nacelle is a small vibration-free motor, while the batteries and speed controller are in the fuselage area.

Electric power can also enhance the realism of a twin. The multi-engine configuration inherently gives more efficient thrust per horsepower. Glow-powered twins, however, usually use larger than normal engines to compensate for the higher structural weight, and they allow a safety margin in the event of an engine failure. The higher wing loading and power loading give most glow-powered twins a very fast, frantic, non-scale flight appearance, not to mention spectacular crashes. The absolute reliability of electrics, along with their better weight distribution and more efficient thrust, allows a somewhat lower-powered system to give the equivalent performance of a single-motor aircraft. An electric twin usually comes out lighter than a glow-powered one with a more scale flying speed and a slower, gentler landing speed. My 1/6-scale, 88-inch, deHavilland Comet weighs 7 1/2 pounds, while the three glow-powered versions that I know about weigh 12, 14 and 15 pounds!

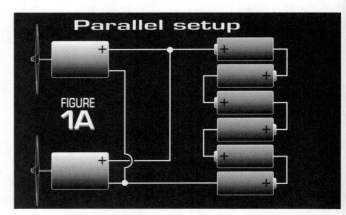

Parallel setup

FIGURE 1A

Design tips for light, reliable multi-engine flying

THE POWER SYSTEM

There are two ways of connecting two motors to a battery pack: in parallel or in series. For the sake of example, let's assume we're using 6-cell motors that nominally draw 20 amps (120 watts).

In a parallel setup, each motor receives the voltage of the 6-cell pack, but since each motor draws 20 amps, the total current drain is 40 amps (see Figure 1A). Even with the best Ni-Cds on the market—the Sanyo* "R" series—a 1200mAh pack would only give a 2-minute motor run. Larger capacity Ni-Cds could be used, but the hidden problem is that, at these high currents, the output voltage of the Ni-Cd pack is quite depressed owing to internal losses. Motor rpm will be lower than normal, and the battery will get very hot. About the only time a parallel power system works well is with small ferrite motors that run at 6 to 10 amps. This keeps the battery current within reason, and it may allow the joy of flying a twin with inexpensive speed controllers and chargers by staying under seven cells.

The other method is to connect the motors in series, with twice the number of cells in the battery pack (see Figure 1B). This would mean the two motors would be wired in series to a

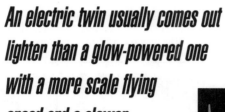

An electric twin usually comes out lighter than a glow-powered one with a more scale flying speed and a slower, gentler landing speed.

12-cell battery. If the motors are reasonably well-matched (same make, size and vintage), they'll each "see" six cells, while the total current drain will stay at 20 amps. Now the Ni-Cds can efficiently deliver power, giving longer motor runs, higher rpm and a lot less heat.

It's important to be able to control the motor power, and this can be done with a simple on/off switch or a speed controller. For small hand-launch twins (maybe up to 12 cells), a servo-operated switch, fuse and arming switch can be inserted into the series loop (see Figure 2A).

A good speed controller, however, would be desirable for aircraft that are designed to take off from the ground (see Figure 2B). The instantaneous power of electrics requires smooth power application to ensure good ground handling. Be sure to use an efficient, high-frequency speed controller that's capable of handling the number of cells and maximum current for your particular design. I've had excellent results with all the Jomar* units and the newer AstroFlight* 205 and 207. Make sure that the arming switch is wired as shown to isolate the speed controller from the battery pack during charging. Many "booster" chargers (the type that's capable of charging 8 to 32

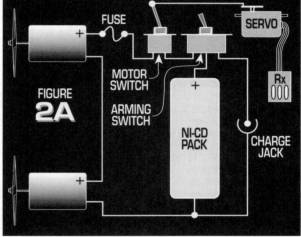

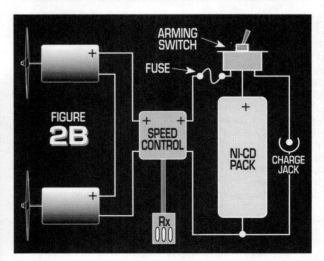

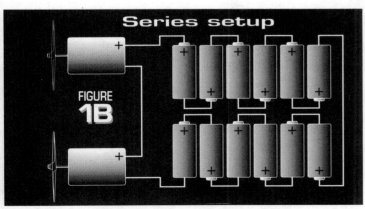

cells) put out high voltage spikes that might damage the speed controller.

Since there are more plugs and wiring in a twin installation, use only the high-tech 12-gauge wire (the stuff with 600+ strands), and low-loss connectors such as those by Sermos*, or the new AstroFlight units. I try to hard-wire as many connections as possible, with plugs only at the battery pack and wing-disconnect point.

About the only limit to the series motor setup is that 28 to 32 cells are the most that the best currently available booster chargers can handle at one time. This maximum system could, however, deliver over 1hp—easily enough to get a 12- to 18-pound aircraft airborne, after which the power could be reduced to cruise level for a longer flight.

SIZE AND PERFORMANCE

The method that I use to estimate aircraft size, power loading and performance is identical to that outlined in "Electric Sport Scale," an article I wrote for *Model Builder* (July 1987).

Be sure to pick a subject to match your flying skills. Many twins don't deserve their bad reputation, since it's usually related to poor handling with one dead engine. A classic example is the P-38, which flies quite well, but is a real nightmare on one engine. You should consider the size, configuration, landing-gear arrangement, weight and performance, and think less about the mythology of the prototype. Could you fly a single-engine plane of this type? If not, gain more flying experience before tackling that project. Many multi-engine aircraft of the 1925 to 1940 era would make excellent Sunday fliers. Of course, military twin fighters, bombers and transport aircraft will require much more flying skill, as would many of today's business aircraft. They're notori-

---

Twin examples and structural considerations

The structure of small hand-launched twins can be very similar to single-motor sport electrics. Simple D-tube wings with one shear-web-braced spar, and sheet-balsa tail and fuselage work very well. The nacelles can be made of sheet balsa and just glued to the wing sheeting. A little glass cloth or $^1/_{32}$-inch-thick ply will protect the bottom of the nacelles or fuselage during landing. An example of this type is Jack Laird's stand-off-scale Westland Whirlwind. It spans 57 inches, has 450 square inches of wing area, weighs 70 ounces and is powered by two Leisure* direct-drive 05 motors on 12 Sanyo 900 SC cells turning Cox* 6x4 props. The power loading is 55 watts per pound with a flight-speed-to-stall-speed ratio of 3:1. With a simple servo-operated on/off switch, it gets excellent, aggressive 4+ minute flights. If it had a speed controller, I guess it would easily achieve 8- to 10-minute flights. The canopy and complex curved fuselage front are made of bead foam that's sanded to shape and covered with $^3/_4$-ounce glass cloth. The finish is Coverite Micafilm* and Perfect Paints*.

Jim McDermott's dream plane was the P-61 Black Widow, on which he was crew chief during WW II. He started out with a set of plans by Frank Baker (*Model Aviation*, February 1982), but he stretched the span by one rib on each side and increased the tip chord somewhat. He also changed the airfoil to a Clark Y, reduced most wood sizes and made the complex fuselage shapes out of blue foam that he covered with silkspan and attached with white glue.

The P-61 is a one-piece airplane with the radio and speed controller in the center pod and the Ni-Cd packs on top of the

Left: the D.H. 88's retract landing-gear towers support the Rhom-Airs, while the lightweight nacelles only contain the small Keller electric motors.

Below: the fuselage is just a shell that contains two servos, and it covers the Ni-Cd power pack; the speed controller; the aileron, flap and retract servos; the receiver and the battery.

ous for their huge fuselages and small wings.

Matching the size of the model to the appropriate powerplant is an iterative process:

1. Obtain a good three-view of your dream plane (hopefully showing cross sections), and guess the size of model you'd like to build. Remember, it has to fit in your workshop and/or car! Then calculate the wing area, length, fuselage cross section, nacelle, spinner, wheel and propeller size.

2. Now determine the desired handling characteristics. For an easy-flying, casual type, try to stay in the 14- to 18-ounces-per-square-foot range. For small hand-launched planes (<350 square inches), keep to lower wing loadings. On very large aircraft (>1,000 square inches), 20 to 22 ounces per square foot still gives gentle handling. More aggressive aircraft, such as fighters and bombers, fly very well with 20 to 25 ounces per square foot— even up to 30 ounces per square foot for the biggies— but better flying skills will be needed. Choose an airfoil to match the intended type of flying. I see little reason to put a "scale," nearly symmetrical wing on a sport-scale airplane unless you plan to do outside loops with it! Mildly cambered airfoils (2 to 3 percent) will have much lower induced drag at the desired scale-like speed. Less drag means lower required power and longer flights. My favorite airfoils are the Clark Y, the NACA 2412, 1412 and 23012.

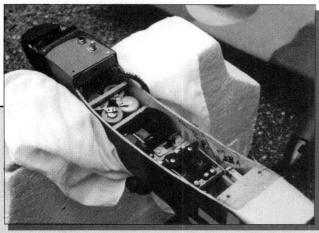

The inside view of Jack Laird's Westland Whirlwind shows Ni-Cds in the nose, the motor switch, the servos and the receiver.

wing under a removable top shell. It has a 63-inch span, a wing area of 570 square inches and weighs 86 ounces. Its power system is two Astro 035 geared motors, 12 900mAh SCR cells, a Jomar SM-4 speed controller and 9x8 props. With a power loading of 40 watts per pound and a flight/stall-speed ratio of 2.2:1, the plane easily lifts off a grass runway in 50 feet, flies very well and is capable of some modest aerobatics. Continuous full-power strafing runs last over 5 minutes, while reduced power prowling can go on for more than 8 minutes.

My deHavilland Comet has been around since 1985 and probably has more than 300 flights on it—a clear indication of the reliability of an electric twin. This $^1/_6$-scale plane has a wing area of 900 square inches, a wingspan of 88 inches and weighs 7.5 pounds. The power system consists of two Keller 25 motors (German 12-cell Cobalt) and 24 Sanyo 1200mAh SCRs

that are controlled by a Jomar SC-4 turning Rev-Up 9x7 props at 9400rpm. With a power loading of 64 watts per pound and a flight/stall-speed ratio of over 4:1, it performs large majestic loops, graceful rolls and a host of other aerobatic maneuvers. The high-aspect-ratio wing and sleek fuselage and nacelles are very efficient, allowing low-power cruising flights of up to 15 minutes, or 6 minutes of full-power aerobatics.

The Comet needed some pretty involved engineering, however. Its high-aspect-ratio wing and slightly swept quarter-chord required a triangulated spar system to enhance torsional rigidity, especially in the landing-gear area. The primary spar is located at 30 percent of the chord and is made of $^1/_8$x$^1/_2$-inch spruce (top and bottom) with full-span shear webs. A similar secondary spar starts out at 70 percent of the root chord and sweeps forward to meet the main spar one rib bay beyond the nacelle.

The retractable landing gear is pivoted near the bottom of a very deep nacelle, but instead of making the nacelle structurally strong enough to support the whole airplane, a plywood and spruce "tower" that keys into the wing spar was designed to support the Rhom-Air* retract unit. The nacelle is then just a very light built-up shell that's held in place by a couple of $^1/_8$-inch dowels in front and a 6-32 bolt near the rear wing spar. Necessary nacelle strength is minimal, as the only thing it supports is a small, vibration-free 8$^1/_2$-ounce motor. With this configuration, the wing must contain the retract system, the aileron and the flap servos. Because of the large wing chord, the radio receiver, switch, battery and speed controller are also included in the wing.

The 24-cell power pack is mounted on hardwood blocks that are keyed into the wing spar. With this tidy package, the fuselage contains only the rudder and elevator servos, and it becomes a light, clip-on shell that's just strong enough to keep the tail in place. The fuselage and nacelles are old-timer truss boxes with some simple bulkheads and $^1/_{16}$-inch-thick sheeting on top. The nacelles each weigh 3 ounces, while the 5-foot-long finished fuselage weighs 14 ounces, including two servos, instrument panels, cockpit detail and two pilots! Had traditional glow-construction techniques been followed, the airplane would probably have been 3 to 4 pounds heavier. Think creatively and look for ways of saving weight.

Jim McDermott's P-61 Black Widow, the "Moonlight Serenade," has a 63-inch wingspan, a wing area of 570 square inches, and it weighs 86 ounces. Twin Astrogeared 035 Cobalt motors are powered by 12, 900mAh Sanyo SCR cells. The speed controller is a Jomar SM-4. The plane flies great and looks particularly sinister on low-level flybys.

> **Total weight** (ounces) =
> **[chosen wing loading**
> (ounces/square foot)**] x
> [wing area** (square feet)**]**

3. I really can't think of any highly aerobatic twins, so modest power loadings are acceptable. Bombers and transports should fly well with 40 to 50 watts per pound. Even fighters with the highest performance should, at most, require 60 to 65 watts per pound. This would allow loops, rolls, climbing rolls, spins, snaps and inverted flight. We're striving for realistic scale-like performance, not turn-around pattern capabilities.

> **Peak power** (watts) =
> **[chosen power loading**
> (watts/pound)**] x
> weight** (pounds)

4. Next, an estimate of the static current draw is needed. This is, of course, related to the size of the Ni-Cd "fuel tank" and the desired full-power flight time. With a fixed-capacity Ni-Cd pack, higher current drain (more horsepower) means shorter flights. The commonly used Ni-Cds in electric flight are the 900mAh, 1200mAh and 1500mAh cells. I prefer the Sanyo "R" cells, as they can deliver the necessary power with little loss or voltage droop. The "E"-type cells run much hotter, are finicky to charge and deliver less

usable power to the motors.

A good starting point is to choose a current that would give a 5- to 5½-minute flight at full power. Since twins are usually quite efficient, this would correspond to a static current of 16 amps for 900mAh cells, 20 amps for 1200mAh, or 25 amps for 1500mAh cells. With some judicious use of the speed controller, flights of 8 to 10 minutes aren't uncommon. Even though my deHavilland Comet can do a very aerobatic 6-minute routine, its flights have several times exceeded 15 minutes just cruising up and down the runway at low throttle.

Good Ni-Cds deliver slightly more than 1 volt per cell to the motor at the indicated currents, so we can estimate the number of cells necessary to create the power calculated in Step 3.

> **Number of cells =**
>
> **peak power** (watts)
> **estimated static current** (amps)

5. The size of the motor will be dictated by the number of cells. If a series layout is chosen, each motor will see half this number of cells. So if you've calculated that 250 to 300 watts would be necessary for your project and you want to use 1200mAh SCR cells (allowing a 20A

static drain), this would imply the use of 12 to 15 cells, or six to seven cells per motor. This would be two 05 motors. I highly recommend the use of Cobalt magnet motors (such as AstroFlight's) not only for their high quality, performance and ruggedness, but also because they're much more stable under high temperatures and aging conditions.

Jim McDermott's P-61 Black Widow.

Many motors are now rated by number of cells and maximum wattage (as they should be), rather than the old glow-equivalent method. To guide you, the Cobalt "035" motors use five to six cells and a maximum of 120 watts, the Cobalt "05" motors use six to eight cells at a maximum wattage of 180 watts, the "15" uses 10 to 14 cells at 250 watts, the "25" needs 12 to 16 cells at 350 watts, and the "40" can use 16 to 20 cells at 450 watts. Remember, these maximum wattages are for the long motor runs in a scale plane, not the short sprints used

by the high-powered gliders.

With the exception of some small hand-launched twins, most motors will have to be geared to turn the larger props necessary for efficient thrust. Some of the expensive European motors are available in a wide array of windings that allow a prop of almost any size to be matched directly to the motor, thereby eliminating the need for a gearbox. Once the

motor size has been chosen, look up the weight (with the gearbox if needed) in the manufacturer's literature. The Ni-Cd pack weight can be estimated, as 900mAh cells weigh about 1.4 ounces, 1200mAh about 1.8 ounces, and 1500mAh about 2.2 ounces. If this results in a power system that you don't own and don't want to purchase, or can't charge, go back to Step 1 and try again.

6. By subtracting the weight of the two motors and necessary number of cells, along with the weight of the appropriate radio equipment, from the total weight in Step 2, we get the finished airframe weight. Choose light servos with sufficient torque to do the job. Don't expect .6-ounce servos to control a 12-pound airplane, and don't cram 1.8-ounce servos into a little hand-launched plane.

A good receiver is essential for electrics, as some of the cheaper units work

Keith's D.H. 88 has an 88-inch wingspan, a wing area of 900 square inches, and it weighs only 7.5 pounds. It's powered by twin Keller 25 motors, and it carries 24 Sanyo 1200mAh SCR batteries, a Jomar SC-4 speed controller, and Rhom-Air retracts.

poorly, if at all, owing to poor rejection of electrical noise. ALWAYS do a thorough range check (with the motors running) before flying any electric. Small models can use a 100mAh receiver battery; mid-size ones use a 270mAh; and even the largest models work OK with a 450mAh pack. Once you become accustomed to field-charging Ni-Cds, the radio battery can also be recharged if you feel it's running low. I'd *never* use battery-eliminator circuitry (BEC) on even the smallest planes; it's not worth the risk. It only "saves" an ounce and can cause major interference problems, since it pipelines motor noise directly into the receiver.

7. Now for the big question: can you build this project to the estimated weight? Most modelers want a plane that flies well, so an exact replica isn't required. Partially sheeted wings and tail surfaces and open-structure fuselages can save a lot of weight. Flat areas on the

kraft paper, or light glass cloth. Because there's little vibration, plywood should be used only in high-stress areas, such as landing-gear bracing, dihedral joiners, or battery pack supports. It isn't worth cutting holes in ribs, as this saves very little weight and weakens the structure too much. The newer lightweight wheels can save many ounces.

Film covering can save a lot of weight, but be careful of some iron-on fabrics, because they're very heavy, especially if painted. If you insist on a painted finish, clear MonoKote* may be painted with a lightly airbrushed coat of Floquil* or other lacquer-based paints. Always clean the surface with acetone first to remove any fingerprints. My 62-inch Spitfire gained 3 ounces with the MonoKote and an additional 3/4 ounce when I painted all the camouflage, roundels and squadron markings. Panel lines, rivets, louvers, latches and a host of other details can be done with permanent

Jack Laird's Westland Whirlwind weighs 70 ounces, and it has a wingspan of 57 inches and a wing area of 450 square inches. Twin Leisure 05 direct-drive motors are powered by 12, 900mAh Sanyo SC cells. The plane uses an on/off motor control, and it's a very aggressive, aerobatic performer.

can make a tremendous difference to performance. Each prop requires a specific horsepower (watts) to turn it at a given rpm. If you wish, a good test rig can be set up with the motor and battery pack, a tach to monitor rpm, a voltmeter to measure motor voltage, and a good ammeter to measure motor current. There are several very inexpensive digital voltmeters available. (Radio Shack has one for about $18.) If you're really serious about electrics, an instrument-quality ammeter is a must. I use a Simpson 0 to 50A panel meter, which is available from electronics suppliers such as Pioneer or Newark for about $50. The

Props of various diameters, pitches and brands may draw the same current, so how do we decide which one would best suit our project? Remember, when we estimated performance in Steps 3 to 5, we only predicted the total wattage, current and number of cells. Once the actual power system has been decided, there will be a specific rpm for the current chosen in Step 4. One approach would be to randomly try all props that meet the desired parameters and see which ones work best. The problem is that some of these props might not be able to get the plane airborne safely. Here's a technique I use to choose a reasonable range of test props.

The stall speed for our models is mostly a function of wing loading, airfoil choice and surface finish. For wing loadings in the 14 to 25 ounces-per-square-foot range and the type of airfoils discussed in Step 2, a reasonably accurate estimate of stall speed is:

Stall speed (mph) **= 3.7 x**

$$\sqrt{\frac{\textbf{wing loading}}{\text{(ounces/square foot)}}}$$

Prop speed is that which a highly streamlined airplane would achieve in level flight, and it's caused by a prop of a certain pitch turning at a known rpm. Sweep-

FIGURE 3

DVM AMMETER

NI-CD PACK

fuselage and tail can be free-hanging covering rather than sheet balsa. Block balsa may be used to reproduce complex shapes but should be hollowed to a wall thickness of, at most, 3/16 inch. White or blue foam may be shaped as desired and covered with silkspan,

markers, MonoKote and creative airbrush shading. Optical illusions can save a lot of weight!

8. The final step is matching the correct props to your airplane. This is where many electric and glow models fail, or seem just mediocre. The right prop

$25 ammeter that's available from some hobby suppliers is much less accurate, but usable for relative performance estimates. (The test-stand layout appears in Figure 3.)

At a given voltage, there's a unique relationship between current and rpm.

ing several canceling effects under the rug, it can be estimated as:

> **Prop speed** (mph) =
> **Pitch** (inch) **x**
> **rpm** (in thousands)

Actual flight speed of most streamlined twins will be at the prop speed or a little faster. This is due to the motor unloading in the air, which allows a higher rpm. A higher-drag airplane, such as one with large radial engine cowls or a large cross-section fuselage, might only achieve 85- to 90-percent prop speed. As an example, a 10x8 prop turning 9,000rpm on a clean monoplane would have a level flight speed of about 70mph.

A level flight speed of twice stall speed is required to just do a nice, round loop. This would be more than adequate for any bomber or transport. At three to four times stall speed, good maneuvering and fighter-type

Keith Shaw shows off his "King Crimson" flying wing at last year's KRC Electric Fly. The wing has a 10.5-foot span, weighs 10.5 pounds and is powered by four Leisure ferrite 05 motors. He advises a different type of design analysis is required for building one of these!

performance is easily achieved.

Finally, the type of aircraft has an effect on the optimum diameter-to-pitch ratio. Aerodynamically clean twins will work best with a ratio somewhere between 1.3:1 and 1.7:1, while "draggier" aircraft such as bombers and transports would probably benefit from a 2:1 ratio.

To help you put all this prop stuff together, an example of prop choice is in order. Let's assume we've chosen a slower transport aircraft that has a wing area of 700 square inches and an estimated weight of $5^1/2$ pounds (18 ounces per square foot wing loading). This plane would have a stall speed of about 16mph, a desired flight speed of 32mph and a required prop speed of about 36mph. For a power loading of 50 watts per pound, 275 watts would be needed; and at a chosen current drain of 20 amps, 14 cells driving two, Cobalt, geared 05s would be adequate. Mounting a geared, Cobalt 05 on our test stand with seven 1200mAh SCR cells, we'd find that a prop would turn at about 6,000rpm at 20 amps. To get a prop speed of 36mph at 6,000rpm we'd need 6 inches of pitch. Mounting several 6-inch-pitch props, we'd find that diameters of about 12 inches would pull 20 amps. Happily, this would be a 2:1 ratio, so a 12x6 prop would be a good starting point for this hypothetical design.

A hidden advantage of electrics is that it's easy to add a little extra horsepower for the test flight. This can ensure an easy takeoff and climb to safe altitude, where handling, stall tests, CG tests and a couple of practice landings at altitude can be done. In the example given, this might mean test-flying with 12x7 or 12x8 props. Once the airplane is trimmed out, you can pursue the perfect prop by trying values near the predicted ones. You might find out that it likes a Rev-Up* 11x8 or a Top Flite* 11x7 better than the predicted 12x6.

Once you're comfortable flying your twin, three- or four-blade props can be tried to enhance scale realism (assuming the prototype had them) at some loss in performance. As a rule of thumb, use a prop of the same pitch, but 10 to 15 percent smaller in diameter.

I've tried counter-rotating props on several of my twins with very little change in performance or handling. Extensive testing is quite limited, since there are only a few really well-matched right- and left-handed props.

> *Most people can't believe how large an airplane can be flown well on such seemingly small motors.*

Flying 10 degrees crosswind induces much worse errors than the slight improvement in tracking with counter-rotating props. It's better to use props that work best on the plane and learn "rudder finesse" to compensate for any tracking errors.

CLOSING THOUGHTS

By now, I hope you can see all the benefits of electrifying multi-engine aircraft. Having built four twins, a tri-motor and a four-motor plane, I can't imagine going back to doing a glow-powered one. Most people can't believe how large an airplane can be flown well on such seemingly small motors. This design technique will help you get used to this phenomenon.

In fact, once some experience is gained at matching correct power systems to an airplane of a particular size, the whole design procedure can be turned inside out. Starting with a given set of motors and an appropriate number of Ni-Cds, and choosing a desired current

(Continued on page 134)

Build a Miniature Electric-Drive System

by TOM DAVIS

6- and 11-minute, full-power flights

This is me tossing the Comet P-38. It has easily made flights of 10 to 16 minutes using the drive system described in this article.

PUSHER CONFIGURATION

47-tooth, 48-pitch spur gear
0.25-inch-o.d. plastic tube
2-56 nut and washer
CA fillet
Rear tube support: balsa, filler, CA
20mm o.d.
approx. 0.06 inch
Kyosho DMC20BB
30mm
0.113 inch
Adapter sleeve
5/64-inch-o.d. shaft
2-56 nut
Threaded
1.02 inches o.d.
0.75 inch
8-tooth, 48-pitch pinion gear
1/16-inch aluminum plate
0.25 inch i.d.
Aluminum support plate
0.59 inch
0.28 inch o.d.
0.48 inch

THE IDEAL MOTOR and gear reduction for electrics that weigh 10 ounces or less should weigh less than 1.5 ounces and have a reduction ratio large enough to keep static prop rpm below 5,000. The system described in this article can put out 20 to 30 watts and spin a rubber-band-powered prop of at least 5.5 inches diameter. The motor must be designed for six or seven cells to allow the use of weight-reducing BEC throttles. Also, for a given target output power, large cell counts, i.e., more than six, keep the motor current below 5 amps. This lower current mini-mizes resistive power losses and battery heating. The Kyosho* Le Mans DMC20BB motor fills the bill perfectly. It's designed for six cells, has ball bearings, weighs only 31 grams (1.09 ounces) and can handle over 20 watts.

The gears and bearings are standard 1/24-scale slot-car parts that should be readily available at local slot-car raceways or hobby shops that handle slot cars.

GEARBOX CONSTRUCTION

This gear reduction can be assembled either as a pusher or a puller. The reason for the two configurations is that the

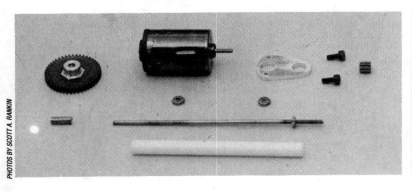

Far left: the components of the gear-drive system before assembly.

Left: the system is partially assembled.

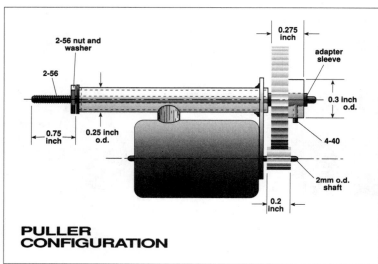

My P-38 uses two DMC20BB motors and weighs about 12.5 ounces with a Sanyo 600mAh AE 6-cell battery pack. It uses an RCD* 535 micro receiver removed from its case, two Cannon microservos and a ModelTronics* BEC micro speed controller.

Gear Drive Specifications
Weight with prop = 1.4 ounces
Reduction ratio = 5.875:1
Gear-hub bore o.d. = 1/8 inch

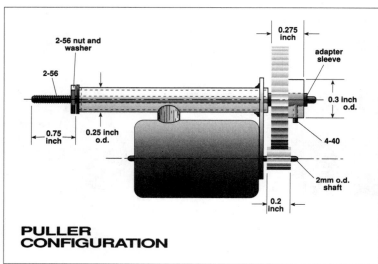

PULLER CONFIGURATION

Labels in diagram:
- 2-56 nut and washer
- 2-56
- 0.75 inch
- 0.25 inch o.d.
- 0.275 inch
- adapter sleeve
- 0.3 inch o.d.
- 4-40
- 2mm o.d. shaft
- 0.2 inch

ILLUSTRATIONS BY JONATHAN T. KLEIN

DMC20BB runs poorly in reverse, regardless of motor timing.

Cut about 4 inches of music wire to make the prop shaft. (A bench grinder works nicely for this job.) Grind the shaft ends flat, finishing with a slight bevel cut to clean up the ends. Clamp the shaft in a vise with 0.75 inch exposed.

Heat the exposed shaft end with a propane torch until it becomes dull red, and then allow it to cool slowly. Now the shaft end can be threaded easily with a 2-56 die. After threading the first 0.75 inch of the shaft, the 2-56 nut can be spun on and jammed where the threads end.

In the pusher configuration, the other end of the shaft will also be threaded to accept a 2-56 nut. This second nut will serve as a shaft retainer. Using the same procedure as before, thread about 0.25 inch of the shaft. To enable the bearings to slide onto the shaft, the threads must be evenly sanded. Remove just enough material to allow the bearings to slide on.

Cut out and drill the aluminum support plate that retains the 0.25-inch-o.d. plastic tube, using the given dimensions. The 0.25-inch hole for the tube must be slightly enlarged to allow the front bearing to be inserted without excessive force. Use a hobby knife to ream the hole. You may have to slot the other holes to allow for gear-lash adjustment. Use a file to finish the plate's edges.

Inspect the gear adapter sleeve (Du-Bro* no. 212 coupler) to ensure that its bore is centered; if it isn't, select one that is. Using a no. 47 or a 5/64-inch drill bit, enlarge the adapter's i.d. to accept the prop shaft. Cut off about 0.35 inch of the sleeve with a hacksaw. Use the uncut end to ride against the inner race of the front bearing.

Press the pinion gear onto the motor output shaft. If it's too loose, you may have to tin its bore lightly with solder. Be careful not to apply force to the motor case. Install the support plate on the motor. Cut the plastic tube to length (see diagram), making sure the ends are cut square. Push the tube through the support plate so that it's flush with the other side of the plate. Insert the bearings, and slide the

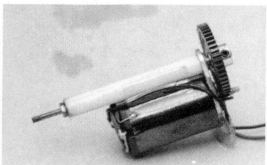

The completed gear-drive tractor system using the Kyosho DMC20BB motor.

IN SEARCH OF A MOTOR

The Klingberg Flying Wing shown in the photos is powered by an AYK Magnum AP racing motor. To my knowledge, this motor isn't available in the U.S., but maybe someone reading this article will know a source. I've heard that in Japan, there's a proliferation of these high-quality 24mm motors. The AYK is a high-performance, precision racing motor in a small, light package. It features a ball-bearing drive, an aluminum front bell, adjustable timing and replaceable brushes. This 50W motor weighs only 1.9 ounces. It's 24mm in diameter, has a 2mm shaft diameter and produces a no-load rpm of about 50,000 on 7.2 volts.

The all-up weight of the half-size Klingberg with the AYK and a Sanyo 600mAh AE 6-cell battery pack is 10.3 ounces. In flight, the motor produces about 40,000rpm and generates much higher rpm in a power dive. Spinning a Peck Polymers 7-inch prop, static prop rpm are about 6,900 (or 36,000 at the motor, given the 5.22 gear reduction). Flight times range from 6 to 15 minutes. The half-size Klingberg performs well with the DMC20BB motor, but its perfor-

AYK Magnum AP racing motor.

mance improves with the AYK Magnum AP.

Miniature Electric Drive System

Materials

- Kyosho Le Mans DMC20BB motor
- Two 2mm-i.d. x 5mm-o.d. x 1.5mm-thick, no-shield, flanged ball bearings (An ABEC 3 precision bearing is adequate.)
- Two 1/8 inch x 4-40 socket-head setscrews
- Two 2x4mm socket-head cap screws
- 5/64-inch music wire
- 0.25-inch o.d. x 0.20 i.d. polystyrene tube
- REH* spur gear: 47 tooth, 48 pitch, 1/8-inch-i.d.
- Pinion gear: 8-tooth, 48-pitch, 0.078-inch-i.d.
- 1/16-inch-thick aluminum plate
- Du-Bro no. 212 coupler: .072-inch-i.d., 1/8-inch-o.d.
- Two 2-56 nuts (The second nut is used in the pusher configuration only.)
- 5/64-inch or 2mm-i.d. washer
- CA, light filler, epoxy, scrap balsa, propane torch, vise, 2-56 die, small round file, flat file, 1/4-inch and 5/64-inch drill bits, hacksaw

shaft and gear into place. Adjust the plate so that just a slight amount of gear lash is detected with the tube parallel to the motor case. Shim the tube with a piece of balsa, as shown. With the tube parallel to the motor, tack the balsa shim and plastic tube to the motor housing with CA. Remove the prop shaft and bearings. Finish gluing the tube into place, as shown. Use a light coat of epoxy to hold the bearings in place. The propeller bore must be drilled out to fit the output shaft. Assemble, and you're ready to go.

270mAh 6-cell pack at 2.9 ounces. Full-power flight times of between 5 and 6 minutes are common. Sanyo 600mAh AE cells are also an excellent choice; they provide nearly twice the flight times

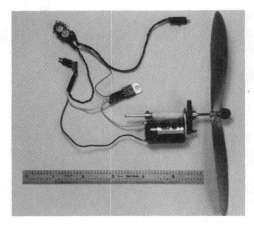

◀ Set-up for the 1/2-scale Klingberg Flying Wing, the Kyosho DMC20BB motor is shown with a pusher gear-drive system and a 7-inch Peck Polymers prop. Connected to a ModelTronics BEC speed controller, the entire system weighs 1.8 ounces.

◀ The Klingberg is shown here with the AYK Magnum AP racing motor, which offers better performance than the DMC20BB. It also uses an RCD 535 micro receiver removed from its case, two Cannon microservos and a ModelTronics BEC micro speed controller.

SPECS AND PERFORMANCE

With a 7-inch Peck Polymers* rubber-powered prop on six cells, 4,000rpm static at 3.5 amps is common. This is equal to a motor rpm of about 23,500. The complete motor with gear reduction and prop weighs a very light 1.4 ounces. With this system, small R/C electrics can fly at an acceptable level of performance for more than 5 minutes at full power. I usually get at least 80, 6-minute flights before the motor brushes wear out.

BATTERY CONFIGURATIONS

The standard battery pack to use with this system is a Sanyo*

of the 270 cells. These cells, if operated at less than 6 amps, perform amazingly well and weigh only 4.2 ounces in a 6-cell configuration. The internal resistances of the 270mAh AA and the 600mAh AE cells are 0.015 and 0.010 ohm respectively. The lower resistance of the 600 cells allows the motor to run at a slightly higher power level. These cells are available from Cermark*.

For a superlight setup, use an Eveready 80mAh, rechargable, 7.2V transistor-radio battery. Be sure to buy only the packs that have two white dots on the case bottom. The other packs have "pile construction," and their high internal resistance renders them useless.

*Here are the addresses of the companies mentioned in this article:
Kyosho/Great Planes Model Distributors,

P.O. Box 4021, Champaign, IL 61824.
Du-Bro Products, 480 Bonner Rd., Wauconda, IL 60084.
Peck Polymers, P.O. Box 710399, Santee, CA 92072.
Sanyo Electric, Battery Division, 200 Riser Rd., Little Ferry, NJ 07643.
Cermark, 107 Edward Ave., Fullerton, CA 92633.
REH Distributors, 4415 Marsburg Ave., Cincinnati, OH 45209.
ModelTronics, 6500 6th Ave. NW, Seattle, WA 98117.
RCD, 9419 Abraham Way, Santee, CA 92071.
Evergreen Scale Models (plastic tube), 12808 NE 125th Way, Kirkland, WA 98034.
National Precision Bearing (bearings), P.O. Box C34140, Seattle, WA 98124. ∎

SELECTING A PROP

Why use rubber-band-powered props and gear reduction for small electrics? Small electrics in general are plagued with several problems, the worst being high weight for their size, low power and pitifully short duration. To help overcome these problems, the model's available power must be utilized to its fullest.

As a rule of thumb, large, slow-turning props are more efficient than small, high-

revving props. This is more pronounced as prop size is reduced and as rpm increase. This can be partially attributed to a propeller's decreasing Reynolds numbers as its size is reduced, and to rapidly increasing parasitic blade drag as rpm increase. To help minimize this effect, small electrics should use rubber-band props with large gear reductions.

As an example, consider my 1/2-scale Klingberg Flying Wing. It has a 39-inch-span

and an all-up flying weight of 8 ounces. Its motor is a Kyosho DMC20BB with a 5.9:1 gear reduction, and it has a 7-inch Peck Polymers prop that spins at 4,000rpm (static). I use either a Sanyo 270mAh 6-cell pack at 2.9 ounces or a Sanyo 600mAh AE 6-cell pack at 4.2 ounces. The former allows full-power flights of more than 6 minutes; the latter, full-power flights of more than 11 minutes.

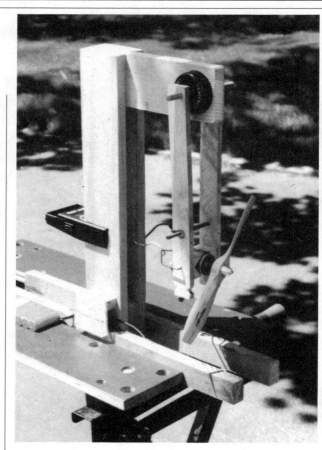

Measure low-pitch prop efficiency

The Thrust Tester uses a swinging pendulum that pivots from a ball-bearing roller-skate wheel. It's nearly frictionless.

Make a Static... Thrust Tester

by JOE BESHAR

WHAT'S THE BEST motor/propeller combination for your model? This frequently asked question is especially important for electric-powered models because they have a lower power-to-weight ratio than glow-powered craft. The Thrust Tester helps to determine the best motor/propeller combinations. (It can also be used for glow engines if you adapt the motor mount to accept the engine.)

Thrust-test measurements performed on a static test rig are useful as comparative data. Actual performance can only be observed during flight when the propeller is unloaded. Static prop testing is most useful when performed on lower-pitch props. High-pitch props (i.e., with a 1:1 diameter-to-pitch ratio) aren't working efficiently until the plane is moving quickly and the prop has unloaded.

Most of the Thrust Tester's parts are wooden. It has a swinging pendulum that pivots from a ball-bearing roller-skate wheel, so there's very little friction, and it can be mounted in a vise or in a Black & Decker Workmate. The thrust measurements are displayed on a Normark* Model 10 electronic digital scale that can measure up to 10 pounds. The amps are measured by a Davey 30A ammeter; the rpm can be taken from any standard tachometer. Just run your motor, and you can read the ounces of thrust, the amperage drawn and the rpm. This information enables you to compare various propellers without guessing or sacrificing efficiency.

I used the Thrust Tester to test props for a cowled electric model I'm building. For a cowled .035 Astro Cobalt motor with reduction gear, a Rev-Up 10x8 prop cropped to 9 inches performed the best, with minimum amps and maximum rpm. These determinations would be extremely difficult to make while flying, and this is why the Thrust Tester is very helpful.

> "THIS INFORMATION ENABLES YOU TO COMPARE VARIOUS PROPELLERS WITHOUT GUESSING OR SACRIFICING EFFICIENCY."

CONSTRUCTION

Don't worry if you can't get the exact measurements that are indicated on the drawings. Wood at lumber stores has designations that are industry standards, e.g., the 1-inch-thick wood that I refer to actually measures 3/4 inch.

To make the cross-member, drill a 2 1/4-inch hole in a 1x3x10-inch piece of wood. The hole should accommodate the roller-skate wheel, which has a 2 1/4-inch o.d. with a 5/16-inch bearing i.d. (standard dimensions for roller-skate wheels). I wrapped masking tape around the wheel's circumference before I inserted it into the hole. This provided a nice fit, and I didn't have to glue it to the cross-member.

Use 1x3-inch wood for the two vertical pieces (see dimensions in the detailed drawing). To make a swing member arm (you'll need two), drill a 5/16-inch hole in a piece of plywood that measures 3/8x1 1/2x12 inches. The hole should be large enough for the 5/16x5-inch dowel that will be the axle. Drill a 1/4-inch hole to accept the threaded rod, and a 1/8-inch hole to accept the hitch. All the holes should be located as indicated in the diagram.

To bend the hitch, use ordinary coat-hanger wire (the standard diameter is about .091 inch). The hitch detailed in the diagram is sized for a .05 or .035 Astro Flight Cobalt motor (its 2 3/4-inch dimension suits this motor). The size of the spacer bushings between the roller-skate wheel bearing and the swing members will also vary

The electronic digital fish scale, made by Normark, provides a quick read-out of prop thrust.

EQUIPMENT
Normark Model 10 scale
Davey 30A ammeter
Standard tachometer

WOOD
1—1x3x10-inch-piece
(cross member)
1—1x3-inch-piece (spacer block)
2—1x3x20-inch-pieces
(vertical member)
2—$^3/_8$x1$^1/_2$x12-inch-pieces
(plywood)(swing member)
2—1x1$^1/_2$x21-inch-pieces
(base member)
4—$^3/_4$x$^3/_4$x1$^1/_2$-inch, 45° corner
moldings (wedge block)

OTHER
1 roller skate wheel
1—$^5/_{16}$x5-inch dowel
1—$^1/_4$-inch threaded rod
2 wing nuts
4—3$^1/_2$-inch wood screws
coat hanger wire
masking tape
spacer bushings
white glue

depending on the motor.

Build the base with two pieces of wood that measure 1x1$^1/_2$x21 inches, and cut the spacer block from a piece of 1x3-inch wood.

ASSEMBLY

Please refer to the assembly drawing for each step. Assemble the base, the vertical pieces and the cross-member using white glue and 3$^1/_2$-inch wood screws. Run the $^5/_{16}$-inch dowel through the roller-skate wheel with the spacer bushings on either side. Glue the wedge blocks to their respective locations on the swing members, then install the $^1/_4$-inch threaded rod and the wing nuts. Insert the hitch into the two $^1/_8$-inch holes, and mount the ammeter and the scale. Then, place the scale's hook over the hitch, and the Thrust Tester is complete.

Run 14-gauge wire from the battery pack's positive terminal to the ammeter.

(Continued on page 135)

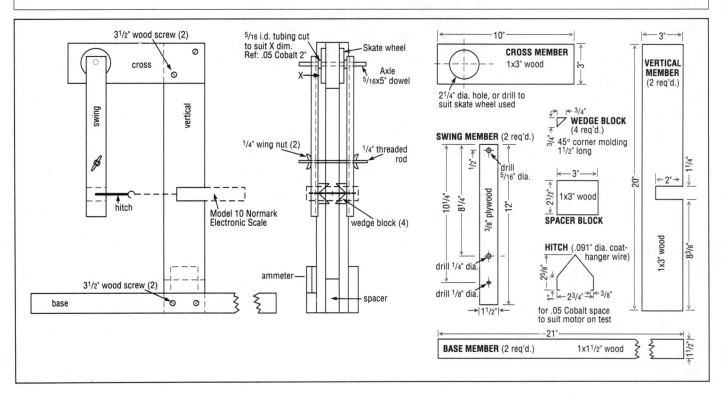

3
STANDS

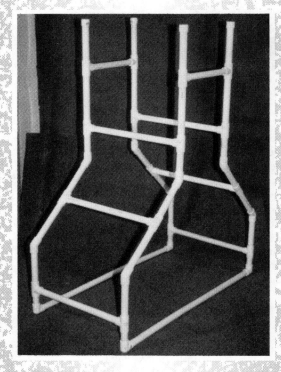

Stands are like chairs. They may not be the subject of the evening news, but when you need one, there's no better solution. If your models and radio transmitters need a rest—at home or at the flying field—give them a break with these simple designs made of inexpensive, widely available PVC pipe.

Build A Handy
TRANSMITTER STAND

by CHARLES D. EVANS

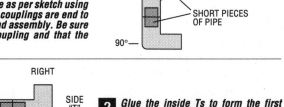

WHEN I SAW that my transmitters were showing excess stress and strain on their cases, I recognized the need for a portable transmitter stand that would help protect them from dirt, sand, wet grass and other hazards at the flying field. Not having any particular stand in mind, but having a surplus of PVC pipe and fittings (which remained from the installation of my lawn sprinkling system), I set forth to create a PVC transmitter stand. The stand worked out well; it's simple to build, costs little and eliminates concern about leaning your transmitter against your flight box or other equipment while it's not in use and not in an impound.

A Pro-Line Ace, single-stick radio sits comfortably in the transmitter stand.

MATERIALS
- 10-foot section of $1/2$-inch PVC pipe
- Two, 45-degree, $1/2$-inch couplings
- Six 90-degree $1/2$-inch elbows
- Six, $1/2$-inch, "T" couplings
- Two, $1/2$-inch endcaps
- Small can PVC cement
- Sleeve of PVC foam insulation

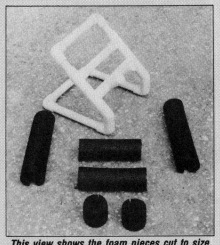

This view shows the foam pieces cut to size. Notice that they've been slit so that they can be fitted to the stand.

1 *All pipes and fittings are $1/2$ inch. Glue as per sketch using short pieces of pipe so that the three couplings are end to end. Make one left-hand and one right-hand assembly. Be sure the T is 90 degrees to the 45-degree coupling and that the assembly is perfectly flat.*

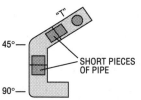

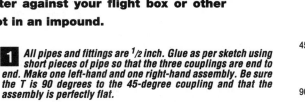

2 *Glue the inside Ts to form the first crosspiece (use short pieces of $1/2$-inch pipe) to the side assembly T. Do this for both the right-hand and left-hand sides.*

3 *Join the two sides with a short piece of pipe so that both inside crosspiece Ts touch each other. Keep the assembly straight and level in relationship to the 90-degree elbows.*

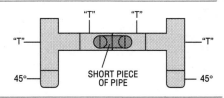

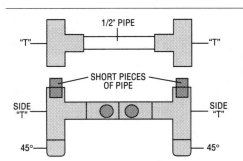

4 *Glue short pieces of pipe into the side Ts on both sides. Assemble (but don't glue) two more Ts on these short pieces of pipe. Cut a piece of $1/2$-inch pipe to fit between these two newly mounted Ts. Use the assembled Ts to measure the length of this $1/2$-inch pipe. Disassemble the Ts, and glue the pipe into the Ts making sure everything is square and level.*

Drill Index and Size Guide

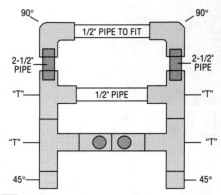

Hole Size	Decimal	Hole Size	Decimal
1/32-inch	0.03125	3/8-inch	0.375
1/16-inch	0.0625	11/32-inch	0.34375
3/32-inch	0.09375	13/32-inch	0.40625
1/8-inch	0.125	7/16-inch	0.4375
5/32-inch	0.15625	15/32-inch	0.46875
3/16-inch	0.1875	1/2-inch	0.500
7/32-inch	0.21875	17/32-inch	0.53125
1/4-inch	0.250	9/16-inch	0.5625
9/32-inch	0.28125	19/32-inch	0.59375
5/16-inch	0.3125	5/8-inch	0.625

Tap Sizes	Drill No./Size	Major Diameter
4-40	43/0.0890	0.1120
6-32	36/0.1065	0.1380
8-32	29/0.1360	0.1640
10-24	26/0.1470	0.1900
10/32	21/0.1590	0.1900
1/4-20	7/0.2010	0.250
1/4-28	3/0.2130	0.250

Decimal Equivalents of Letter-Size Drills

Letter	Size	Letter	Size
A	0.234	N	0.302
B	0.238	O	0.316
C	0.242	P	0.323
D	0.246	Q	0.332
E	0.250	R	0.339
F	0.257	S	0.348
G	0.261	T	0.358
H	0.266	U	0.368
I	0.272	V	0.377
J	0.277	W	0.386
K	0.281	X	0.397
L	0.290	Y	0.404
M	0.295	Z	0.413

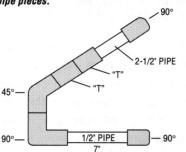

5 Cut two pieces of pipe 2½ inches long and glue into top Ts on both left and right sides. Assemble (don't glue) the 90-degree elbows to the 2½-inch pieces of pipe. Cut a piece of ½-inch pipe to fit between the two 90-degree elbows. As in all PVC construction, the pipe must mate inside the couplers. Disassemble the elbows, and glue the pipe and elbows into an assembly keeping everything straight and level. Glue the elbow/pipe assembly to the 2½-inch pipe pieces.

6 Cut two 7-inch pieces of ½-inch pipe, and glue into the 90-degree elbows on the forward bottom of the stand. Assemble (but don't glue) two 90-degree elbows to a 7-inch piece of pipe. Cut a piece of ½-inch pipe to fit between the two 90-degree elbows. Disassemble the elbows, and glue the pipe between the elbows; ensure that the assembly is straight and level. Glue this assembly to the 7x½-inch pipes that form the base.

A Cirrus PCM transmitter rests in the PVC transmitter stand.

7 Cut two short pieces of ½-inch pipe, and glue them into the two remaining openings in the Ts on the first crosspiece. Add the two endcaps to complete your transmitter stand.

8 Cut the foam sleeve to fit the stops, the side pieces and the crosspieces. It will be necessary to slit the foam sleeve to attach it to the stand.

It took a total of two hours to build the first stand. I'm sure it will be much easier to assemble the next one. Enjoy! ∎

A Stand For All Seasons

by CLIFF & LANELL SANDS

Cliff uses the stand as he repairs the MiG.

I'VE BEEN AN airplane-watcher for 26 years, and I especially appreciate the realistic flight characteristics that the giant-scale models capture. In the air, they're graceful birds, but when the time comes to take them home, they become unwieldy crates—prime targets for hangar rash.

As my appetite for big models grew, the size of my shop shrank. I was having a space crisis. Then I remembered meeting H. L. Skates when I visited my son at Moffett Field in Mt. View, CA. Mr. Skates collects giant models, and he's quite an innovator. At the time, he was building a giant scale that was sitting on a very practical stand.

It dawned on me that a stand could be the solution to my space *and* my transporta-

GIANT-SCALE SPACE-SAVER

tion problems. Skates's stand was made out of PVC pipe, but I couldn't recall exactly how it was built, so I decided to build my own. I went to a plumbing outlet and purchased about 60 feet of ³/₄-inch-diameter, heavy-walled PVC pipe, a large array of Ts, caps, 45- and 90-degree elbows and adhesive.

My expectations were high, so I took my time with the plans. I'm over 6 feet tall, so the stand had to be high enough so that I could use it without breaking my aching back, and it also had to be sturdy. I wanted it to be convertible so that I

could use it with different aircraft, e.g., high-wing and mid-wing, and the top had to be removable so that the bottom would form a "cradle"

PARTS

36 feet of ³/₄-inch PVC cut into the following sizes:
- 2 pieces of 3 feet
- 3 pieces of 11 in.
- 4 pieces of 18 in.
- 4 pieces of 9 in.
- 4 pieces of 8¹/₂ in.
- 4 pieces of 5 in.
- 4 pieces of 3 in.
- 12 pieces of 7 in.

4 90-degree elbows
8 45-degree elbows
16 Ts
8 caps
5 feet of gray pipe insulation foam

that I could use to hold the plane at the workbench or to transport the plane to the field.

The stand's dimensions of 39x52x20 inches accommodates most giant-scale planes. First, make a 39x20-inch base with the PVC pipe, then assemble the legs. Each leg consists of the following pieces, used in this order: a 90-degree elbow; a 3-inch piece of PVC; a T; a 7-inch piece of PVC; a 45-degree elbow; an 8¹/₂-inch piece of PVC; a T; a 7-inch piece of PVC; a 45-degree elbow; a 5-inch piece of PVC; a T; a

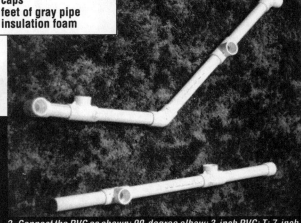

1. Cut the thick-walled PVC into the lengths listed.

2. Connect the PVC as shown: 90-degree elbow; 3-inch PVC; T; 7-inch PVC; 45-degree elbow; 8¹/₄-inch PVC; T; 7-inch PVC; 45-degree

9-inch piece of PVC; a T; a 7-inch piece of PVC; and a cap. After you've built the four legs, join two of them at the bottom with a 3-foot section of PVC; join them again at the first T from the top, with the 11-inch PVC piece to form the back. Build the front in the same way. With a helper, hold the back and the front so that they face each other, and connect them with the 18-inch PVC pieces.

You can reinforce the cradle by installing two more Ts and some 9-inch PVC pieces to make a cross-member (optional).

The foam pieces on the cradle are optional, but they're great for cushioning and steadying the airplane.

You have to decide how permanent you want your stand to be. At first, I didn't glue any of the joints. This is fine if you're just going to use the stand as a storage unit, but if you're going to use it as a building support or as a means of transportation, some of the joints should be glued. I ended up gluing the bottom joints, up to the second 45-degree elbow. I didn't glue any of the top joints, because I use the stand with different models, and I wanted to be able to adjust the

The floats stay clear of the gravel.

stand accordingly. When I remove the top, I install four caps on the bottoms of the 5-inch legs. If I want the cradle to be taller, I replace the 5-inch legs with longer ones.

This stand is ideal for float flying. At the site, it suspends the floats above the rocks and gravel; in the shop, it provides excellent storage for wings and floats.

This stand certainly has alleviated my space and transportation problems, and it's a real asset in building. ■

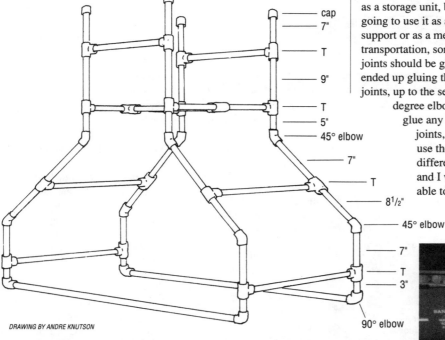

cap
7"
T
9"
T
5"
45° elbow
7"
T
8¹/₂"
45° elbow
7"
T
3"
90° elbow

DRAWING BY ANDRE KNUTSON

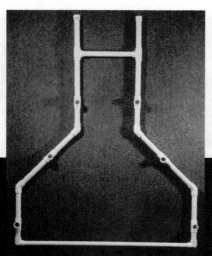

3. Join two of the legs using a 3-foot piece of

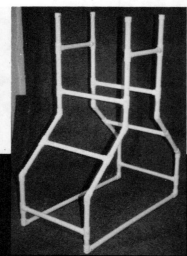

4. Join the front and the back using the

5. In the shop, the stand is a handy place to store wings and floats

4
CONSTRUCTION—GENERAL

Most modelers are tinkerers—people who like to build, solve engineering problems and create models that function well. Some like to go the extra mile and create scale models that are true works of art. The articles in this section offer a range of techniques for died-in-the-wool modelers who love to work with their hands.

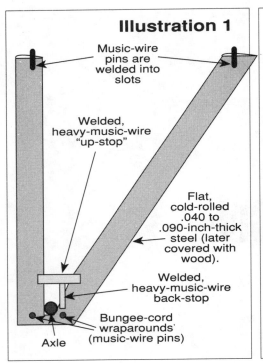

Illustration 1

Music-wire pins are welded into slots

Welded, heavy-music-wire "up-stop"

Flat, cold-rolled .040 to .090-inch-thick steel (later covered with wood).

Welded, heavy-music-wire back-stop

Bungee-cord wraparounds (music-wire pins)

Axle

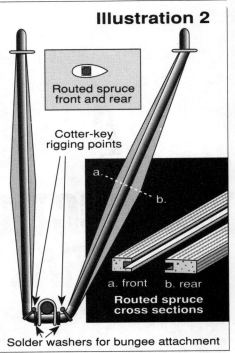

Illustration 2

Routed spruce front and rear

Cotter-key rigging points

a. front   b. rear

Routed spruce cross sections

Solder washers for bungee attachment

Make WW I Scale Landing Gear

by CLARKE SMILEY

MODEL AIRPLANE landing gear might be nothing more than balsa sticks, or they might be as complicated as the systems found on full-scale aircraft. When you're out of the featherweight class, landing gear must fulfill two functions:

- They must let the craft move along the ground under control.
- They must be able to absorb and

Achieve strength and scale looks

dissipate the energy generated as the airplane touches down (the gear flexing that you've seen on the student pilot's trainer is the most obvious example). If the gear can't handle the loads generated on landing, the gear and, quite possibly, the plane will break!

When making WW I landing gear, there's one main problem: how do you engineer gear that will dissipate the energy of landing, yet retain a scale landing-gear appearance?

In Sketch 1, I show the Sopwith-type landing gear, which works well if you want super strength and good shock absorption. The gear "V" is made out of flat, cold-rolled steel. The pins in the top fit

▲ 3. These washers limit how far the gear legs can go into the fuselage. The top ends will be trimmed to ¼ inch. The lower washers center the axle and hold the "bungee" cords.

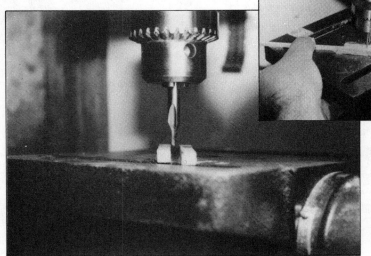

▲ 2. The drill press should be set at its top speed. The wood is passed slowly through the guide, leaving a channel for the music wire.

◄ 1. A close-up of the router system I use for cutting slots in hardwood. The two pieces of spruce are glued to the drill-press table to act as a guide. A router bit is used.

into holes in the bottom of the airplane. These pins should protrude from the top of the gear legs about ¼ inch—no more than that. They're welded into slots that have been cut in the legs.

No adhesive is used to hold the pins in their mounts in the fuselage. I believe in letting the rigging hold the gear tightly to the plane. (I use 15-pound test, stainless-steel, nylon-coated fishing leader.) This way, the whole gear will come off in a hard landing, and I only have to replace some rigging points. The back-stops and the up-stops are made of heavy music wire and are welded into slots cut in the rolled steel.

Almost any sheet-metal shop will shear some stock for you, and if you make the notches for all the pins, they'll "weld up" your gear. I've used this type many times and have found that .040- to .060-inch-thick steel works well. After this has been assembled, it can be covered with balsa or hard wood and sanded to an airfoil shape. On

PHOTOS BY CLARKE SMILEY

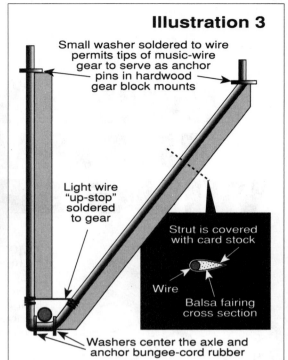

Illustration 3

Small washer soldered to wire permits tips of music-wire gear to serve as anchor pins in hardwood gear block mounts

Light wire "up-stop" soldered to gear

Strut is covered with card stock

Wire

Balsa fairing cross section

Washers center the axle and anchor bungee-cord rubber

5. Looking up into the bottom of the fuse-lage, you can see how the washer acts as a gear stop. The extra blocking is spruce. A fishhook rigging point can be seen just to the left of the landing-gear leg.

4. Here, I've covered the wire legs with routed spruce and sanded them to shape.

6. & 7. These pictures show the extended axle at rest. The amount of "give" is determined by the number of "wraps" of rubber. This type of suspension allows the rubber to center the axle. In Photo 6, just behind the forward strut, you can see the loop of a rigging point. (They're soldered at the same time as the lower washers.)

larger aircraft, .090-inch-thick steel wouldn't be considered overkill.

Sketch 2 shows my favorite gear design for .20- to .40-size vintage planes. I use the heaviest music wire and enclose it in routed spruce. Photos 1 and 2 show a routing jig that you can make using a drill press. You can make your own bit by sharpening a piece of music wire of the same size that you use for your gear. I bought a Sears 5/32-inch pin router and have had good luck using it with a guide that's glued with CA to my drill-press table. This way, I can make my own stock for struts and the like.

Photo 3 shows the start of a gear "V." I've soldered small washers to the top of the gear legs as stops for my gear anchor "pins." At the bottom of the "V," I've soldered two more washers that center the axle. In Photo 4, I've covered the wire with routed spruce, which I've sanded to shape.

Photo 5 shows the bottom longeron to which I've added extra blocking against which the gear can rest. If you look closely, you'll see a rigging point just to the left of the wire leg. I use the eyelet ends of cut-off fish hooks for this. They're made of a very hard steel and, when glued into place, they

provide strong attachment points for rigging wire. During a hard landing, they'll pull out without causing any significant damage, and they can be quickly glued back into place. It's best to drill the holes for the rigging points slightly oversize and use gap-filling CA in them.

Photo 6 shows the amount of "give" in the rubber that anchors the axle to the wire-covered gear. You can adjust this by varying the number of "wraps" of rubber. The

rubber should be wrapped inside the washers so that they'll be centered; the rubber also provides further shock absorption.

Sketch 3 shows a different way to produce a streamlined strut. Balsa is used to make an airfoil shape, then it's covered with card stock. I've also tried using aluminum tube for landing gear, but I've had only limited success. The tube doesn't withstand compression unless it's supported by a dowel or a hardwood insert.

I hope that I've given you some ideas on making scale landing gears for WW I aircraft. If I can be of further help, feel free to contact me: Clarke Smiley, 23 Riverbend, Newmarket, NH 03857. ∎

BUILD THE ULTIMATE WING SPAR

by MIKE LACHOWSKI

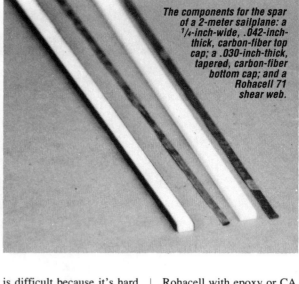

The components for the spar of a 2-meter sailplane: a 1/4-inch-wide, .042-inch-thick, carbon-fiber top cap; a .030-inch-thick, tapered, carbon-fiber bottom cap; and a Rohacell 71 shear web.

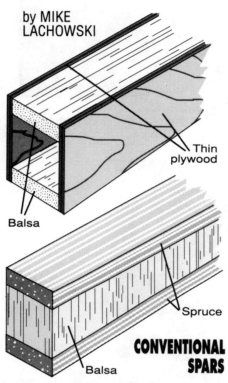

CONVENTIONAL SPARS

Conventional spars are built by gluing balsa between the two spars or by gluing balsa or plywood to their edges.

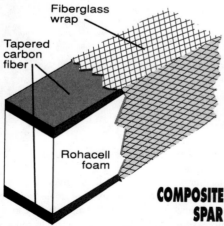

COMPOSITE SPAR

The composite spar is built by gluing Rohacell between the two carbon-fiber spar caps and wrapping the spar with fiberglass or Kevlar.

MOST WINGS have spars that strengthen them. Many of you are familiar with applying a thin carbon-fiber laminate to an existing spar to enhance its strength, but you can make the wing even stronger—yet lighter—by using an all-composite spar.

The spar has three parts: a top, a bottom and a shear web. The top and bottom parts of an all-composite spar are carbon-fiber laminates. The .007- or .014-inch-thick laminates you use for conventional spar reinforcements aren't thick enough to strengthen the spar sufficiently and make it resistant to buckling. Composite Structures Technology* (CST) offers laminates (with tapers or without them) in thicknesses up to .060 inch. In addition to strengthening the wing where it needs it most—in the center—tapered laminates reduce weight and save you money. Tapering conventional spars is difficult because it's hard to make the taper gradual and even. The taper is built into a composite during the laminating process, and because the spar requires less carbon fiber, it costs less to make.

Make the shear web of Rohacell instead of balsa.

Stronger and lighter!

Rohacell provides the necessary strength, but it's lighter and easier to work with than balsa, e.g., when you taper such a web you don't have to worry about the grain. Glue the carbon fiber to the Rohacell with epoxy or CA. If you use CA, make sure that the bond is good. Epoxy gives you more time in which to work and reduces the likelihood that you'll make a mistake.

A fiberglass or Kevlar spar wrap applied to the center section will strengthen the spar even more and prevent the carbon fiber from pulling away from the Rohacell. I tack-glue the fiberglass to the spar by spraying the spar with 3M 77 adhesive and wrapping the fiberglass around it. Then I apply epoxy with a foam roller to "wet out" the cloth and complete the spar. I usually attach the spar to the foam-cores at the same time.

CST offers carbon fiber in a variety of thicknesses and widths. You can design the spar to carry the entire wing load, and this permits you to reduce the weight of the wing sheeting or cloth lay-up when you vacu-bag. The cloth lay-up can be as little as one layer of 1.8-ounce Kevlar and one layer of .75-ounce fiberglass. The Kevlar is a good choice here, because it provides a thicker, more durable finish. In the end, the carbon fiber/ Rohacell spar is stronger, yet lighter, than one made of spruce, carbon fiber and balsa. This approach will result in a lighter wing with a spar that carries the entire load.

*Here's the address of the company mentioned in this article: CST, P.O. Box 4615, Lancaster, CA 93539.

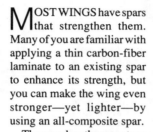

The spar is wrapped with fiberglass cloth along its entire length to prevent the laminates from coming apart.

MODEL AIRPLANE CONSTRUCTION NEWS MAGAZINE

DESIGNING MODEL planes is my favorite part of the hobby, and because I fly electric, most of my designs are intended for maximum speed at minimum power. To obtain this speed, the model must be clean and light, and this suggests retractable gear.

In half of my designs, the main gear retracts into the fuselage instead of into the wing. Since no one sells a mechanism to do this, I created one (similar to the retract action on single-engine Cessnas) that folds the main gear down so that the gear legs are first parallel and then extended. It then retracts the legs by pulling the gear together and up into the fuselage.

To model this design, I built a retractable Midwest* Aerostar 40, and my modifications required a substantial departure from the kit plans. For power, I chose Hobby Lobby's* Ultra 1600 motor that runs on 14 1700mAh SCE cells. Spinning a 10x8 prop at about 8500rpm, this system pulls about 23 amps static and is good for 4 to 5 minutes of fairly fast, full-throttle flight. (See photos 1 and 2.)

PHOTOS BY LLOYD SCHULZ

■ *1. Above: Speed increases and the glide flattens when the gear are retracted.*

■ *2. Left: The Aerostar approaches landing with gear deployed.*

Build In-line Fuselage Retracts

by LLOYD SCHULZ

ABOUT WEIGHT

You'd like all these pieces to be weightless but, of course, they aren't, nor can they be as light as fixed gear. My gear add about 6 ounces to the overall weight, which I found acceptable in a .40-size model. (If you substitute a light servo for a portion of the steering mechanism, you can save another .7 ounce.) This prototype Aerostar weighs 108 ounces, which is light for wet power, but heavy for electric. I could have built it lighter by scratch-building the fuselage instead of using the kit's plywood, but the whole idea was to adapt my gear to an existing trainer.

■ *3. The nose gear and landing gear retract forward into the fuselage. The fairing added to the chin plate covers the bottom of the nose-gear wheel.*

This design can be adapted to many different planes. Of course, certain parts will have to be "eyeballed" and customized to fit. I'll discuss the project in building sequence.

Pull up your wheels Cessna style

FUSELAGE

To provide space for the retracted gear, join the fuselage sides at the bulkhead nearest the wing's leading edge. Then, add the firewall, and join the aft fuselage at the very end of the tail. To accommodate the 2-inch-diameter main-gear wheels, widen the bulkhead to about 3 1/2 inches, which is 1/2 inch wider than is called for in the plan. (This

■ *4. The author shows off his modified Aerostar. With an electric drive system (Ultra 1600, 14 Sanyo 1700mAh SCE cells and a 10x8 Top Flite* prop), the plane weighs 6 pounds, 12 ounces.*

■ 5. Above left: The nose-gear mounting plates are glued to the square-stock verticals, to the firewall triangle verticals and to the longeron sections that run between the verticals along the fuselage bottom. Note the reinforcing ply doubler behind the axle hole and the 3/32-inch-ply cross block that serves as a nose-gear downstop. ■ 6. Above right: The main gear-mount plate is installed. Note the vertical square stock that was added to fuselage side. The 1/4x1/2-inch spruce cross brace absorbs the main gear loads. (See photo 9.)

1. Swing-arm axle
2. Main-gear vertical
3. Main-gear mount plate
4. Actuation arm
5. Down-lock cross-brace
6. Main-gear vertical
7. Gear-up hard spot
8. Main-gear leg
9. Main-gear wheel
10. Outside guide plate
11. Main-gear swing-arm plate
12. Main-gear mount axle
13. Gear-down hard-spot block
14. Center guide plate
15. Vertical guide plate
16. Idler-mount brace
17. Idler post
18. Steering cable
19. Nose-gear steering arm
20. Nose-gear mount axle
21. Nose-gear swing-arm plate
22. Nose-gear actuation arm
23. Nose-gear vertical
24. Nose-gear mount plate
25. Nose-gear vertical
26. Nose-gear strut
27. Idler control arm

isn't noticeable in the finished model.)

Next, prepare the fuselage for the gear pieces. Glue 1/4-inch balsa square-stock verticals and longeron segments to the inside of the fuselage to serve as nose gear and main-gear load distributors. (See the illustration to identify these pieces.) The nose-gear and main-gear mounting plates distribute the landing load to the fuselage. What I call the "swing-arm axles" pivot in the mounting plates. The nose gear rotates on this axle during retraction,

and the main gear is actuated when the main-gear swing-arm pivots on its axle. Glue the 1/16-inch-ply nose-gear and main-gear mounting plates to the verticals and longeron segments. (See photos 5 and 6.)

BUILDING THE NOSE GEAR
● **Location of the nose-gear swing-arm axle.** The 1/8-inch-ply nose-gear swing-arm plate holds the nose strut and rotates around the pitch axis for retraction. Using the kit's plans as a

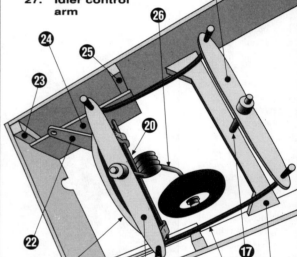

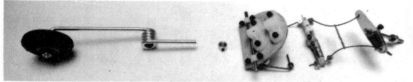

■ 7. Above, from left to right: nose gear, nose-gear swing-arm plate, steering horn and idler horn. Note the pull/pull cables.

■ 8A. Above left: installed nose gear in extended position. ■ 8B. Above right: the nose gear installed in the retracted position. Light-duty nylon straps anchor the landing-gear strut.
■ 9. Right: the main gear is fully extended. Note the close fit of the swing-arm plate.

Build In-line Fuselage Retracts

ILLUSTRATION BY JONATHAN T. KLEIN

reference, place the nose-gear swing-arm plate axle $1/2$-inch above the fuselage bottom. To determine how far back from the firewall to mount this axle, allow room for the nose gear and the wheel in its retracted position; then choose an appropriate mounting point.

As you can see in photo 8A, this axle is located on the nose-gear swing-arm plate just below the lower nylon strut support. I used a 1.5-inch wheel for the nose gear.

• **Nose-gear strut.** Use the nose-gear strut from the Aerostar kit. It projects above the top of the moveable swing-arm plate to attach to a double-armed control horn (pull/pull linkage) for steering, and it's mounted with light-duty-nylon landing-gear straps so they'll break away on hard landings instead of damaging the retract mechanism.

• **Nose-gear down lock.** The nose gear swings up and forward to retract, and

Fuselage retracts detail

■ **10.** *Left: The main-gear legs are attached to the mounting axle with keepers and a washer. To anchor the keeper, be sure to file a flat in the axle. This inside view of the extended main gear reveals the gear-down hard spot that supports the extended main-gear legs.* ■ **11.** *Above: The nose gear and main gear are fully retracted. Outside and center guide plates are visible on the bottom of the fuselage. Vertical guide plates hold the retracted gear in position and support the cabin floor above the retracts. Also visible is the cross-brace used to support the bottom of the idler shaft.*

Build In-line Fuselage Retracts

■ 12. Nose gear and main gear fully extended.

down and rearward to extend. Place a 3/32-inch aircraft-plywood cross block on the rear of the firewall so that the top half of the nose-gear swing-arm plate braces against it when the nose gear is fully extended. (See photo 5.) Remove just enough wood from the firewall so that the nose-gear leg can retract through it.

BUILDING THE MAIN GEAR

The main-gear swing-arm is a 1/8-inch plywood plate that rotates on a piano-wire axle around the model's pitch axis. It carries a second piano-wire axle (the main-gear-mount axle) longitudinally to hold the inboard ends of the main-gear legs. The swing-arm was made to just fit inside the mounting plates. (See photo 9.)

Using the kit plans again, place the main-gear swing-arm axle 1/2 inch above the fuselage bottom and the length of the swing-arm plate back from the normal gear location shown on the plans. This will position the extended gear correctly.

● **Down-lock cross brace.** Made of 1/4x1/2-inch spruce, this cross brace absorbs main-gear loads in three directions. It cushions the rearward and upward shock of landing, and it anchors the moveable end of the swing-arm so that the main-gear side loads are transferred to the cross-brace. (See photos 6 and 9.)

● **Gear legs.** Use the gear legs supplied in the Aerostar kit. Bend the inside end of each gear leg into an eye for mounting on the main-gear-mount axle. These eyes wrap around the axle at the end of the swing-arm plate, and they're secured by washers and a keeper. (See photo 10.) Be sure to file a "flat" in the mount axle to anchor the keeper.

● **Main-gear guide plates.** These are made from 1/16-inch-thick aircraft ply. Cut a single plate to fit the bottom of the fuselage; then cut the grooves that define the outside plates. (See photos 11 and 12.) This yields three pieces: a center guide plate and two outside guide plates. The center guide plate holds the gear-down hard-spot block, and the outside guide plates hold the gear-up hard spots. (See photo 10 and illustration.) The center guide plate's width is determined by installing the main-gear legs (with wheels attached) on the swing-arm plate and letting them hang down in parallel so that the wheels touch. The center plate must fit between the legs without touching. The grooves between the center and outside guide plates must allow for friction-free travel of the gear legs.

The guide plates guide the main gear during the middle of its up/down travel. The "hard spots" guide the main gear during its first few inches of up-travel and the last few inches of down-travel. The vertical guide plate (which is located at the forward edge of, and is perpendicular to, the center and outside guide plates) guides the gear during the last few inches of up-travel and first few inches of down-travel. (See photo 11.) The 1/16-inch-ply vertical guide plate also supports the cabin floor directly above. In the Aerostar, install a 1/32-inch-ply cabin floor directly above the compartment that houses the retractable landing gear. The floor holds the motor packs or a fuel tank. (See photo 15.)

The center guide plate extends aft to the trailing-edge point and forward to a point that enables the retracted wheels to safely clear the guide plate by 3/8 inch. The guide grooves are cut parallel at the front edge of the guide plates. Near the aft end of the guide plates, the grooves curve 90 degrees toward the fuselage sides to allow for full extension of the gear.

● **Gear-down hard points.** These top outside edges of a small hardwood block are mounted atop the

(Continued on page 135)

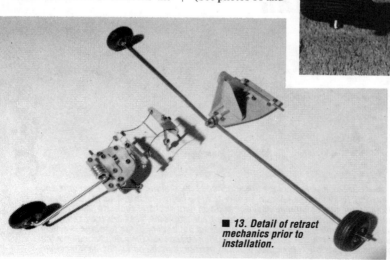

■ 13. Detail of retract mechanics prior to installation.

■ 14. Above: A top view of the idler arm, which is used for nose-gear steering. A piano wire push/pull rod connects the idler arm to the rudder servo, and another links both swing-arm plates (only the nose-gear plate is visible here). ■ 15. Below: Top view shows the cabin floor after installation. Center cutout allows clearance for the retracted main landing gear legs and mount axle.

The P-38 looks majestic as it comes in for a landing with its Fowler flaps deployed.

PHOTOS BY ROBERT M. ALMES

Build
Fowler Flaps

by ROBERT M. ALMES

A simple, functional design for giant-scale R/C aircraft

HARLAN FOWLER JOINED the Lockheed Aircraft engineering staff in late 1935. There, Fowler introduced the flap design that has become widely known as the "Fowler flap." Lockheed was so impressed with Fowler's flap idea that they underwrote a patent on it. The test bed for the flap system was the Model 14 Super Electra in January 1937. The Lockheed Hudson, P-38 Lightning, Constellation and Consolidated's B-24 Liberator employed Fowler flaps. Numerous aircraft, including modern-day jets, use Fowler flaps.

A practical application of Fowler flaps has long been the quest of avid scale enthusiasts, particularly of P-38 fans. Note the photo showing a Lockheed P-38, with its sizable flaps fully deployed, coming in for a landing.

Fowler flaps were a distinctive feature of this famous aircraft. Imagine the sight of those large flaps hanging from the trailing edge of your scale P-38 as it comes in for a landing.

In the full-scale P-38 Lightning, four flaps are linked together by pulleys, cables, pushrods and screw jacks. The mechanics and linkages involved don't lend themselves to plug-in wings and other disassembly requirements for transporting R/C aircraft to and from the flying site. After careful consideration of the design requirements, I developed four flap units for a giant-scale P-38. These are linked together by a single air line. These flap units are integrated pneumatic/mechanical devices; the design provides support

Detail of Fowler flaps installed on Yellow Aircraft P-38.

and carriage for each flap. A Robart* air-line quick-disconnect is used at each wing plug-in point.

I flight-tested the design with a modified Ace R/C* "Big Bingo." Two 14x4-inch flaps were installed, as well as conventional ailerons. Three pilots have flown the aircraft and uncounted airborne extensions and retractions have been made. One of the distinctive features of Fowler flaps is that the horizontal and downward angles are

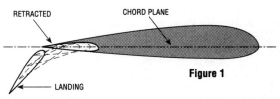

Figure 1

Action of Fowler flaps (flaps have constant chord and airfoil).

always in perfect balance. Therefore, very little force is required to operate the flaps. At full extension, each cylinder spring exerts a 1-pound retraction force, and the flaps retract easily, regardless of aircraft speed.

The photographs show flaps in a $\frac{1}{6}$-scale P-38. A different scale or a different aircraft will require slight modifications, e.g., a $\frac{1}{5}$-scale P-38 has a flap chord of 4 inches. The air cylinders used have a stroke of 4 inches, and the mechanical linkage provides a progressive downward angle of 40 degrees. On the other hand, a $\frac{1}{6}$-scale P-38 has a flap chord of 3 inches. In this case, the air cylinders have a stroke of 3 inches, but the mechanical linkage must still allow a progressive downward angle of 40 degrees. The smaller scale allows for a shorter crossbar, thus, the cylinders can be closer together. The shorter stroke and crossbar result in a smaller unit. A careful examination of the Figure 2, which is for a $\frac{1}{5}$-scale P-38, will reveal the nature of the operation. Appropriate adjustments can be made for other applications.

FOWLER FLAPS

The plans show the flap unit with the flap retracted and with the flap extended. For clarity, the bottom panel has been removed and the view is of the underside of the wing. Note that the 10-degree forward sweep of the wing's trailing edge requires that there be two right-wing flap units and two left-wing units (the plan shows a left-wing unit). Right-wing units require a reversal of the forward sweep and linkage.

CONSTRUCTION

Bimba* or Clippard* air cylinders and fittings are available through various distributors listed in the "Yellow Pages" under "cylinders-air & hydraulic." I use Bimba 0074 cylinders for $1/5$-scale and Bimba 0073 for $1/6$-scale in my P-38 designs. I recommend the Clippard RC-0581 clevis for both versions because it's smaller than the Bimba unit. All other parts for the Fowler flap units are available at a hobby shop near you.

Begin by preparing two identically sized pieces of $1/32$-inch-thick ply with an angle of 10 degrees at the forward and aft ends. (The 10-degree angle will match the trailing-edge sweep of the P-38 after the unit has been installed.) As shown on the plans, these pieces will form the top and bottom walls of the removable module that contains the retract mechanics.

Select one piece to work on and put the other aside (you'll use it as a cover for the finished

The flap unit is shown deployed (above left) and retracted (above right).

unit). The size of the ply work piece will depend on the model you're building; in turn, its size will dictate the size of all spruce rails. Use CA throughout. Cut and fit the spruce rails along the outer edge of the ply floor.

Attach a Clippard hose fitting to the ends of both Bimba air cylinders. Be sure to use the gasket provided. Thread the 10-32 nut and Clippard clevis over the piston rod (inner shaft) at the other end of each cylinder. With the cylinders retracted, turn the nut and clevis all the way down to the barrel of the cylinder. Check to see that 4 inches of piston-rod extension are available. Lock the nut and the clevis together so that they don't turn on the piston.

Lay each cylinder in place with its air-vent hole facing upward. Apply CA to two or three

places along the crevice formed by the cylinder and the spruce rail. Don't obstruct the air vents. You must drill a $7/32$-inch hole into the side of one of the inner rails (see plan). Mount the butt end of a Du-Bro* ball post in this hole with CA. Cut out and fit all other spruce pieces into place.

Make a crossbar according to the dimensions shown on the plans. Mount the crossbar and a Du-Bro nylon hinge to the appropriate cylinder clevis using a steel rivet. Use a small washer at each end of the rivet as a spacer. The washer should be mounted between the rivet head and clevis at one end of the rivet, and between the crossbar and rivet burring at the other end.

Fasten a Du-Bro nylon hinge to the other cylinder in a similar manner, but omit a crossbar connection. Place the brass tube (or piano wire) hinge axle through the nylon hinges, with the Du-Bro collars mounted in the hinges as shown in the plan (4-40 bolts will later anchor the flap to these collars).

In the retracted mode, the flap-hinge axle forms the proper 10-degree sweep angle for the flap. Later, before you mount the flaps on the retract mechanism, coat the clevis cavity with CA so that the hinge can't pivot sideways.

Make a restraining rod out of a threaded 2-56 rod that has a steel Kwik Link* at one end and a nylon socket at the other end. The ball link that you mounted on the retract assembly side rail will fit into the socket. Make a 10-degree bend in the rod at the nylon connection before the Kwik Link is connected to the crossbar. You may cover

FOWLER FLAP OPERATION

The unit's two $5/16$-inch-bore air cylinders have stroke lengths that accommodate the flap chord involved. The cylinders are connected to the flap hinge and provide suspension for the flap. A crossbar is attached to the piston of one of the cylinders. The other end of the crossbar is connected by way of a Kwik Link to a restraining rod that extends diagonally across the frame and is anchored to a ball socket. A flap drag link connects the crossbar to the flap aft of the hinge line. As air extends the pistons aft, one end of the crossbar also moves aft. This action causes the crossbar and the restraining link to be extended, changing the angle of the crossbar. The flap drag link is somewhat restricted in its travel, causing the flap to rotate downward across the hinge line. The flap has been extended aft the required 4 inches and progressively angled downward the required 40 degrees. The air cylinders are the spring-return type, so removal of the air supply causes the flaps to return to the retracted position. I use B&D Enterprises'* flow-control valve because of the rapid air exhaust when the control is moved to the flap-up position. Only two of the operation ports are used. A short piece of air line runs between the unused ports.

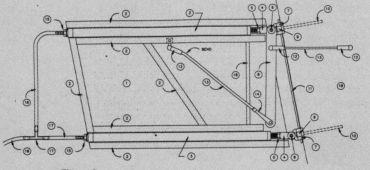

Figure 2

1. $1/32$-inch ply, top and bottom
2. $1/4$x$5/8$-inch spruce rail
3. $5/16$-inch-bore Bimba air cylinder, no. 0074
4. Clippard clevis, no. 0581
5. 10-32 nut
6. $1/8$-inch steel rivet
7. Du-Bro nylon aileron hinge
8. Crossbar
9. Du-Bro $3/32$ collar
10. $1^{1}/2$-inch 4-40 bolt
11. $3/32$-inch brass tube hinge axle (or piano wire)
12. Du-Bro nylon ball link and post
13. 2-56 threaded rod covered with heat-shrink tubing
14. Du-Bro 2-56 steel Kwik Link
15. Clippard 10-32 to $1/16$-inch hose fitting, no. 11752-2
16. $1/16$-inch-i.d. plastic tubing
17. Plastic or brass tee fitting
18. $1/8$-inch square spruce or bass wood
19. Flap

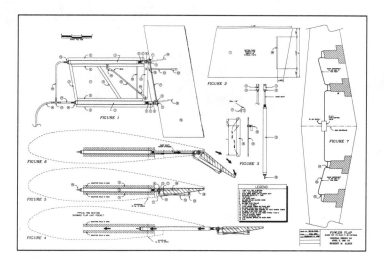

the threaded area of the restraining rod with heat-shrink tubing.

Adjust the Kwik Link so that the crossbar is at a 90-degree angle to the cylinders, i.e., directly across the aft edge of the retract assembly (see plan). Screw a $1^1/2$-inch 4-40 bolt into each of the $^3/32$-inch collars. Clip off the heads of the bolts when you're ready to fasten the flap into place.

Wing construction should provide for a flap-unit pocket (the plans show wing-mount rails into which the flap mechanism slides) and a flap cavity. The flap cavity should have a floor (assuming you're looking at an up-side-down wing) upon which the rivet heads can slide freely throughout extension. As indicated in Figure 6 on the plan, the rivets support the flap mechanism when air loads

The prototype flap mechanism was tested on an Ace Bingo. Countless trouble-free extensions and retractions have proven the design's reliability.

Here, Fowler flaps are deployed on the $^1/8$-scale P-38 sold by Yellow Aircraft* of Lexington, MA.

are in effect. The round rivet heads also facilitate retraction by sliding cleanly under load.

Fit the flap retract unit (not the flap itself) into the wing pocket, and position the 4-40 bolts parallel to the flap floor. The position of these bolts at the collar dictates the locations of the holes in the leading edge of the flap that will accept the bolts. When installed in the flap, the bolts must be positioned at a 90-degree angle to

the wing's trailing edge (not the cylinders).

Once you've fitted the flap into place, manually extend it by pulling it at the brass hinge line. When free operation is assured, you may apply epoxy to lock the bolts into the flap. Make a flap drag link of a 2-56 threaded rod with nylon sockets at each end. You may cover the threaded area with heat-shrink tubing. Snap one end of the drag link onto the ball post on the crossbar. Snap a ball post into the nylon socket at the other

end. With the flap retracted, position the ball post on the flap, and mark the center. I suggest that you fasten the ball post to a 1-inch-square piece of $^1/16$-inch plywood and that you prepare an insert in the flap surface for mounting the ply and ball post.

On the plan, note the screw center line that has been drawn through the bottom spruce rails of the wing into the outer spruce rails of the flap unit (see "Center line of no. 20 screw"). Two screws are used, one on each side. Sheet-metal screws will firmly anchor the flap unit in the wing. Thus, the unit can easily be installed or removed from the wing. Be sure that you attach a quick-disconnect plug to the air line at the plug-in wing separation point.

The total cost per unit is about $40 for a $^1/5$-scale plane and a little less for a $^1/6$-scale. If you have any questions regarding adaptation of this flap design to different scales or types of aircraft, please feel free to contact me at Apt. 1525, 12660 Jupiter Rd., Dallas, TX 75238; (214) 348-5193.

*Here are the addresses of the companies mentioned in this article:
Robart Mfg., P.O. Box 1247, 310 N. 5th St., St. Charles, IL 60174.
Ace R/C, 116 W. 19th St., Box 511C, Higginsville, MO 64037.
Bimba Mfg. Co., P.O. Box 68. Monee, IL 60449; (708) 534-8544
Clippard Instruments Laboratory, 7390 Colerain Rd., Cincinnati, OH 45239; (513) 521-4261.
Du-Bro Products, 480 Bonner Rd., Wauconda, IL 60084.
Kwick Link; distributed by Du-Bro Products
B&D Enterprises, Route 81, Box 7, Ballard, WV 24918.
CBA Models, 1620 N. Leavitt Rd. NW, Warren, OH 44485.
Yellow Aircraft, 203 Massachusetts Ave., Lexington, MA 02173.

Authentic Aluminum

by CLARKE SMILEY

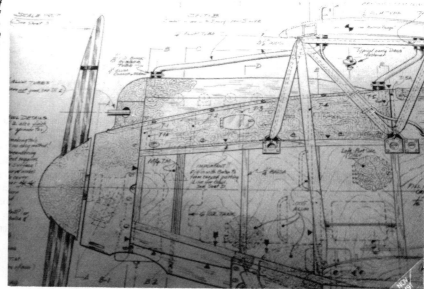

1

1. The fairing over the top of the engine is the trademark of the Albatros D-11 (Airdrome plan). The chin fairing on the underside of the cowl is the piece shown in this article.

CREATE A SCALE, BURNISHED FINISH

FOR ME, ONE of the more difficult facets of scale modeling has been how to simulate round or compound-curved metal surfaces. Some WW I aircraft had many such curves, and many had tooled or burnished surfaces. Such is the case with the Austrian built Albatros D-11, a scale version of which I am now building from Airdrome* plans.

A mixture of aluminum powder (which usually comes in paste form) and clear dope can be used to simulate the appearance of these surfaces very realistically. This type of mixture is also used to "sun-proof" fabric on full-scale aircraft. Aluminum paste is available through many airports and from Aircraft Spruce & Specialty*. A little of this goes a long way.

There are a couple of things worth noting about aluminum. It oxidizes rapidly, which means it seals itself off from further oxi-

dation. This makes it a long-lasting, protective medium. Natural aluminum panels are gray to almost white. An aluminum panel will only stay very shiny if it's polished and waxed often. The technique shown here will result in a shiny surface that makes your model look as if it has just emerged from the factory, and it will retain its finish—no polishing necessary. The pictures tell the rest of the story!

*Here are the addresses of the companies that are mentioned in this article: **Airdrome**, P.O. Box 1425, FDR Station, New York, NY 10150; (212) 421-1440. **Aircraft Spruce and Specialty Co.**, Box 424, Fullerton, CA 92632; (714) 870-7551.
Sig Manufacturing Co., 401 S. Front St., Montezuma, IA 50171; (515) 623-5154.
Randolph Products Co., 701 12th St., Carlstadt, NJ, 07072; (201) 438-3700. ∎

2

∎ 2. This is the balsa-sheeted chin fairing before it had been finished.

3

∎ 3. First, apply three coats of Sig* Supercoat clear dope to the balsa.

4

5

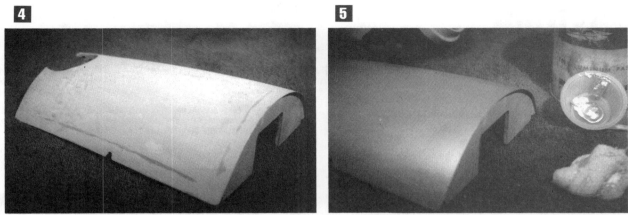

■ 4. Next, add a light coat of surface primer (I use Du Pont no. 30S). Fill nooks and dents with body putty, and sand the surface smooth. I use 400-grit wet sandpaper with water and a drop of dishwashing liquid. ■ 5. To cover a section of this size, mix about ¼ teaspoon of aluminum paste (Randolph* no. 701) with 1 ounce of clear dope. The photo shows the paste before I had added dope. Brush on two coats.

6

7

8

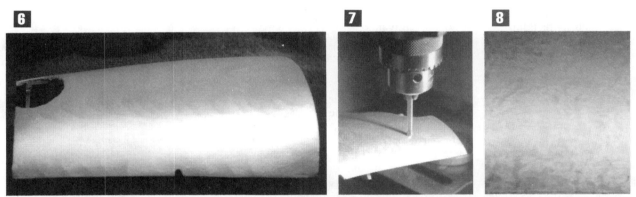

■ 6. After the coats of aluminum and dope have dried, apply aluminum paste directly to the fairing surface. If you use a drop of thinner on a small rag to apply the paste, it will go on like shoe polish. In the photo, you can see little swirls where the cloth was rubbed on the surface. Coat the surface twice with aluminum paste. Your workplace should be well ventilated. I recommend that you use a respirator as well. ■ 7. Here's the enjoyable part! Mount a piece of very soft ⅛-inch-square balsa in a drill press or a Dremel tool. Keep the end of the balsa wet with thinner. (I keep a capful of thinner nearby and wet the balsa often.) The secrets here are to turn the balsa very slowly, and to use little pressure. You'll be rewarded with a very scale, random, swirling pattern. This technique can be used to create other burnished-metal patterns as well ■ 8. This is the fruit of my labor. Don't forget, there's burnished aluminum powder on the surface, so you must protect it. Rub the surface lightly with a soft cloth to remove any aluminum dust. If you want a dull, weathered finish, apply a coat of Sig flat dope, flat epoxy, or another flat finish.

9

■ 9. I wanted a shiny finish, so, after adding some copper rivet heads, I sprayed two coats of Sig clear dope onto the fairing. This left a finished surface with a pleasant, random swirled appearance to which the camera can't really do justice. You'll find all sorts of uses for this aluminum paste. Example: to create different metallic sheens for metal wing panels, mask off an area on a wing, add a drop of black pigment to the paste and rub it into the surface.

Positive pullers

Good for models of any size

by H. DAN MOSER

IN THE LAST two years, I've installed pull/pull cable systems in over a dozen small sports trainers, old timers and kit planes, and I'm convinced

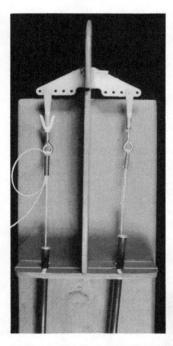

■ *Above: two back-to-back nylon control horns are all that's needed. Make sure the horns' holes are lined up with the hinge line and that both clevises are equidistant from the hinge line.* ■ *Right: the wing nut, which is made out of a nylon clevis, makes it possible to make adjustments at the field without tools. Safety loops should be used at the servo ends and at the control-surface ends.*

that this is the ideal elevator and rudder system for any R/C plane. Positive action, lightness, easy installation, the absence of radio interference, minimal friction with adjacent pushrods or formers and the absence of trim variations caused by temperature changes are some of the obvious advantages.

I've found that Sullivan's* no. 521 Pull/Pull Assembly provides the most convenient assortment of pull/pull hardware. It includes plastic guide tubes, tube-end eyelets, soft-copper terminal sleeves, eyebolts, locknuts, Sullivan's Golden clevises and companion safety clips, and Kevlar cable. Other sources of pull/pull hardware include fishing-tackle shops and Proctor* for the $^{1}/_{4}$-scale builder.

To make the T-bar control horns on the control surfaces, mount two standard control horns back-to-back (one on each side of the surface) with no. 2 screws or 2-56 machine screws of the proper length. To eliminate geometric errors, the clevis holes should be on the hinge line and at an equal distance from the line. The effective ratio of control-surface movement

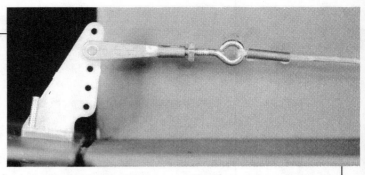

All the small components here are available in Sullivan's no. 521 package—very convenient. After the safety loop has been tightened, the copper terminal sleeve should be crimped at two or three points.

Cable Linkage Systems

to servo rotation can be adjusted by selecting the clevis mounting holes at the servo and/or control horn.

Straight-line cables between the servo and the T-horn provide the ideal setup, though you can offset the cables through the guide tubes where necessary to avoid formers or other interference. To determine guide-tube routing, study the plane's top

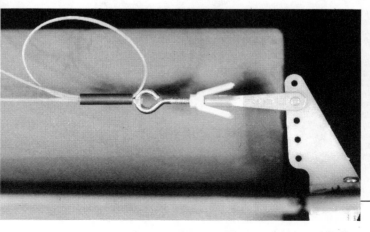

and side views while it's under construction. By drawing straight lines on each view between the servo arm and the control horn, points of entry into the fuselage can be established. Light balsa sheeting should be installed in these areas to support the covering. To insert the guide tubes at the correct angle, drill angled holes with a long $^{3}/_{16}$-inch drill bit. The top and side views will also establish the location of the guide-tube supports at a former near the servos. No other supports should be necessary in a straight-line installation.

After installing the control horns, the servos and the guide tubes, the

Cable Linkage Systems

final location of guide supports can be verified by inserting a straight 0.040-inch wire through the guide tube from the T-horn to the servo. After the points of entry have been covered, install and permanently anchor the guide tubes.

Once you've assembled and covered the fuselage and control surfaces, you can start on the final installation of the cables. The cables are first connected to the servo arms with the clevis, the eyebolt and the locknut where space permits. Alternatives may be necessary in some

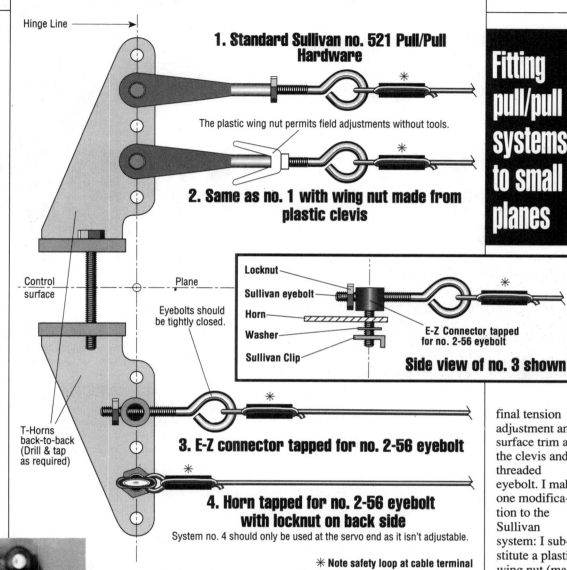

Hinge Line

1. Standard Sullivan no. 521 Pull/Pull Hardware

The plastic wing nut permits field adjustments without tools.

2. Same as no. 1 with wing nut made from plastic clevis

Control surface

Plane

Eyebolts should be tightly closed.

Locknut
Sullivan eyebolt
Horn
Washer
Sullivan Clip

E-Z Connector tapped for no. 2-56 eyebolt

Side view of no. 3 shown

T-Horns back-to-back (Drill & tap as required)

3. E-Z connector tapped for no. 2-56 eyebolt

4. Horn tapped for no. 2-56 eyebolt with locknut on back side

System no. 4 should only be used at the servo end as it isn't adjustable.

＊ Note safety loop at cable terminal

Fitting pull/pull systems to small planes

situations. To eliminate the possibility of slippage, make safety loops in the cables at all the terminal fittings. When the assembly is firmly in place and the terminal fitting is against the eyebolt, the terminal sleeve should be crimped at two or three points.

Feed the cable through

Using a Du-Bro EZ connector, the wing-nut adjusting method can be used at the servo end of the cable control system.*

the proper guide tube to its respective control horn, and connect it to the clevis eyebolt after centering the servo and the control surface. Adjust the clevises at the approximate center of the threaded portion on the eyebolt. Before you crimp the final terminal fitting, adjust the tension on the cable. Allowing 1/64 inch to 1/32 inch of free movement should prevent servo pre-loading and excessive battery drain. Make the

final tension adjustment and surface trim at the clevis and threaded eyebolt. I make one modification to the Sullivan system: I substitute a plastic wing nut (made from a plastic clevis) for the locknut, and this allows me to make field adjustments without using tools.

I'm convinced that after you install and fly your own planes with the pull/pull system, you'll never revert to the pushrod setup again.

Here are the addresses of the companies mentioned in this article: Sullivan Products, P.O. Box 5166, Baltimore, MD 21224. Proctor Enterprises, 25450 N.E Eilers Rd., Aurora, OR 97002. Du-Bro Products, 480 Bonner Rd. Wauconda, IL 60084. ∎

Don't Trash Your CRASH

by ROY DAY

YOU CAN REPAIR IT

AFTER A BAD CRASH, there's a terrible temptation to just dump the whole mess in the trash can. Don't. There's a good chance it can be repaired at minimum expense and in much less time than it would take to build another plane. Here are some helpful hints on how to repair that next crashed plane.

KEEP ALL THE PIECES

First, carefully gather all the pieces at the crash site. Even a scrap of balsa may save you time by serving as a template for a new part. Maybe it can be glued back into place with a doubler.

ASSESS THE DAMAGE

Next, remove the radio and the engine, and carefully check them for damage. If none is apparent, then check that both still operate. Do this right away, in case there's a long wait for replacement parts or repairs. It's surprising how today's radios and engines survive terrible crashes.

Assess airframe damage. Remove the covering and sheeting to reveal the "broken bones." Check for loose servo mounts, broken hinges, and wiggle the tail to see if it's loose.

1. The secret of strong and straight repairs: splices that are eight to ten times the thickness of the material. Begin by making the first cut with your saw on the new material.

2. Place the new member over the damaged one, and mark it for the mating splice cut.

PHOTOS BY ROY DAY

3. Cut the old member as marked.

4. Voilà! A splice that's strong and straight (cross-hatching added for clarity).

CRASH

5. To make new parts, use old broken ribs as templates.

6. Slip the new rib parts into place and glue.

REPAIRING THE BEAVER

Liberal use of doublers can make the repair of damaged lite-ply or balsa-sheet structures generally easier than the repair of damaged stick construction, which often requires splicing. Here, I'll concentrate on repairing the wing of my Beaver, which is of stick construction. The techniques I'll use are applicable to all built-up construction.

REPAIRING THE WING

There are two keys to the successful repair of a structure like a built-up wing:
● dimensional accuracy and alignment
● strength

When the covering and sheeting have been removed and the damaged areas identified,

7. With the fuselage and the wing repaired, the Beaver is ready for covering.

jig-up the wing on your building board so that it's straight and has the correct dimensions. Weight it down with bean bags or sand bags.

● **Splicing hints.** The trick to making strong and straight repairs to longerons, spars, and leading and trailing edges is to make good splices. For strength, a splice must be eight to ten times longer than the thickness of the material to be repaired. For 1/4-inch square stock, that means a splice that's at least 2 inches long. Decide on the length of the replacement piece, and then, to be safe, cut it a couple of inches longer. With your razor saw, make a splice cut on one end, remembering the length criteria mentioned.

Lay this new part on the old part, align it carefully, and then mark the required splice cut on the old member. Make that cut carefully with your saw. If it's done correctly, the result will be a good fit.

Now, make the splice cut on the new part at the other end. Clamp the first splice joint, and mark your cut on the old member for the second cut. When the four splice cuts have been made (both ends), clamp both joints and apply thin CA. The result will be a joint that's as strong and as straight as the original. Repeat until all the members have been repaired.

● **Repairing ribs.** Use the broken ribs as templates to cut new ones, which can either be doubled over the old ones or slipped in as replacements.

In a surprisingly short time, you'll have your "crash" ready for covering. You'll amaze people at the flying field with your completely rebuilt plane. So, next time you crash, stay away from that trash can! ■

8. Anyone for flying?

by MICHAEL LACHOWSKI

—beats blind nuts!
Use Threaded Inserts

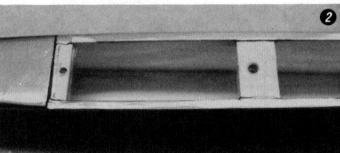

1. Threaded inserts are made of brass with machine threads on the inside and a coarse, self-threading exterior. Small quantities of inserts in sizes that are suitable for modeling can be bought from Du-Bro* and most hobby dealers.

2. Drill holes for the threaded inserts. The inserts should be installed in a hard material like hardwood or plastic. The proper hole sizes are listed on the package.

Nylon bolts are commonly used to attach wings and other parts to models. The bolts can be screwed into a variety of mounts, such as threaded hardwood or blind nuts. Threaded inserts provide another technique with several advantages:

● You don't need special tools like a tap to thread the hole.

● Mounting is very easy: just drill a hole of the proper diameter.

● The inserts provide a better permanent mount and won't come out of the holes like blind nuts.

These step-by-step photos show how to install threaded inserts to mount a wing.

3. Screw the threaded inserts into the holes. A steel machine screw can be used to drive in the insert. For extra security, apply a thin coat of epoxy to the outside of the insert before screwing it in.

4. Remove the steel screw, and your bolt mount is now complete. Mounting is especially easy in restricted areas where there would be an access problem if you tried to install a blind nut from the rear.

5. The modified Mini Challenger. A pan-head 10-32 bolt is mounted flush with the wing's surface near the spar. The rear bolt is a 6-32, so it can easily shear if a wing tip hits hard, and this will allow the wing to rotate. Be sure to add a hard surface to the wing for the bolt to be tightened on. (Plywood or epoxy/glass plate work well.)

6. The finished model, ready to fly.

*Here's the address of the company featured in this article: Du-Bro Products Inc., P.O. Box 815 Dept. EP, Wauconda, IL 60084.

OWING TO HANDED-down, tried-and-true methods, the installation of landing gear, retracts, steerable nose wheels, pushrods, wheel pants, etc., hardly fazes modelers of land-based R/C aircraft. Unfortunately, common knowledge about floatplanes isn't as widespread. I suspect that many modelers avoid float projects because they believe that they're too complex, and they won't "get them right." Well, cheer up! You can easily make floatplane conversions with parts and materials that you already have.

There are many ways to approach float-gear, rudder and linkage fabrication. I doubt that this article and five others like it could list every existing method, and I'm sure there are more on the way! If there's one thing you should know, it's this: if it works, it's OK. Converting a plane to floats lets you be an inventor. All the hard stuff, e.g., aluminum gear, threaded rods, brass and aluminum tubes, connectors, bellcranks, cables, pulleys, hinges— you name it—is already out there! Just study these pictures and captions, visit your local hobby shop, and put it all together. Have a good time, and see you at the lake!

Floatplane Conversions and Gear

Simple solutions with handy hardware

by JOHN SULLIVAN

▲ A water rudder driven directly off the air rudder can be very effective. This one has been clamped to the air rudder with the nylon rudder-control horn, wrapped around the music-wire down shaft and soldered.

▲ This Williams Brothers rudder is one of the few commercially available units. Its size restricts it to use on .20- and .40- size models. Although disconnected, the ball link suggests that this rudder was slave driven from the opposite float.

▲ A pushrod exiting the hull drives a bushed-nose wheel arm. This soldered metal rudder uses a rubber band stretched around pins to provide a kick-up/return action. All the work shown here can be done with tin snips, a drill, a Zona saw, and a sol-

▲ A pair of nylon hinges was bolted to the stern tab on a Gee Bee float, and the rudder was bent on top to form a control horn. This water rudder

Floatplane Conversions and Gear

The pull/pull arm appears to be splined to the rudder post and held in place with a spring connected to a long, wheel-collar set-screw. The rudder plate has been stiffened with a short length of music wire soldered to the plate, and a rubber stern gasket prevents water from seeping in around the screws.

▼ A V-shaped stern block houses a brass tube for this system's rudder shaft, which is bent at the bottom and soldered to the rudder plate. The sheet-metal pull/pull arm was soldered to a wheel collar. The rudder can take a fair amount of abuse without failing, yet it's not overbuilt or heavy.

▲ To build a rudder quickly, laminate two pieces of 1/16-inch ply over EZ hinges. The bottom forward skeg blends into the float bottom so that it won't catch on weeds. Plans for six sizes of this type of rudder are available from Model Airplane News (plan no. FSP10893).

The drive side of this slave rudder system uses two nose-wheel arms to form an adjustable bellcrank. Push-rods crossing from stern to stern, as these do, don't seem to get swamped by spray. The rigid, nylon hold-down clip that's screwed into the fiberglass on the stern deck does the job.

Flattened Proctor tubes were pop-riveted to aluminum tab plates to complete this "N" strut/spreader bar juncture. This is a clean, light and sturdy system. Black, non-skid bathtub tape was used for the deck walk material.

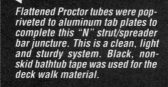

The deck foot on this system was made out of stock aluminum channel. The spreader bar is actually heavy aluminum tube that has been threaded internally on the ends with drilled-through sections as spacers. A round-head machine bolt holds it all together, and four Phillips-head wood screws secure the foot to the deck. Notice the pushrod hold-down.

▲ A nose-wheel block was used to secure music-wire gear in this setup. A flat wooden spreader is trapped under the gear system to limit float twisting. Many modelers elect to test their systems before completely filling and finishing the floats, and that explains the pinholes and bare glassed surfaces on a few of our subjects.

▼ The strap aluminum gear leg and spreader are stacked and held with two wood screws to an embedded wooden deck plate. Simulated rivets, panel lines and an aluminum finish add realism and really make this float system stand out.

▼ The wooden deck plates and airfoil-shaped spreader bars have been finished with glossy varnish. The neatly wrapped, soldered gear leg and "N" strut terminate in a nylon nose-wheel block. Three wheel collars hold the gear leg firmly in place. Setups like this can break all conventions and still look great.

▲ The aluminum "N" struts and spreader bar terminate at an internal hard-point on this Byron Husky float. Seal these entry points with silicone to keep out water. Note the turnbuckle and threaded rod used for cross-bracing. This is an extremely rigid setup.

▶ In this setup, a music-wire spreader pierces the aluminum gear blank and terminates in a nylon block. The four hold-down screws are staggered to provide strength and to prevent the float from twisting. The 1/64-inch ply strips simulate deck well plates.

▼ This setup is a tinkerer's delight. A sub-fin has been hung from the tail group with mating brackets. A pair of ball links on a swing arm ties off water-rudder cables. To complicate matters further, two stab struts end in the same area; an air rudder pushrod and a horn are in there, too! If you can finish something like this, you're ready for anything!

▲ This modeler used a stock landing-gear blank and achieved additional float spread by bolting it even with the inboard edge of the float deck. The connection between the gear leg and the spreader was made with a fabricated "T" section, but a stock aluminum section could have been used. Notice the glassed-over wooden deck plate embedded in the float.

▲ These pull/pull water-rudder cables have been reversed by threading the cables through swept brass tubing sections that are soldered to the rear music-wire gear legs. Proctor multi-strand leader wire is coated, so it doesn't bind. This system eliminates the complexity of pulleys, and line tension is less critical.

▶ This single-shaft, tail-mounted drop rudder is driven by two opposing nylon control horns mounted on the air rudder. It's difficult to see, but the shaft holder is screwed into the fuselage's underside, making the whole unit easily removable for land conversions. Single, aft, water rudders should be submerged only when the model is at rest

▲ The nose-wheel gear wire on this setup has been bent 90 degrees, flattened, and drilled to accept a metal clevis that drives a steel strand cable to a single stern-mounted water rudder. Music-wire float gear is attached to the fuselage's bottom with nylon hold-downs and wood screws. To convert this to a land system, drop the float system and screw in the trike gear.

Floatplane Conversions and Gear

This modeler clipped off his nose-wheel-gear wire and added a second swing arm. Stock aluminum gear blanks are attached with cap screws and blind nuts. One of the cap screws is also a pushrod hold-down.

▲ This is a good way to drive water rudders off the air-rudder servo. A threaded rod with ball links pushes an L-shaped music-wire shaft that penetrates the fuselage floor. Many modelers simply run another flexible pushrod through the fuselage, down a rear gear leg, and out to the stern of the float.

▲ Here's the other half of the servo-driven down shaft. The sha__ is housed in a brass tube and terminates at a swing arm that soldered to a wheel collar. The multi-strand Sullivan thrott__ cable controls the water rudders. An extra ⅛-inch ply plate is a__ you need to reinforce the fuselage's bottom for float-gear a__ tachment, because fore and aft gear spread the load.

▼ To make a rubber bow, cut the piece you need out of a rubber mallet with a band saw. The bumper was secured to the float with silicone. The heavy rubber also served as a needed nose weight in this application.

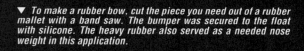

CHRISTEN HUSKY

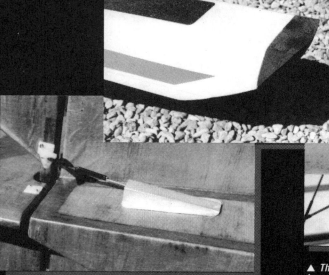

▲ Aluminum flashing was used to fabricate this L-shaped cable standoff. Two screws hold the standoff in place, and a rubber gasket prevents leaking on this built-up float. The dark circle is a piece of inner tube that was glued with contact cement over a deck inspection hole. The rubber cover can be peeled off and re-installed.

▲ Sometimes, water can enter the fuselage through pushrod exit slots. Make a spray deflector out of light aluminum flashing material and attach the shield with silicone. Aluminum flashing is available through builders' supply outlets. One small roll could last a whole club for a lifetime!

▲ This view highlights an "N" strut hard point on the fuselage of a Byron Husky. A remote on/off switch is located just above the plane's logo. The one-piece strut tab was bolted to a bulkhead bracket inside the fuselage. The modeler has burnished the gear legs with a swirl pattern—nice touch!

Note: for information about Sullivan Products, contact Swenson Specialtie__
P.O. Box 663, 2895 Estat__ Ave., Pinol__, CA 94564

MANY TIMES, I've been asked how hard it is to fly off water. A surprising number of modelers seem to think that there must be some magic involved, but I actually find it much easier than flying off land. My first R/C model was a deBolt Live Wire Champion that was powered by a Cox 14 and guided by an Orbit single-channel radio with a Bonner escapement (circa 1959). I've flown off a few runways in my time, but since my first flight off water in 1984, I've been almost exclusively a float flier. Consider this: when you land on a lake, you have more than 50 acres. How many runways have that much room?

From time to time, I hear people say that water is as hard as a brick. Last time I drank some it seemed pretty soft! The point is that as you go faster, water gets "harder." My planes have taken off, stalled and gone straight in, cartwheeling through the water—and behold!—not a scratch. I've yet to get a water scratch on one of my planes! If you keep your speed down, you'll suffer little damage in a crash.

When I talk to fellow fliers at meets, they ask all kinds of questions about the peculiarities of flying boats; they especially want to know how to make the landing gear work and how to keep water out. This article addresses these questions and, I hope, answers *your* questions about flying boats and amphibians.

by Air, Land, or Sea

by BILL PRICE

Amphibian and Flying Boat Set-Up and Operation

LANDING GEAR

Making amphibious landing gear is a tricky project. The key is to avoid anything that will work through or become detached from the hull and allow water to enter. I designed my amphibians so that their landing mechanisms are mounted on the outside of the fuselage in the wheel wells, which are built into the hull. Only the mounting bolts and air lines go through the hull, and the holes can be sealed with silicone glue.

Designing the landing gear and the fuselage will always be easier if you tackle the landing gear first, the wheel wells second, and then design the fuselage to accept the assembly. If you look at the drawings of the Albatross landing gear, you'll see that if the wheel well isn't designed and installed correctly, it simply won't work.

When I began to design amphibious landing gear, it soon became quite obvious that there's not a lot of "off-the-shelf"

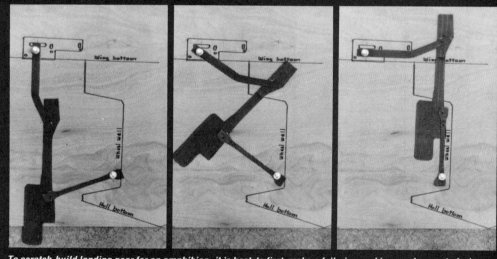

The construction of amphibian landing gear consists of basically simple parts, but component placement, arm bends and lengths are critical. These two views of the Albatross gear can be applied to many amphibious models for fabricating scratch-built retract units.

To scratch-build landing gear for an amphibian, it's best to first make a full-size working mock-up out of plywood and cardboard. Here, the Grumman Albatross landing gear sequence is checked in model form. (See text.)

hardware from which to choose. This necessitates either designing the gear from scratch, or using parts of existing gear hardware to get the job done. A landing-gear system has two basic components: the load-carrying mechanism and the power-actuation system. I rejected jack-screw systems because of the tremendous amount of work involved and because they're very heavy.

I watched others use the servo-actuated type. With this gear, there isn't usually enough room in the retractable gear area to mount servos; there are all kinds of goofy angles to deal with; and, as always, water is a problem. I didn't put servos in my PBY's wings because of the radio interference associated with running long servo leads to the wing tips. My only alternative was a pneumatically operated landing-gear system. It provides a good deal of water resistance; requires only one or two air lines to actuate; and, in the case of the Spring Air system, provides an automatic extension if pressure is lost.

Next, I designed and built the prototypes. After "sketching around" for a while, it occurred to me that I should make wood-and-cardboard models of my ideas. First, I drew a full-size cross-section of the fuselage on a piece of 1/8-inch plywood. Next, I drew the wheel (actual size), the axle and the lower strut on a piece of cardboard. I then cut 1/2-inch-wide cardboard strips to the length I thought the pivot arms would be, and I used thumbtacks to pin the strips onto the fuselage's profile in the approximate places where they would be on a full-size aircraft. At the points where the arms join the lower strut, I inserted the thumbtacks from the bottom so that the tack's heads would slide on the plywood.

The photos show the setup that I made for the Albatross gear. This is quick to make, gives you a scale-like model of the system, and all that needs to be done to determine the dimensions is to measure from thumb tack to thumb tack for the

part lengths. I machined articulating joints as shown in the isometric drawing, and then I silver-soldered them onto 5/32-inch piano wire to make the struts. I'm currently working on a 9-foot PBY, and the scale landing gear will be powered by Robart air cylinders.

ABOUT AMPHIBIANS

A flying boat is just that. The fuselage is usually shaped like a boat, at least in the front. Another component of the hull is the step, which is usually located near the CG to provide hydroplaning capabilities and the ability to rotate for liftoff. Be-

cause the hull is in the water, it's very important to seal it. My remedy is very sophisticated: I place a sponge under a rubber band that's fastened to the bottom of the hull *on* the CG. Imagine my terror when I flew one of my first PBYs with a half-pint of water sloshing around inside the hull. When I pulled the nose up, the water ran to the back, and it became tail-heavy. When I pointed the nose down, the water ran forward and it became nose-heavy. I was all over the sky trying to control pitch!

Another little problem can occur if you have water inside the fuselage: it can wet

PIVOT D
PIVOT B
PIVOT D
PIVOT C
PIVOT A
PIVOT A
PIVOT C
PIVOT B

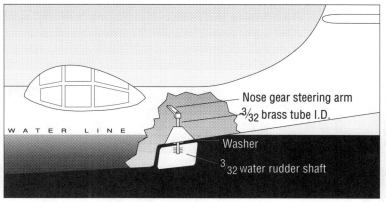

Nose gear steering arm
$3/32$ brass tube I.D.

Washer

$3/32$ water rudder shaft

WATER LINE

Water rudder details for out-of-the-water tail-section hulls like the one on the Consolidated PBY.

a connector and cause the servo to shut down. I once had to land my PBY with rudder only because the aileron connector was wet. Fortunately, when it quit, the aileron's control was in neutral. It's very handy to have a $3/6$-inch hole drilled somewhere above the water line so that you can drain water out without having to remove the wing or hatches.

WATERPROOFING

To keep water out of the hull, run a line of silicone glue around the surfaces to be sealed, put wax paper on the bottom part, and bolt the two pieces together. This will make a custom-fit seal that can be improved after the glue has dried if you put a thin film of petroleum jelly on the join.

I install water rudders on all of my amphibians, and I construct them as shown in the drawing. When I build a flying boat, I always waterproof all the surfaces. As an amphibian accelerates, it rotates its nose up as it gets up onto step. This brings the tail down, and quite a bit of spray can go up over it. Be sure to seal

FLYING

Landing amphibians isn't difficult. The PBY should be landed with just a little power. It makes the controls more effective, especially the elevator and rudder. Hold the aircraft just off the water until near the stall; then, holding full up-elevator, cut the power and let it settle onto the water.

With the Albatross, as soon as it touches the water, release the elevator to neutral to avoid "porpoising." The Canadair needs 15 to 20 percent more power. The Canadair is an extremely efficient flying machine, but its boxy fuselage and large engine cowls, nacelles and

level. This is the only real trick to flying an amphibian rather than a "land" plane, and it's only a concern during the first part of the takeoff run, because as speed picks up, the floats tend to skip off the water and the wing keeps itself level.

I was pleased to find that flying twins wasn't nearly as difficult as I had imagined. The biggest problem is just plain old intimidation. If you follow a few flying rules, a twin can live a long time. I put 55 flights on my first PBY before I retired it. Two cautions about props: wooden ones will be destroyed instantly if they hit water spray; and three-blade props are inef-

Canadair CL-215 taxiing to shore.

Canadair CL-215 taxiing out of the water.

the edges of the MonoKote well, and overlap the seams at least $1/4$ inch.

Test your hull in the bathtub to ensure that it's sealed. I've found that when I join fiberglass hull halves, the bond tape tends to suck resin out of the joint, and this causes leaks. Sometimes, these leaks are a pain because the water enters at one point and exits to the inside of the hull at another point. To prevent this, run a small line of resin along the joint so it fills the crack, let it cure, and then add the bonding tape with resin. After you've finished water flying, be sure to spray the retractable landing-gear system with WD-40 to prevent rusting and corrosion of the gear parts.

tail group cause drag. Without power, this machine comes down! The Canadair's bow is more blunt than that on the PBY and the Albatross, and it doesn't skip off the water as easily as the other planes. Keep feeding in up-elevator until the plane sinks onto the water; keep the elevator in the up position and the nose high. If the plane is allowed to come down too quickly, it will plant its nose straight into the water.

Takeoffs are slightly different in that the wings should be kept level on the takeoff run to prevent the wing floats from digging into the waves. It takes concentration to keep the plane going in the proper direction while keeping the wheels

ficient on these twin amphibians. It's easiest to get up on step with 9x6 two-blade props, because they cut through the water spray much better. The Albatross won't get up on step with three-blade props, but it jumps right up with 9x6 two-blades and ASP .46s.

I was always intrigued by the PBY Catalina, and after I had built one, I went on to explore other amphibians. It seems that every week I hear about—or see—another amphibian. The subjects for modeling these flying boats are nearly endless. So many planes and so little time (sigh)! ∎

ROGALLO WING

by STEVE STAPLES

The author salvaged his Air Scout by adding a Rogallo Wing. This easy-to-control, flex-wing airplane flies, climbs and dives at about the same speed!

A REN'T BUILDING and flying model airplanes supposed to fun? I think so, and like so many modelers in Little Rock, AR, I enjoy showing up at the flying field with extraordinary flying machines. The flexwing—or Rogallo wing—has been around since the '40s and was one of the first wing designs used for modern hang gliders. Hanging a model airplane under one of these wings isn't really a new concept, but it *is* fun.

WINGING IT

With a main wing structure of only three spars and a brace, the Rogallo wing is an easy project. I volunteered my old Ace Air Scout—with its O.S. .20 and 3-channel radio—as the main sled. First, I built a base and pylon mount from ¼-inch scrap plywood, although ⅜-inch would have been better. I built the mount

It may look ungainly, but this is a very efficient configuration that's easily adapted to most high-wing models.

to fit the Air Scout's wing saddle, so I didn't have to modify the plane, and I can change wings in a few minutes.

My greatest concern was finding suitable material for the wing spars. Wooden dowels flex too much, as did the plastic material I found. I decided to use aluminum arrow shafts in two sizes. By telescoping them to the appropriate length and joining them with epoxy, I had exactly the spars I needed.

The shafts are secured to a triangular wooden nose block. (A clamp-and-bolt setup would work equally well.) The center shaft literally becomes a keel, while the two on the outside act as outriggers. Approximately a quarter of the length of the keel back from the nose block, I mounted an arrowshaft cross-brace to hold the outriggers at the proper angle. I then made an aluminum clamp with which I bolt the "keel" to the plywood pylon.

By now, you should be

getting the idea. The parameters for this project aren't strict: you can use almost any material to cover the framework; just remember that the wing area is three to four times that of a conventional wing. I chose "rip-stop" nylon, which was originally developed for racing-yacht sails and is almost indestructible!

With the help of my wife, a sewing machine and some careful measuring, I covered the wing in about 1 hour. If you cut the nylon with a hot soldering iron, it should fray very little. I used nylon thread to sew all the seams. The covering material should be slack between the spars. (This was the first wing I'd ever built for which the covering didn't have to be

taut.) After pulling on the covering, I attached the cross-brace. When everything was assembled, I used braided nylon for shroud lines. Although this works well enough, it seems to stretch too much, and I plan to change to C/L braided-steel cable.

OFF TO THE FIELD

With the assembly ready to be attached to the victim—I mean, to the plane!—it was time for a field trip. The angle of incidence was set at approximately 15 degrees; the weather was perfect; and the crowd—refraining

and attitude; at idle, the other controls were almost nonexistent. After I had adjusted to these quirks, touch-and-gos were easy and amazing. Hovering into a 5 to 10mph breeze is just a matter of tweaking the throttle, and I can make blazing, 10mph flybys.

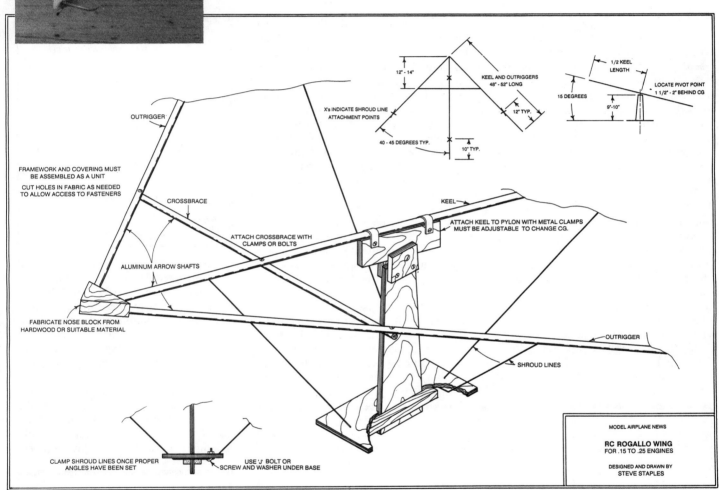

12" - 14"

KEEL AND OUTRIGGERS
48" - 52" LONG

12" TYP.

X's INDICATE SHROUD LINE
ATTACHMENT POINTS

40 - 45 DEGREES TYP.

10" TYP.

1/2 KEEL
LENGTH

15 DEGREES

9"-10"

LOCATE PIVOT POINT
1 1/2" - 2" BEHIND CG

OUTRIGGER

FRAMEWORK AND COVERING MUST
BE ASSEMBLED AS A UNIT

CUT HOLES IN FABRIC AS NEEDED
TO ALLOW ACCESS TO FASTENERS

CROSSBRACE

KEEL

ATTACH KEEL TO PYLON WITH METAL CLAMPS
MUST BE ADJUSTABLE TO CHANGE CG.

ATTACH CROSSBRACE WITH
CLAMPS OR BOLTS

ALUMINUM ARROW SHAFTS

FABRICATE NOSE BLOCK FROM
HARDWOOD OR SUITABLE MATERIAL

OUTRIGGER

SHROUD LINES

CLAMP SHROUD LINES ONCE PROPER
ANGLES HAVE BEEN SET

USE 'J' BOLT OR
SCREW AND WASHER UNDER BASE

MODEL AIRPLANE NEWS

RC ROGALLO WING
FOR .15 TO .25 ENGINES

DESIGNED AND DRAWN BY
STEVE STAPLES

from comment—hung back politely in awe. The initial flight was a success!

A hand-launch at full throttle gave a surprisingly good climb-out, and rudder and elevator control were mushy, but adequate. The throttle proved to be the main control of altitude

The Rogallo wing can be made quickly for very little money, so if you're tired of your plane, try a flex-wing. It's fun—and isn't that what our hobby is all about? ∎

THE
MECHANICS OF LANDING GEAR

MUSIC WIRE VS. SHEET METAL-BOTH SIDES OF THE COIN

by JIM STOCKE

LANDING-GEAR MECHANICS are one of the most misunderstood aspects of R/C airplane design. During my 20 years in the hobby, I've seen landing gear ripped from fuselages countless times; modelers repair them, only to have them ripped out again on the next hard landing. Apparently, there's a lack of understanding about just what we're asking these legs to do.

Whether the aircraft is a tail-dragger or has tricycle gear, most of the trouble is with the main gear. The nose wheel is less susceptible to problems, so I'll confine my discussion to the main gear, of which there are two types: music wire and aluminum. (Retracts have wire legs and a metal or hard-plastic mount, so they're a combination of wire and aluminum, but they closely resemble aluminum in their mechanical behavior when landing.)

My first R/C airplane was the Goldberg Senior Falcon, which I built in 1967. Its main gear and nose gear were made of 5/32-inch-diameter wire. The main gear used the torsion-bar principle, which I thought very clever at the time (and still do). During landing or takeoff, the gear flexes in two directions. The part of the wire that's embedded in the fuselage is tortionally deflected (twisted). In addition, the wire is also deflected vertically along the exposed length that extends from the fuselage. (Figure 1 shows this type of landing gear; Figure 2 shows how this gear flexes on landing.) As long as the degree of bending is below the yield point of the steel in the wire, the gear retains its shape. We all know that in practice, however, the gear tends to lean somewhat rearward after several landings (depending on how smooth they were). We also know that on a less-than-perfect landing, the gear could flex and bend until the fuselage literally touches the ground. The gear would, of course, take a new, static position, but it could be bent back to its original shape, and, if we're lucky, there won't be any damage to the airplane.

I've had many less-than-perfect landings, but I've never ripped the gear from an airplane equipped with wire landing

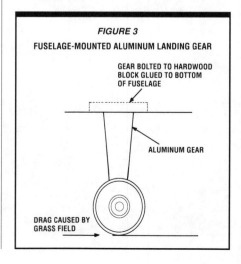

FIGURE 2
SIDE VIEW OF FUSELAGE-MOUNTED WIRE GEAR

DIRECTION OF FLIGHT

GEAR BENDS BEFORE MOUNT BREAKS

DRAG CAUSED BY GRASS FIELD

gear. On a low-wing airplane, I've bent wing-mounted gear far enough backward to push the wheels into the wing's bottom covering and, once, even through the top!

Enter the aluminum landing gear, which mounts rigidly to the bottom of the fuselage, as shown in Figure 3. These gear readily flex vertically, but not longitudinally. On a hard landing, they rely on strength to prevent gear-mount breakage. The problem is this: on a hard landing, the impact exerts high forces on the landing-gear system. The forces build up rapidly in longitudinal and vertical directions, es-

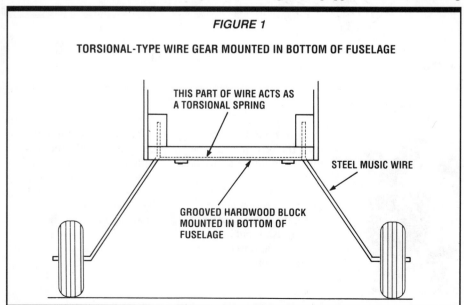

FIGURE 1

TORSIONAL-TYPE WIRE GEAR MOUNTED IN BOTTOM OF FUSELAGE

THIS PART OF WIRE ACTS AS A TORSIONAL SPRING

STEEL MUSIC WIRE

GROOVED HARDWOOD BLOCK MOUNTED IN BOTTOM OF FUSELAGE

FIGURE 3
FUSELAGE-MOUNTED ALUMINUM LANDING GEAR

GEAR BOLTED TO HARDWOOD BLOCK GLUED TO BOTTOM OF FUSELAGE

ALUMINUM GEAR

DRAG CAUSED BY GRASS FIELD

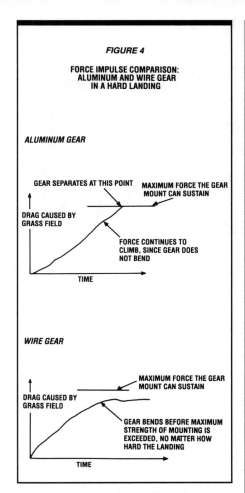

FIGURE 4

FORCE IMPULSE COMPARISON: ALUMINUM AND WIRE GEAR IN A HARD LANDING

ALUMINUM GEAR

GEAR SEPARATES AT THIS POINT

MAXIMUM FORCE THE GEAR MOUNT CAN SUSTAIN

DRAG CAUSED BY GRASS FIELD

FORCE CONTINUES TO CLIMB, SINCE GEAR DOES NOT BEND

TIME

WIRE GEAR

MAXIMUM FORCE THE GEAR MOUNT CAN SUSTAIN

DRAG CAUSED BY GRASS FIELD

GEAR BENDS BEFORE MAXIMUM STRENGTH OF MOUNTING IS EXCEEDED, NO MATTER HOW HARD THE LANDING

TIME

pecially on grass fields. Sometimes, the the mount, which is weaker than the gear itself, can't resist these forces and rips out the bottom of the fuselage.

This isn't true of wire gears. The forces build up rapidly, but only to a point where the gear begins to bend and twist. In other words, the maximum force the landing-gear mount sees is equal to the force necessary to bend the gear out of the way. This usually isn't enough to break the mount. Figure 4 shows a force/time diagram that illustrates this principle using both wire and aluminum gear assemblies.

I've seen millions (well, maybe hundreds...or would you believe dozens?) of aluminum gear fail at the mount. A few years ago, at Byron's "Striking Back," at least 70 percent of the gear broke on landing during very gusty conditions—honest: 70 percent. Most of these were retracts that appeared to have a shear pin to protect the mount and the gear, but several didn't, and the results were what you'd expect. This experience clearly showed the problems of a mount-rigidly-and-try-again approach, which, of course, always adds weight.

I watched a friend rip the gear off a Byron Glasair three times. After each disaster, he reinforced the mount, only to have it fail again. I saw his plane for sale

in the local hobby shop with its gear reinforced beyond your wildest dreams. I bet the gear will be ripped out again—and take a large portion of the fuselage with it. When I try to explain to my flying buddies what the mechanics of the system are, most simply don't believe me. Rejection of my explanation has been unanimous, and I don't understand why. Some R/Cers even haughtily proclaim that they *never* have hard landings. Well, I bet they don't fly very much; unless you're a Chip Hyde, you have a hard landing once in a while.

Lest the makers of aluminum gear string me up from the highest tree, I must make a few very important points. The strength-to-size ratio is very favorable in planes up to approximately 5 or 6 pounds (and this covers the majority of craft flown). Smaller planes can survive most hard landings with their aluminum gear intact, but gear on the larger planes have problems. The strength-to-size ratio is less favorable, and you see many gear failures on these larger airplanes.

So, what to do? After I broke the gear on my 1/3-scale Rousch Laser for the second time, I mounted it on a brass plate, which bends enough to reduce the force below the "rip-out level." (Figure 5 shows this design.) Since I installed the plate, the

gear on my Laser hasn't broken, even though I've had a few rough landings.

This plate design truly absorbs energy by bending the plate to which the gear is mounted, rather than transferring high-impact loads directly to the structure (as is the case with gear mounted directly to the plane). When the plate is bent, though, you must remove it and re-bend or replace it, but this sure beats repairing a ripped-out mount. The plate shouldn't be too heavy, or the forces will overcome the strength of the mount. The Laser weighed 16 pounds, and the brass plate was only 1/16 inch thick. Smaller aircraft should probably have an aluminum plate that's approximately 1/64 inch thick, or even thinner. Some experimentation is necessary here. Start with a very thin plate, because you've nothing to lose if the plate bends too much. If you start a plate that's too thick, you risk breaking your gear mount. It would be even better to apply something like R/C car shock absorbers to landing-gear systems. These shocks are real energy absorbers, and I can visualize beautifully smooth landings with proper use of them in R/C landing-gear design. Wire gear store landing energy because they're springs, and this is what makes for a bouncy landing...well, better bouncy than broken!

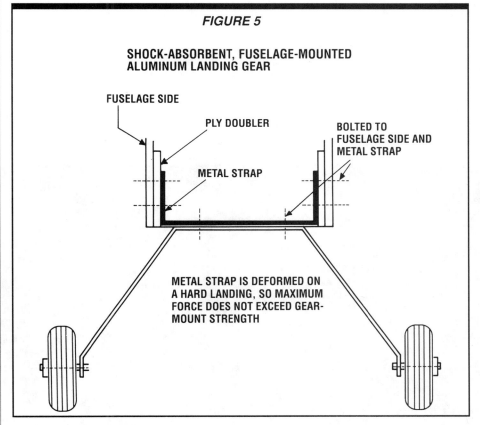

FIGURE 5

SHOCK-ABSORBENT, FUSELAGE-MOUNTED ALUMINUM LANDING GEAR

FUSELAGE SIDE

PLY DOUBLER

BOLTED TO FUSELAGE SIDE AND METAL STRAP

METAL STRAP

METAL STRAP IS DEFORMED ON A HARD LANDING, SO MAXIMUM FORCE DOES NOT EXCEED GEAR-MOUNT STRENGTH

SERVO-TRAY INSTALLATION

The stuff that stops the leaks also damps the vibrations!

by MIKE LEE

I'VE DISCUSSED sevo installation in fiberglass fuselages by using plywood trays and silicone adhesive. (Silicone adheres aggressively to fiberglass and provides excellent vibration-damping for the radio gear. It also makes it very easy to remove the tray.) Now I'll tell you how to install a tray in a wooden fuselage using the same materials.

Wooden fuselages have several advantages over fiberglass ones: they damp vibration well, they absorb sound much better, and they're stiffer. On the other hand, they take longer to build, they must be carefully aligned for true flight, and they may weigh more than a fiberglass fuselage, depending on how well it has been assembled and sanded. Even though (in pattern, at least) fiberglass models are a little more common, there are many wooden ones out there, and in the sport category, wood is dominant.

Mounting a servo tray in a wooden fuselage takes only slightly longer than mounting one in a fiberglass fuselage. Start by fitting the tray into the fuselage. Make sure that there's a gap of approximately $1/16$ inch between the sides of the tray and the fuselage, and mark the tray's position on the fuselage sides with a pencil. Attach two pieces of $3/8$-inch triangle-stock balsa to the sides of the fuselage with CA. Position them so that they lie just below the tray's final position.

When they're securely in place, run a generous amount of silicone adhesive over the top of the tri-stock balsa. Put the tray immediately into position, and press it down firmly, seating it into the silicone. *Don't* let it touch the tri-stock. When the tray is in position, run another bead of silicone adhesive along the line where the tray meets the fuselage sides, and allow the adhesive to cure overnight.

GYROSCOPIC EFFECT AND SHUCKED BLADES...

Many pilots use the new, soft motor mounts to minimize vibration and noise. The mounts work well for this, but there's at least one problem with them, and it concerns the prop.

Mac Patterson of Mac's Models in San Jose, CA, has noticed something about the gyroscopic effect of the prop on a soft engine mount and the flexing that occurs. Several APC props have lost a blade in flight for some unknown reason, but their aircraft had one thing in common—a beam-style soft mount (manufacturer unknown)—and their pilots all reported that blade separation occurred when the aircraft were accelerating and pitching hard through a maneuver. (This action is common in FAI flight; most of us fly at half-throttle during level flight, yet throttle-up when pitching up to vertical.)

You can reproduce this effect by spinning a gyro or a vertical bicycle wheel. Hold the spinning wheel like a propeller in straight and level flight. Now, attempt to tilt it sideways; it will resist. This is a gyroscopic effect. The prop on your engine behaves similarly; it resists the movement when the plane pitches its nose upward or downward.

I saw a prime example of this at the 1982 Lincoln Nationals when Dean Copeland flew his CAP 21 from the runway during a scale flight. His takeoff maneuver included a snap roll, and when he did it, his Quadra engine's crank-shaft snapped. The cause was determined to be the gyroscopic effect of the engine's flywheel resisting the changes in the angle at which the plane was flying.

That's interesting, but our engines don't have anywhere near the mass of a Quadra flywheel. Nevertheless, the APC prop is heavier than any other pattern prop on the market. The gyroscopic effect of any spinning object is a function of its mass and, to some degree, its rate of rotation. With the APC prop, a certain mount allows the engine to flex in a plane of movement that's highly resistant to the gyroscopic effect created by the prop. This happens when the aircraft is made to pitch upward, and the resistance is amplified under acceleration. The result is catastrophic prop failure.

Wow! You'd better accelerate first and then pitch up. It works for me; I haven't popped one yet!

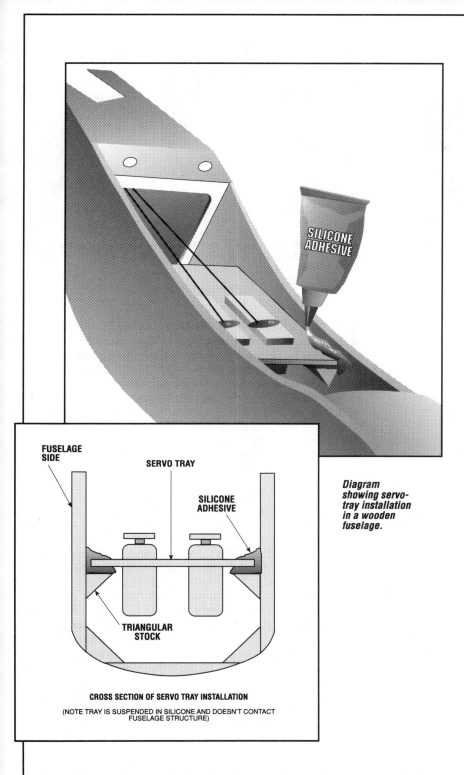

Diagram showing servo-tray installation in a wooden fuselage.

FUSELAGE SIDE

SERVO TRAY

SILICONE ADHESIVE

TRIANGULAR STOCK

CROSS SECTION OF SERVO TRAY INSTALLATION

(NOTE TRAY IS SUSPENDED IN SILICONE AND DOESN'T CONTACT FUSELAGE STRUCTURE)

You now have a vibration-damping tray that won't come out unless you want it to. (To remove the tray, simply slit the silicone along the corner joint with a sharp razor blade, and pull it up.) The best thing about this type of installation is that you can put all the servos into the tray, position the tray fore and aft until the servos are where you want them, then let the silicone set.

If you're concerned about whether this installation is rigid enough for the servos, don't worry. The force applied to the servos as they control the flying surfaces is resisted by the tray, which is securely attached to the fuselage. The fuselage will crumble like an accordion before the tray will break loose! ■

Airframe Alignment

by MIKE LEE

The Robart incidence meter is used to measure the wing incidence on this Beetle. Ensuring proper wing alignment is a must for achieving a straight-flying aircraft.

No question!
Straight birds fly
better; here's how.

That small, dark block inside the fuselage is the wing-incidence adjuster in the Beetle. Absolute alignment can be achieved using these devices, and they can also help to correct the airframe for incidence of the wing to the engine or to the stab.

The incidence meter at work again, this time on the horizontal stab. Before permanently gluing a stab into place, make sure that it's set correctly relative to the wing. This is one way to do it.

ON A PATTERN bird, a little twisting or warping will cause the plane to change its flight characteristics as its speed changes. This is true of any model, but the effect is more pronounced on faster-flying pattern models. Precise alignment is the ultimate solution to this problem.

The most important "tool" for building a true wing is the building surface, which must be flat, uncluttered and big enough to hold the entire wing. I bought a piece of Formica counter top (which is very flat and "bulletproof") at a local hardware store for about $2 a foot. Many builders use a wooden door core. Whatever you use, make sure it's twist-free and level.

For the actual construction of the wing, it's wise to invest in some building tools. Many modelers use a wing jig to align the ribs and hold them while building, but this isn't absolutely necessary. The tools I value most during build-up are a straightedge and building triangles. These enable me to keep the edges straight and the ribs perpendicular when they should be. On foam wings, I use the ruler to measure the chord angle of the tips of the cores compared with that at their roots; this comparison tells me whether the core is warped. When the build-up is completed, I move on to bigger and better things.

One of my most useful tools is the incidence meter. (Robart* has been offering one for years; mine is 10 years old.) First, I put it to work on the wing. I block up the wing on sandbags and then weight it down with more bags until I know it won't move easily. With the incidence meter, I measure from the wing root to the tip once more. When I'm satisfied with both wing halves, I mount the wings to the fuselage.

My Pattern Tek Beetle has a plug-in wing, and both halves share a common tube spar. For alignment to the fuselage, pins are used at the leading edge of the wing-root saddle. One of the photos shows that these pins are adjustable, so they provide the ability to correct wing halves that may be misaligned. Used on both wings, the adjusters can be used to change the entire wing incidence in relation to the fuselage, stab, or engine thrust line. This feature allows the precise alignment we're seeking, and even though it's no longer variable once the proper setting has been achieved, it's worth its weight in gold the first time you use it.

To arrive at the correct wing-to-stab incidence, builders usually mount the wing first and then align the stab. This is particularly true with a fiberglass bird, because the wing saddle is already molded in, and changing it leaves an unsightly

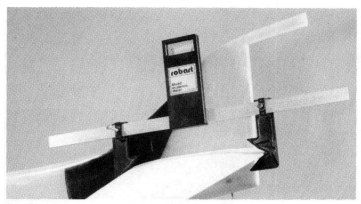

The Beetle features an adjustable stab, an alternate method of ensuring proper stab-to-wing alignment. You might only use it once, but that one time pays off in big dividends!

Sighting down the fuselage from the tail is the way to check for twists in the fuse. You can also check for the horizontal alignment of the stab and wing from this point of view. The alignment must be correct for the plane to fly correctly.

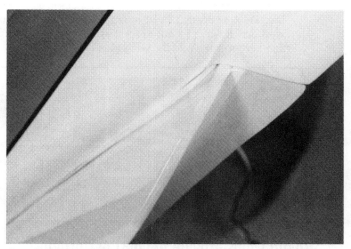

This view of the wing-to-fuselage joint shows how the wing saddle had to be shimmed to correct the incidence of the wing to the stab. Such measures make for an unsightly joint, at best.

This is the most difficult type of horizontal stab to align: the anhedral stab. In this case, the tail belongs to the prototype Excelsior. Misalignment here will cause a multitude of problems in flight.

mess. If you don't believe me, look at the photo of the prototype Excelsior, which required a wing-incidence correction of 3 degrees relative to the stab. Yes, I mounted the stab first, and the wing second. Don't make the same mistake! Sandbag the fuselage with the wing mounted to it, measure the wing incidence, and mount the stab to the tail in accordance with the plans, making sure the incidence is correct.

The Beetle has another lovely alignment feature that helps to deal with this problem: its adjustable stab allows changes in the stab incidence. A small screwdriver slot on the underside of the plane permits the stab to be adjusted easily when required. This feature also allows the stab to be removed. As you can see, this is a rather versatile aircraft! If your bird doesn't have this feature, ensure that the alignment is correct the first time, or be prepared for less-than-optimum performance.

Now for the fuselage. Of course, a wooden fuselage allows no room for error. After it has been built, it's extremely difficult—if not impossible—to correct twists or bends. There are several fuselage-building jigs on the market, and these are an immense help in building the fuselage straight.

On a fiberglass fuse, it's easier to correct a slight problem. While using a heat gun, I twist or bend the fuselage in the opposite direction, but the results aren't wholly satisfactory. The fuselage will usually have a dent where the fiberglass has been compressed by the opposing twist. The fuselage is straight, but not cosmetically pleasing.

For engine alignment, I usually use the plans as my starting point for any variations from zero in thrust settings. On a fiberglass bird, most manufacturers "mold-in" the correct thrust settings by getting you to align the engine-spinner backplate with the fuselage spinner ring. This works most of the time, but I always allow extra distance between the spinner plate and the spinner ring, just in case an adjustment is required.

When the airframe has been completed and aligned to your satisfaction, the only items still to be inspected are the flying surfaces. Elevators, ailerons and rudders are easy to warp, particularly when you use an iron-on covering. Just be careful to maintain the straight-and-flat look.

At any rate, whichever model you're building, take time to ensure the bird is straight. It's essential for consistent performance.

*Here's the address of the company mentioned in this article:
Robart Manufacturing, P.O. Box 1247, St. Charles, IL 60174.   ■

Measure 1 inch in and drill one ¹¹/₆₄-inch clearance hole in each end of block 2. Using a ³/₁₆-inch drill, countersink the holes ½ inch.

Drill one ¹¹/₆₄-inch clearance hole in the center of each block.

For each block set, lay block 3 over block 2, mark the location of the hole, and drill a starter hole in block 2.

by LEE KUFCHAK

WHETHER SCRATCH-BUILDING or building from a kit, it isn't easy to build a straight wing, and a wing jig really helps. I've been using the one described here for more than 15 years, and it's as accurate and easy to use today as when I first made it.

Although my workbench is made of ³/₄-inch plywood, over time, it might have sagged or warped without my noticing, so, to ensure that the jig is as straight as possible, I attached the jig blocks to a piece of pressboard shelving. This means that I can move the jig, with the wing attached, off my workbench when I want to set it aside (even on end). I can then work on another project while the wing glue is setting.

Place one block 2 at the end of the particle board, then mark and drill two ⁵/₆₄-inch pilot holes in the board. Using two screws (4), attach the block to the particle board. Repeat for the other block.

BUILD A WING JIG FOR LESS THAN $5!

Straight wings provide the best performance. Here's how to build 'em that way!

You'll need the following parts to assemble your jig:
1. Two 36-inch-long, ¹/₄-inch-diameter steel rods (drill rod is best, but music wire also works well); cost, approximately $3.25.
2. Two 12-inch lengths of 1¹/₂-inch-square wood (pine or fir).
3. Two 12-inch lengths of wood (pine or fir), approximately ¹/₂ inch thick and 1¹/₂ inches wide.
4. Four no. 8 by 1¹/₂-inch round-head wood screws.
5. Two no. 8 by 1¹/₄ inch round-head wood screws.
6. One 36-inch length of 1x12-inch *straight* particle-board shelving; cost, approximately $1.25.

Cut the wooden blocks (nos. 2 and 3) out of a knot-free piece of 2x4 using a hand-operated circular saw with a rip fence. Measure each (2) to ensure their sides are parallel. If you don't have a saw, your local lumber yard can supply you with stock of the right dimensions that you can cut to length. Don't buy wood that's less than 1¹/₂ inches square for block 2. You'll need the clearance under the wing ribs when you use the jig.

Before assembling your jig, paint the top of the particle board white. Using a permanent-ink pen, draw reference lines in a 2-inch grid. Take care to make *absolutely* sure the lines are square. These grid lines will be useful when you're assembling a wing.

Set the two rods (1) on the assembly, then, using one screw (5) each, attach block 3 to block 2. Tighten just enough to clamp the rods between the blocks.

The finished jig.

WING JIG

Cut one root rib and one tip-rib template out of plywood.

Clamp the rib blanks between the templates with bolts, then sand the rib blanks to match the templates. Cut openings for the spars as necessary.

Completed ribs.

Slide the ribs onto the rods, line up, and tighten upper blocks. Add the leading edge, trailing edge, and spars. After checking everything for alignment, glue into place. Add landing-gear blocks and sheeting, and your wing half is finished.

JIG USE

With your new wing jig assembled, the next step is to use it. Whether you're scratch-building or building from a kit, you use the jig in the same way. Drill two $^1/_4$-inch holes in each rib, slide the ribs onto the steel rods, then clamp the rods onto the jig by tightening the upper blocks. This holds the ribs perfectly square so that you can completely assemble the wing and add top and bottom sheeting without worrying about warping.

If you're scratch-building, cut root and tip rib templates from $^1/_8$-inch plywood. Draw a center line on the ribs, then carefully drill two $^1/_4$-inch holes in the templates. If you have a small model and are using $^3/_{16}$-inch rods, you obviously use a $^3/_{16}$-inch drill. Try to put the holes where they won't weaken the structure of the wing. I usually put one hole between the leading edge and spar, and the other approximately a quarter of the chord's width ahead of the trailing edge. Be sure the holes are the same distance apart on both the tip and root rib. This makes it easier to slide the finished ribs onto the rods.

Cut enough $^3/_{32}$-inch balsa blanks for one wing half, then lay one template over each blank and drill two holes to match the jig holes in the template. Use a sharpened piece of brass tube to drill holes in the rib blanks. Clamp the templates and ribs together with $^1/_4$-inch bolts (or $^3/_{16}$-inch bolts for $^3/_{16}$-inch rods) and sand the balsa ribs to the shape of the templates. Repeat this for the other wing, and you now have enough ribs.

If you are building a tapered wing as shown in the photos, you'll have to touch up the finished ribs with sandpaper to remove the sharp edge from the leading edge and sides of the ribs.

When building from a kit, clamp the ribs together and drill two holes for the rods as described. To ensure alignment on the jig, be sure the holes are in the same place on each rib.

Slide enough ribs for one half of the wing onto the steel rods, line up the rods with one of the reference lines on the particle board, then tighten the upper blocks. Mark the rib locations on the wing's leading and trailing edges, and pin or clamp them into place. Sight the ribs to ensure they're aligned with the reference lines, then glue the assembly together. Add leading-edge and trailing-edge sheeting as required. Don't add the center-section wing sheeting until after the wing has been joined and the dihedral braces are in place.

To work on the other side of the wing, loosen the upper blocks and turn them so that the rods can clear the blocks. Keeping the rods in the wing, turn the wing over, then tighten the upper blocks again. This way, you can work on both sides of the wing (even apply sheeting) without waiting for the glue to set.

Repeat for the other wing panel, and you've finished. Now you've built the jig and a warp-free wing; you'll probably never again build in any other way! ■

Make a
BUDGET ★ FLIER
Tail-Wheel Assembly

by BILL HAYWOOD

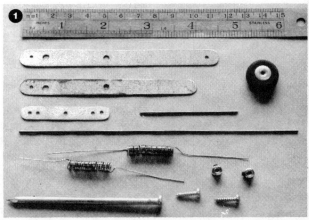

1. You'll need: a piece of 20-gauge sheet metal that's at least 4½ inches long and 2 inches wide (you'll use it to make two, 20-gauge leaf springs and one 20-gauge tiller arm); a suitable tail wheel; 1/16-inch music wire; 1/64-inch music wire (for tiller springs); a 3-inch nail; two mounting screws; two 1/16-inch wheel collars.

OFTEN, A MODELER will spend huge chunks of his spare time on building and finishing a beautiful aircraft. He will fit it with a good prop, scale wheels, a sturdy main landing gear and even wheel pants. But when he visits the local hobby shop in search of a scale, or scale-like, tail-wheel assembly, his real difficulties begin. Good, inexpensive tail-wheel assemblies of the correct size are very difficult to find, and he must usually either build one himself or screw a humdrum, awful-looking, plastic assembly onto the back of his model. No more! Build one of these state-of-the-art, tail-wheel assemblies for your next model—and all the others.

2. Cut two, 3/8-inch-wide strips out of the sheet metal; one strip should be 4½ inches long and the other, 4 inches long. Use the strips to make two leaf springs.

TAIL-WHEEL GEOMETRY

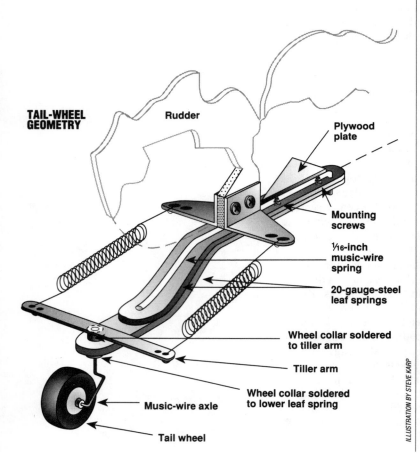

- Rudder
- Plywood plate
- Mounting screws
- 1/16-inch music-wire spring
- 20-gauge-steel leaf springs
- Wheel collar soldered to tiller arm
- Tiller arm
- Wheel collar soldered to lower leaf spring
- Music-wire axle
- Tail wheel

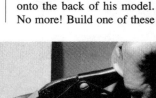 

3. Mark the positions of the four holes you'll need, and then center-punch them (see illustration). Drill two 1/8-inch holes (for the mounting screws) and two 1/16-inch holes—one for the tail-wheel axle and one to secure the central music-wire spring. 4. Put the sheet-metal strips (leaf springs) over a piece of wood, and then drill the holes. Make sure they're centered along the strips' length.

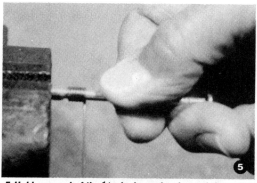
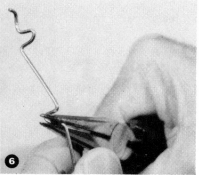

5. Hold one end of the 1/64-inch music wire and the nail in a vice, as shown, and make two tiller springs by tightly coiling the wire around the nail for about 1 inch. (To do this, you must first capture the music wire between the nail and the vice jaw.)   6. Bend the music-wire spring you just made as shown. The two bends will allow the spring to be held in place by the mounting screws.

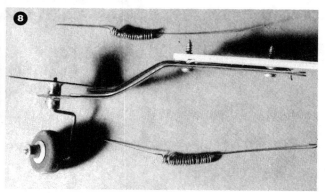
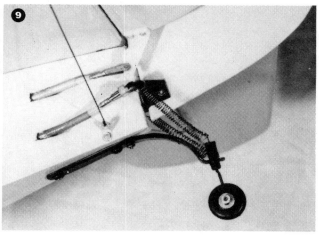

7. Here, the spring is held by the two mounting screws. 8. The finished tail-wheel assembly. Note how the music-wire spring protrudes through the front ends of the leaf springs. 9. A version of the completed tail-wheel assembly on a smaller plane.

The tail-wheel assembly described here is sturdy, good-looking and very easy to build. It takes very little time to make it, and you'll need only simple tools and materials that are probably already at hand. It can be built in almost any size, and another outstanding feature is its low cost.

Tail-wheel leaf springs are usually made out of spring steel, which is expensive, brittle, hard and difficult to work with; and most of us don't have the right tools or facilities to work with it. This tail-wheel assembly is made out of ordinary, 20-gauge, galvanized sheet metal, which can be cut and bent easily. This mild steel can be used only because 1/16-inch music wire is integral to the assembly. The wire is strong enough to support the model on the ground and flexible enough to cushion it when it lands. Don't leave out this most important component! The music wire is the secret to the success of this light, rugged, tail-wheel assembly! ∎

5
CONSTRUCTION—GLASS, FOAM AND COMPOSITES

Even as CAs and iron-on coverings revolution-ized model building in past years, foam, fiber-glass, laminates and carbon fiber are enabling us to build truer, stronger, lighter designs today. This section (and the "Building Secrets" section that follows it), covers several key techniques. If you want your models to look more like the prod-ucts of a NASA contractor and less like an old stick-and-tissue job, then read on.

QUESTION: WHY DO you need carbon-fiber rods? Answer: *flex!* Carbon fiber rods don't flex as much as other types of rods and cables. Therefore, carbon-fiber rods allow true elevator movement under pressure, i.e., the movement of the control surface isn't distorted by unwanted flexing in your control rod. Carbon-fiber rods also

Carbon fiber rods don't flex as much as other types of rods and cables.

reduce the possibility of flutter when your plane is flying at high speeds.

PUSHRODS
Yes, it's possible that you've been using carbon-fiber rods and haven't known it! For example, Dave Brown Products* offers pushrods that use carbon fiber. Aerospace Composite Products* makes carbon-fiber rods, both solid and hollow, in a large variety of useful sizes.

The most commonly used carbon-fiber rod is the hollow elevator pushrod

(see photo). There are a million-and-one ways to set up your control linkage system. Dave Brown Products offers a plastic plug that can be used to attach the metal-threaded pushrod connector(s) for either a straight single rod or a split pushrod elevator system. It's all included in the package. You could also epoxy a small length of dowel rod into one end of the hollow carbon-fiber rod and then drill a hole into which you can thread the metal-threaded pushrod wire (apply a thin coat of CA to the inside of the hole in the dowel to ensure that the threaded wire will be anchored firmly).

I prefer to use the new carbon-fiber pushrod method from Aero Sport Products*. This is set up for split elevators using a machined-aluminum support that guarantees both rods push straight and evenly—a hot setup!

PLUG-IN STABS
Carbon-fiber rods are also used frequently for plug-in stabs on pattern and 1/4-scale planes. You use a hollow carbon-fiber rod for fuselage and stab inserts, and slide a solid connecting rod into the hollow rods to anchor the whole assembly

The two outer carbon-fiber rods are hollow; the center rod is solid. Carbon-fiber rods are available in a wide variety of sizes.

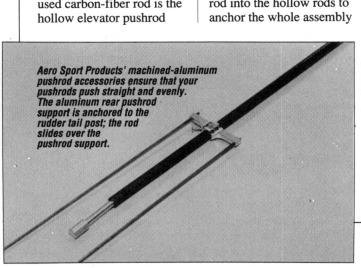

Aero Sport Products' machined-aluminum pushrod accessories ensure that your pushrods push straight and evenly. The aluminum rear pushrod support is anchored to the rudder tail post; the rod slides over the pushrod support.

Using Carbon-Fiber Rods
by GREG POPPEL & JOHN JUNDT

For better control and increased strength

Using Carbon-Fiber Rods

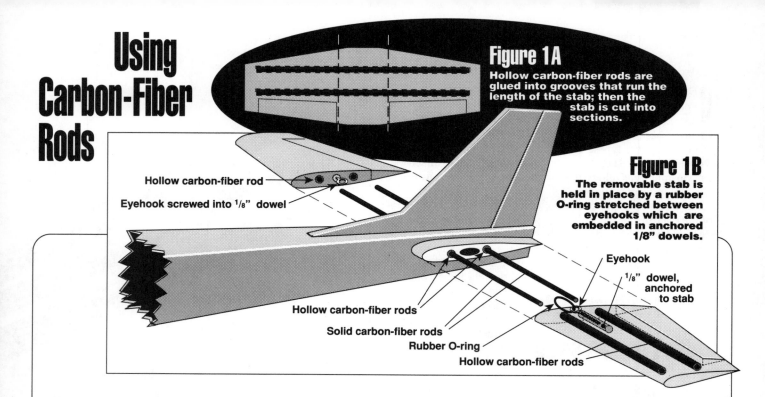

Figure 1A
Hollow carbon-fiber rods are glued into grooves that run the length of the stab; then the stab is cut into sections.

Figure 1B
The removable stab is held in place by a rubber O-ring stretched between eyehooks which are embedded in anchored 1/8" dowels.

Hollow carbon-fiber rod

Eyehook screwed into 1/8" dowel

Eyehook

1/8" dowel, anchored to stab

Hollow carbon-fiber rods

Solid carbon-fiber rods

Rubber O-ring

Hollow carbon-fiber rods

(Figure 1). Build the stab in one piece and use a router to rout out two grooves parallel with and about 20 percent of the chord from the leading and trailing edges. Lay a larger hollow rod in each groove and epoxy it into place (be careful not to get epoxy in the holes at the end of the carbon-fiber rods!). Fill in any remaining space in the groove with a solid piece of lightweight balsa, and sand to shape.

Next, cut out the stab center (the piece that will nest in the fuselage) with a band saw. Cut this center section so that its end pieces will protrude about 1/2 inch from the fuselage sides; then block-sand the edges flat, and glue a 1/16-inch plywood plate to the

end pieces to cover the foam interior of the stab section. Glue plates to the end surfaces of the outside stab pieces as well. Now insert the solid carbon-fiber rods into the hollow rods and rejoin the entire stab. Tape the whole assembly together and epoxy it into the stab saddle in the fuselage. This ensures proper alignment of the stab in the fuselage.

BRACING A WING
Another use for carbon-fiber rods is as braces in thin foam or cored-out wings. This provides enough strength to withstand almost anything you could give it in a rigorous

Figure 2
This shows the position of the carbon-fiber support rod, which protects against wing failure.

flight. I learned about this technique from the "glider boys."

We used a Dremel tool to rout out a groove in the wing (Figure 2). It doesn't matter if you use the top or the bottom of the wing. Put the rod in the groove (solid or hollow rod, although hollow is recommended, as it saves weight). Then spread a little epoxy over the rod and into the groove. Let it dry, then sheet the wings. This idea has been proven in Quickee 500 planes. It's a tremendous aid in the prevention of wing failure.

"TRICK" FUN-FLY PLANES
You can also use carbon-fiber rods in the new

"trick" fun-fly airplanes. They use a larger, hollow, carbon-fiber rod for a "boom" that serves as the fuselage! I know that you've seen them, e.g., the "Yard Dart," the "Smith Special" and the "Schtick." Well, the carbon-fiber rod is all that holds them together!

COMBAT AIRCRAFT
Last, but not least, a bulletin just in from "R/C Central": people are using carbon-fiber rods as leading edges in their bats! Humm!!! Yes, I said *bats*. They're back and they're great! Could be one of the most enjoyable things you can do to relax and unwind.

Till next time! Fuel 'em, flip 'em and fly 'em!

Here are the addresses of the companies mentioned in this article:
Dave Brown Products, 4560 Layhigh Rd., Hamilton, OH 45013.
Aerospace Composite Products, P.O. Box 16621, Irvine, CA 92714.
Aero Sport Products, 6150 E. Main St., Columbus, OH 43213. ■

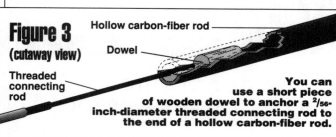

Figure 3
(cutaway view)

Hollow carbon-fiber rod

Dowel

Threaded connecting rod

You can use a short piece of wooden dowel to anchor a 2/56-inch-diameter threaded connecting rod to the end of a hollow carbon-fiber rod.

Sheeting with Obechi

by MICHAEL LACHOWSKI

Try this balsa substitute

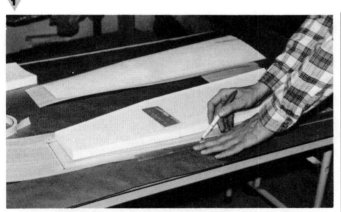

Using tape, outline the area that you want to cut, and then measure the dimensions and draw the actual cut line. Keep a roll of masking tape handy. A clear work space will lessen the chance that the wood will be bent or split.

Cut the obechi on the taped line with a sharp knife blade. A sharp blade is especially important when you cut across the grain. Left: spread out the epoxy—you need only a little!—with a plastic scraper.

IF YOU SHEET foam-cores, then you know that it can be a challenge to find good, contest-grade balsa that's suitable for use as sheeting. Moreover, the work required to splice balsa sheets together can be a real pain. On most powered ships, you have to glue multiple sheets of 3- or 4-inch-wide balsa together to create a panel that's wide enough to cover the wing. On sailplanes, you have the additional work of building a 6-foot-long sheet. Thin hardwood veneers are a good alternative to balsa. Obechi is one of these woods, and it works well on models.

ABOUT OBECHI

Obechi is an African hardwood that's harder and heavier than balsa. It's available, e.g., from Dave's Wood Products*, in long (more than 6 feet), fairly wide, e.g., 15 inches, sheets—a definite advantage. Many European modelers use obechi because it's inexpensive, and it's strong, yet light.

To ensure that your wing will weigh the same as it would if it were sheeted with balsa, you use thinner sheets of obechi. It's available in a .025-inch thickness—less than half as thick as normal ($^{1}/_{16}$-inch) balsa.

AVOID SPLITTING THE WOOD

Working with obechi isn't much different from working with balsa. You can use the same adhesives and finishing techniques. However, you must be careful not to split the wood. Remember, this sheeting is very thin, so it's easy to split it along the grain before you apply it to the wing. Be sure to keep masking tape nearby while you work with obechi. Always put a strip of tape across the ends of obechi sheeting so that the veneer won't split. To fix any splits that do develop, simply put tape over them to hold them together until you've applied the sheeting to the core. (Be sure to apply the tape to the *outside* of the sheeting.)

CUTTING AND BONDING OBECHI

You'll also use masking tape to prevent the sheeting from splitting when you cut it. Simply apply the tape along the approximate outlines of the shape you plan to cut, and then draw the precise outline on the tape. Be sure to use a *sharp* knife so that you'll cut through the tape.

You can use your favorite method to attach the obechi to the core. I use epoxy and a vacuum bag; the bag holds the sheeting in

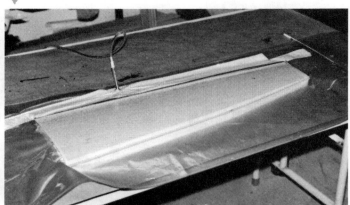

Left: For extra reinforcement, carbon-fiber mat and fiberglass cloth can be put between the foam and the obechi. Right: A vacuum bag is certainly easier on the work table than a huge stack of magazines! It's particularly useful for complex tip shapes or for sheeting a panel with multiple tapers all at once. The bag holds the wood down over all compound curves.

place until the epoxy has cured. Vacu-bagging equipment is relatively inexpensive; you can purchase a complete setup (including pumps) for approximately $80 from Composite Structures Technology* or Aerospace Composite Products*.

Use a thin laminating epoxy such as that offered by West System*. Apply it to the wood carefully, and remember that you only need a little; anything extra will just add weight. Brush it on a small area, and then spread it out by scraping it as shown. (A 3-inch plastic scraper with a clean edge works well.) After you've applied the epoxy and scraped it, the wood should look almost dry and there shouldn't be puddles. Don't pour a substantial amount of epoxy onto the wood and spread it out; rather, apply it a little at a time. This technique will prevent excess epoxy from "sitting around" and soaking into the wood.

Next, put the sheeting on the core, tape it in place along its ends and, if you plan to vacu-bag, put the wing into the bag. If you don't plan to vacu-bag, be sure not to let the epoxy seep through the sheeting to the core beds. Put wax paper or plastic between the sheeting and the beds, otherwise the

sheeting will adhere to the beds.

Because obechi veneer is thin and relatively hard, you may have

> **"Obechi is an African hardwood that's harder and heavier than balsa."**

to cut a few slits in it to work it over curves. This technique can be useful if you want to sheet a complex tip shape with one piece of sheeting. As noted, you can finish obechi just as you would balsa. You can create a "fine-furniture" look by applying a clear, colorless finish.

TRAILING EDGES
You might be concerned about the strength of the obechi on thin trailing edges. My favorite strengthening technique is to put a layer of 0.5-ounce carbon-fiber mat between the top and bottom sheets when I bag the wing. I use a little extra epoxy to "wet out" the carbon fiber, because I've found that, when it has cured, resin-impregnated carbon fiber is stiffer than fiberglass. If there are any cutouts in the wing, consider putting a layer of light fiberglass between the obechi and foam in

Here, the foam-core rests inside the obechi panels. You can see the carbon-fiber mat at the trailing edge. Note the masking-tape remnants on all the edges.

Here's a sample wing sheeted with obechi. The techniques used to finish obechi are the same as those used for balsa. Obechi is easy to sand and will accept most model finishes, paints and film coverings.

these areas. This will make it easier to cut the sheeting when you're completing the wing, and it will do a better job distributing flight stresses around these areas. For very thin airfoils, you should also fiberglass the outside of each obechi trailing edge to stiffen and strengthen it. (After I've sanded each edge to shape, I apply a strip of ³/₄-ounce fiberglass.) I hope you find this technique useful.

*Here are the addresses of the companies mentioned in this article:
Dave's Wood Products, 12306 Bergstrasse, Leavenworth, WA 98826.
Composite Structures Technology, P.O. Box 4615, Lancaster, CA 93539; (805) 723-3783.
Aerospace Composite Products, P.O. Box 16621, Irvine, CA 92714; (714) 250-1107.
West System Epoxy; distributed by Weston Aerodesign, 944 Placid Ct., Arnold, MD 21012; (301) 757-5199. ∎

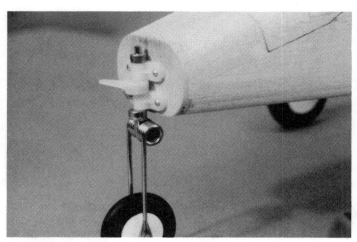

THE PROBLEM:
how to finish the nose of the fuselage of my new airplane.

by VERNON WILLIAMS

THE SOLUTION:
custom-make a fiberglass cowl that rivals the best made from a cowl kit.

STEPS TO A FIBERGLASS COWL

SINCE I prefer to scratch-build model airplanes, the problem of how to build cowls came up early in my career. I've devised my own construction method that makes a cowl that's easy to repair. First, I make the basic shape; then I add the necessary parts. Epoxy, aliphatic resin, or one of the odorless CAs can be used to glue the foam, and fillets and repairs can be made with model filler.

A simple way to custom-make a cowl.

In 10 steps, I'll show you how I finished the nose of my new electric twin. The quality of my one-off fiberglass cowl rivals that of the best cowl kits.

You'll need: foam, epoxy finishing resin, glass-cloth, filler, primer glazing putty, paint, wood, gloves and sandpaper. Note that the foam is a closed-cell Styrofoam that's usually blue.

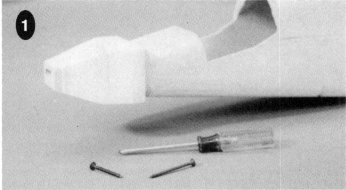

Cut the foam roughly to shape, and attach it to the fuselage. The wooden piece that's attached to the front of the nose will form the air inlet. (This could be a spinner ring on a power cowl.) You can attach the foam with screws or tack-glue it.

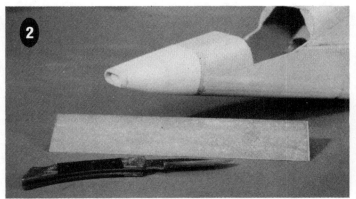

Carve and sand the foam to shape. (Do this outdoors, if possible.)

Attach ⅛-inch balsa to the rear of the foam plug, and sand it to the plug's contour. This forms the part of the cowl that overlaps the fuselage. The idea is to sand the wood so that it has the same shape as the fuselage.

10
STEPS TO A FIBERGLASS COWL

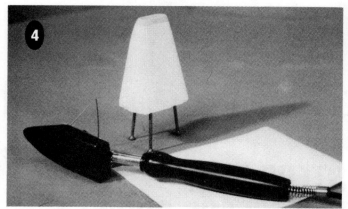

Cover the plug with "low-temp" covering. When the foam has been removed, the slick covering leaves the inside of the cowl with a smooth finish, and it also makes it easier to remove the foam. Note that the balsa for the air inlet isn't covered.

Rough-cut your fabric. I used one layer of 2-ounce fabric, two layers of 6-ounce fabric and a final layer of 2-ounce fabric. I only used the 2-ounce cloth over the wood in the air inlet.

Mix the epoxy resin according to instructions. Using gloves, apply the fabric and the resin to the plug. Try to stagger the overlaps, and use only enough resin to wet the fabric. Slit any puckers or air bubbles with scissors, and flatten out these areas to smooth the surface.

Mix enough filler, e.g., talc, with the remaining resin to form a fairly thick slurry, and apply this immediately, before the fiberglass starts to cure. (Most of this will be sanded off in the next step.)

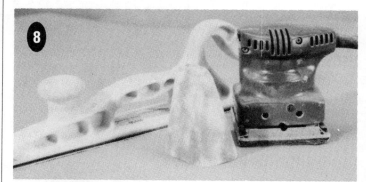

Let the resin cure for several hours. When it's fairly hard, trim the rear flange and nose opening with a sharp knife, and sand the exterior to shape. I use an auto-body hand file and 80-grit sandpaper to do most of the rough shaping, and I finish with a pad sander and 120-grit sandpaper.

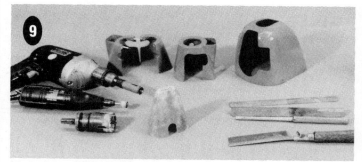

I try to do any drilling that's necessary before I remove the foam. Pictured are several cowls and the tools that I used to make the cutouts. I prefer to dig out the foam. You can dissolve it with solvent, but this method is messy and exposes you to the solvent's fumes.

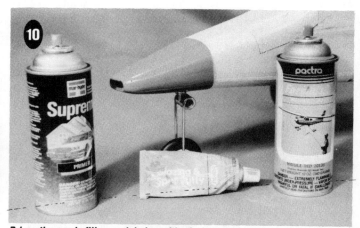

Prime the cowl, fill any pinholes with glazing putty, and sand with 220-grit sandpaper. Paint it with the color of your choice. ∎

FIBERGLASSING
FOAM FLOATS

by JOHN SULLIVAN

Completed Savoia floats ready for mounting and prime coat. Tops are covered with 5-ounce Kevlar, while the bottoms received 6-ounce glass-cloth. Finishing epoxy resin is applied directly to foam.

ONE SURE-FIRE METHOD of constructing floats is to apply fiberglass cloth directly onto a foam core using epoxy finishing resin. This method has the best strength-to-weight ratio; it's puncture-proof; and it has no interior voids. Glassed floats seem to offer the best of everything—including the quickest path from the bench to the lake!—yet many float fliers shy away from using this method because they're unfamiliar with the glassing process.

Making a natural flotation medium even better for our models

MATERIALS

● *Polystyrene foam:* The best polystyrene foam I've found is cast from BASF 322 virgin small bead with a vacuum-assist that eliminates internal stressing in the finished product. This small-bead foam is available from plastic suppliers in big cities, or you can buy slabs with larger beads (used for insulation) from a building supply yard. The polystyrenes used in construction are usually sold in standard and utility grades, and they contain recycled foam or large beads. They'll work for floats, but they react differently to sanding, and it's more difficult to get a smooth, uniform surface.

● *Fiberglass cloth:* I recommend 6-ounce fiberglass cloth. You can buy the "heavyweight" cloth from Sig*, K&B*, or PEC's*, or a package of "Bondo," which is available from hardware and auto-supply stores. At first glance, the heavy cloth seems to be *too* heavy, but if you cut a sample strip off a finished float, it would be almost as thick as $1/64$-inch ply and have superior tensile strength.

● *Finishing epoxy:* I prefer West System's* finishing epoxy. Many companies use fillers in their epoxy formulas to provide users with easy-to-measure ratios of 3:1, 2:1, or 1:1. For superior strength

and resilience, West Epoxy mixes its epoxy at a ratio of 5:1, and it supplies an automatic metered pump to ensure the correct mixing ratio. You can use epoxies that have lower ratios, but thin them with alcohol until they're the consistency of a high-quality varnish.

SAMPLE FLOATS

The floats shown are for the Savoia-Marchetti that Mike Johnson and I are building for the 1990 Schneider Race. They have a more complicated shape and component makeup than most sport floats, so I suggest that you disregard the "extras" in these instructions if a sport float is all you're after. We used the Savoia float for this article to give readers an overview that will help them deal with special situations; we included a float-proportion-and-layout plan to help those of you who cut your own floats. This plan was first published in the September '87 float issue of *MAN*, and hundreds of readers have written to express their satisfaction with the design.

First, the Savoia floats were cut to top and side profiles. This view shows center web ready for lamination. Note rudder pushrod sheath embedded in half-core stern section.

Float on right has been shaped to a 45-degree angle, while the one on left has final $22^1/2$-degree tangents cut in. Note $1/64$-inch-ply keel plates glued into place.

FOAM FLOATS

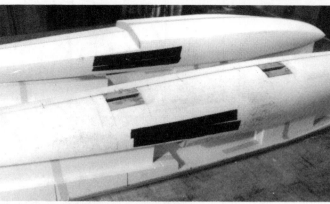

These floats have been finished to shape. Note .003 carbon-fiber reinforcement and redwood landing-gear blocks.

FLOAT PREPARATION

Preparation of a foam float for glassing usually involves the installation of hard-point, or "strong-back," material (to take abuse where it's encountered most), a light sanding, and vacuuming to remove loose material. Hard-point material usually consists of a deck plate to accept land-ing-gear screws, a stern plate on which to mount a rudder, and a stiffener on the step's vertical wall (to reinforce that area and to prevent the step from being distorted or crushed when you lay the floatplane down on a rocky beach or a workbench full of tools).

For the deck plates, 3/8-inch material is sufficient, and 1/8-inch ply will work for the stern and step. Never round the edges at the bottom of the float or in the step and stern area, as this will dramatically reduce the float's efficiency—much like curving the sharp edges of snow skis.

What about reinforcing the float longitudinally? In a usual sport float that's up to 48 inches long, the 6-ounce cloth will provide all the strength you'll need for normal service. The Savoia floats, however, are 5 to 7 1/2 feet long, will support a total aircraft weight of 30 pounds, and will probably take a pounding at Havasu. To prevent failures when venturing into the unknown, I used three reinforcement methods.

After making two primary cuts for the top and side profiles, I split the Savoia float down the middle. Then, I drilled the 1/8-inch mahogany ply templates (which were used for hot-wiring the side profile)

to lighten them, and I sandwiched them between the float halves to provide a full-length, full-depth web reinforcement.

I epoxied two, 1x10x.003-inch, carbon-fiber ribbons to each float side just above the step and cutaway juncture. I then glassed the entire top and the sides with 5-ounce Kevlar, which is at least three times as strong as 6-ounce glass-cloth. If these floats break, it won't matter, because the plane will be impossible to identify!

It's important to keep sport floats light and maintain a balance between strength and weight. Reinforcing the side step area with carbon fiber or a strip of 1/64-inch ply is probably the strongest, lightest and most effective method available to modelers. Installing a full web for reinforcement will practically turn the float into an I-beam when glassed, so, if you use this method, consider using 2-ounce (medium) cloth for covering to make up for the weight of the web.

CUTTING QUANDARY

Even if you don't own hot-wire-cutting equipment, you can still use foam floats. Several ready-cut foam float cores are available through hobby distributors, and polystyrene foam can be machined and shaped easily with band saws, table saws,

hand-held hacksaw blades, Surform® tools, sanding blocks, etc.

While shaping the Savoia floats, I made a surprising discovery. To round the floats from their hot-wired, two-dimensional shape, I had to cut successive facets along their full length. I went to the kitchen and came back with an arsenal of butcher knives. To my surprise, the oldest one, which is about 11 inches long and 1 inch deep and *not* hollow-ground, cut the foam smoothly and without tearing out beads. Apparently, a hollow-ground blade makes an entry cut that's too fine to allow the shank to pass through the foam, while a thin, uniformly sided blade slices through accurately and almost effortlessly. With practice, I was able to shave off wafers of foam that were so thin you could see the knife blade *through* them!

GETTING STARTED

Before glassing, collect the following tools and materials: glass-cloth, epoxy, a tape measure, a marking pen, scissors, a straightedge, spatulas or squeegees, filler, brushes, mixing cups, newspaper, rags and acetone for cleanup. It's best to glass the float's top and sides in one operation, and do the bottoms after the tops have cured. To begin, put the floats up on blocks on your workbench so that the excess cloth hangs freely past the float sides. Measure and cut the glass-cloth leaving extra all around, and draw a line down the center. Next draw a center line down the float top, and roll up the cloth on the longitudinal axis.

Now you're ready to pump the resin and hardener into a cup and mix it thoroughly. *Use as little epoxy as possible.* One of the best ways to do this is to paint the epoxy directly onto the foam, and then roll the cloth out onto the float, using the centerlines as a guide.

Gently dry-brush the cloth around the

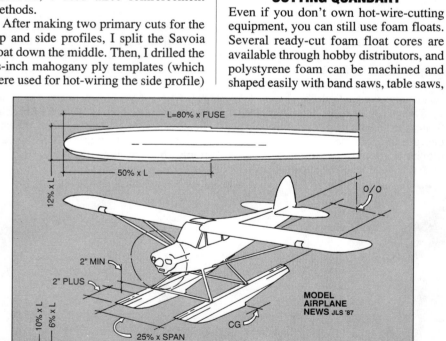

PHOTOS BY JOHN SULLIVAN

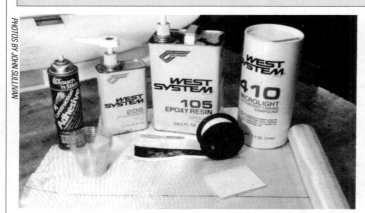

Partial array of materials, which are assembled before glassing. Note center line drawn on Kevlar cloth.

Floats are blocked up before glassing. Kevlar cloth has been glued to foam core with spray adhesive because of side undercamber. (See text.)

curved sides of the float. If you don't rush, the cloth will conform to a bias easily. You'll notice that the resin will wick up into the cloth and make it semitransparent. Using a spatula or squeegee, continue to press the cloth onto the wet foam core until all surfaces are of the same transparency. *Do not* apply additional epoxy unless it's absolutely necessary. You should use just enough to change the color of the cloth fibers without creating a glossy surface or puddles. If done properly, the glass-cloth will feel rough when cured and have microscopic pores throughout.

After the initial curing (about 16 hours), use a razor blade to trim the excess cloth off the float sides, and block-sand the edges flush with the bottom. Now, invert the floats and block them up again. I had previously glassed float bottoms with four pieces—for the rocker, step, cutaway and stern—because I found it impossible to make the cloth stay down around the 90-degree corners at the step and stern. I've since discovered a spray adhesive call "Spray & Stick"* that allows me to use one piece. Here's how:

After cutting the cloth, marking the center lines and rolling up the cloth, spray a light coat of adhesive onto the float bottom. Immediately roll on the cloth, using a spatula to press it into the corners and around the step edges. Although the spray adhesive is compatible with epoxy that's either wet or cured, it's best to let the bond dry for an hour to ensure permanent contact at the sharp edges.

Now it's time to wet the cloth on the float's bottom. If you haven't used the adhesive spray, coat the foam directly, as outlined in the procedure for covering the top, and then apply the four pieces of glass-cloth. If you *have* used the adhesive, the epoxy must be brushed on and then scraped off with a squeegee or spatula to remove as much resin as possible. Remember: when the cloth has become translucent, applying more resin will just add useless weight to the float. Allow the bottom to cure for 16 hours, trim it, and block-sand the edges just as you did for the float's top coat.

The primary glassing has been completed, and you now have a pair of floats that have a hard skin and no longer have to be handled carefully. Roughly sand the floats to knock off the glass hair that's left standing and to provide extra "tooth" for the filler coat. Unlike polyester resins, epoxy sands easily and won't accumulate on the sandpaper. For rough-sanding, 60- or 80-grit paper is adequate, and each float can be finished in minutes.

KEVLAR

The Savoia float tops were covered with Kevlar—a completely different ball of wax! The first change in the process occurred when covering the float tops. Because the

After glassing, convert the core-bottom excess into a stand. Plastic wrap protects the floats during application of spray foam, which duplicates contour of float bottoms. Excess foam is later trimmed away.

Counterbalanced water rudders are mounted on the Savoia's canoe sterns with Robart Super Hinge Point hinges. Rudders can be removed for static display.

After glassing, servo compartment for rudder control is cut out of float. Servo is located just aft of rear strut receiver block.

Savoia float is round in section and develops undercamber below the hull

(Continued on page 135)

1 *Some of the items you can use: top, left to right—3M Press-in-Place caulk for sealing the bag; MityVac's hand vacuum pump to create the vacuum; bagging tubes. Middle: Bondo paddles to spread the epoxy; unidirectional S-glass and unidirectional graphite, which can be substituted for fiberglass. Bottom: no-fray, unidirectional, carbon-fiber tape.*

LIKE MANY composite construction techniques, vacuum bagging wings is easy, and anyone can do it. It's one of the fastest methods of constructing a strong, perfectly finished, accurately shaped wing, and it doesn't require many special tools, or cost a lot of money. There are different approaches to vacuum bagging, just as there are to other building methods, but I've found that the following works well for beginners.

Many different materials can be used to sheet a foam wing. I'll describe a fiberglass-covered wing that's reinforced with carbon-fiber tape. Balsa sheeting can also be laminated to the foam core with or without the application of glass-cloth. If balsa sheeting is used, 1/2-ounce fiberglass provides ample strength. If the sheeting over the foam cores is fiberglass alone, then either 3- or 6-ounce cloth can be used.

The Sucker Kit from Composite Aircraft Engineering & Supply* (list price $59) is one of the easiest kits to use. It includes a hand vacuum pump of the type com-

2 *Contents of the epoxy finishing kit from Aerospace Composite Products. Top, left to right: E-Z LAM epoxy, mixing cups and trays, mixing sticks, 15 feet of satin-weave, 3-ounce cloth and five pairs of latex gloves.*

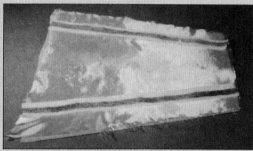

3 *Three-ounce fiberglass cloth with two strips of no-fray tape all cut to size.*

One of the fastest methods of constructing a strong, perfectly finished, accurately shaped wing.

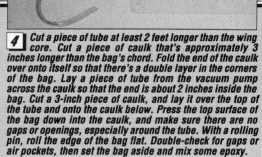

4 *Cut a piece of tube at least 2 feet longer than the wing core. Cut a piece of caulk that's approximately 3 inches longer than the bag's chord. Fold the end of the caulk over onto itself so that there's a double layer in the corners of the bag. Lay a piece of tube from the vacuum pump across the caulk so that the end is about 2 inches inside the bag. Cut a 3-inch piece of caulk, and lay it over the top of the tube and onto the caulk below. Press the top surface of the bag down into the caulk, and make sure there are no gaps or openings, especially around the tube. With a rolling pin, roll the edge of the bag flat. Double-check for gaps or air pockets, then set the bag aside and mix some epoxy.*

5 *Place the fiberglass on top of the Mylar, and pour a line of epoxy onto the glass-cloth.*

6 *Using a Bondo Paddle, or a credit card, spread the epoxy around until all of the glass-cloth is wet. Next, go back over the glass-cloth with the paddle, scrape up the excess epoxy, and put it back in the mixing cup. Continue this process until most of the epoxy has been removed and the glass-cloth takes on a flat, almost dry look. In the photo, the top section has already been done; the bottom section still has excess epoxy to be removed. The more epoxy you remove, the lighter your finished wing will be, so take your time and do it right. Make sure there are no wrinkles or air pockets in the glass-cloth.*

Vacuum
FOR TRUER, LIGHTER,

7 *Lay one strip of carbon-fiber tape about one third of the way back from the edge of the glass, and make sure that it's straight. Lay the other strip the same distance from the other edge. The carbon fiber will reinforce the high point of the spar location on the finished wing. Pour some more epoxy along the carbon fiber, and "wet it out" as described earlier. Remove the excess epoxy. The photo shows loose carbon fiber, but I recommend no-fray tape.*

8 *Lay the foam core on the epoxy/glass about 1/8 inch from the (center) trailing edge. Fold the edge of the Mylar/glass over the top surface of the wing (think of a taco). Make sure that the wing's trailing edge hasn't moved forward. Smooth the top of the Mylar down over the wing core, and move the wing and cardboard to the side. The total time from mixing the epoxy to bagging the wing is 10 to 15 minutes.*

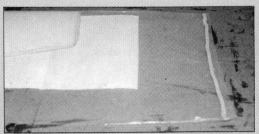

9 *Before you lay the vacuum bag out on your bench, make sure there isn't any spilled epoxy on the bench. Lay the Mylar on a long sheet of paper towel. Slide the whole thing into the bag, and to help ensure a straight trailing edge, place the core's trailing edge against the crease in the edge of the bag. Make sure the core hasn't shifted in the Mylar and that you haven't created any wrinkles. Do this now because it can't be fixed once the bag is sealed. Take your time. When everything is properly placed in the bag, seal the open end with caulk, and roll it shut. The paper towels under the core help air wick through the bag and soak up the excess epoxy that's forced from the glass by the vacuum.*

10 *Smooth the bag with your hand to get out most of the trapped air. Now suck the remaining air from the bag. I strongly recommend using a Dust Buster or household vacuum to do this. Don't suck the air out with your mouth; epoxy fumes can be dangerous to your lungs. Hook-up the hand vacuum pump to the tube, draw a test vacuum, and check for leaks. If everything is satisfactory, release the vacuum.*

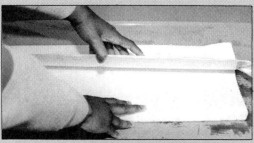

11 *Put the bag in the top cradle from which the core was cut, and lay it on the bench with the curved side up. Place the core—bag and all—into the cradle. Smooth out any wrinkles, and hold the core down firmly in the cradle (don't press too hard and dent the core). Draw a vacuum of about 3 inches of mercury. To help remove any trapped air and to stick the glass-cloth to the wing, roll the core lightly with a rolling pin.*

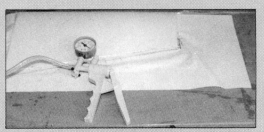

12 *When you're satisfied that there are no wrinkles or trapped air, draw about 7 inches of mercury vacuum. (Use about 5 inches for white foam, 7 inches for pink foam and 10 inches for blue foam.) Remove the bag from the cradle. If the wing was straight when you pulled the vacuum, it will be straight when you take it out of the bag.*

monly used for automobile brake bleeding and enough plastic bagging to make several wings. You can also buy a hand vacuum pump from an auto parts store (e.g., National Auto's MityVac brake bleeder pump, which lists for $25). I used one of these pumps and bought bagging material from Composite Aircraft Engineering & Supply (photo 1). I also recommend their fine video on vacuum bagging.

Aerospace Composite Products* offers an Epoxy Finishing Kit (photo 2) that includes all the glassing materials needed to build several wings. Write to them for a complete catalogue.

PREPARATION

It's easier if you have all your equipment ready before you mix the epoxy. Make sure that all the pushrod tubes, spars and wing joiners are installed properly in the foam core and that the tip and root ribs are also attached. Fill any imperfections in the foam core with spackle. Lay out some newspaper to cover your work-

by BILL GRIGGS

Bagging
STRONGER WINGS

bench; then place cardboard over your working area. Cut two pieces of Mylar (one top and one bottom) that are ¹/₂ inch larger overall than your foam wing core. Place the two pieces of Mylar side by side. The edges that correspond to the wing's trailing edge should have about a ¹/₁₆-inch gap between them. Tape the Mylar pieces together along the center.

Lay down the fiberglass cloth, and cut one continuous piece that's the same size as the attached pieces of Mylar. Put the glass aside for now.

Next, measure two pieces of carbon-fiber tape that are 1 inch longer than the Mylar span. I recommend Aerospace Composite Products no-fray tape (photo 3)—a 1-inch-wide, unidirectional, carbon-fiber tape sandwiched between two strips of light, nonwoven, glass fabric. It won't unravel when cut, and it's easy to "wet out" with epoxy. If you use another brand, make sure you apply masking tape over the carbon-fiber tape before you cut it. (Cut only on the masking tape, or the carbon-fiber tape might unravel).

For the rest of the procedure, see photos 4 through 17 and their related captions. I think you'll find that

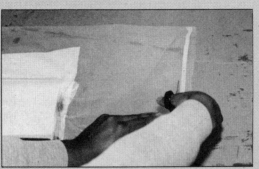

13 *Clamp some spruce spars along the trailing edge Put the bag aside while the wing cures (at least 24 hours). To ensure that the bag is holding a vacuum, check the vacuum gauge for the first hour or so. Some drop will be normal because of the trapped air that escapes. The most critical time to maintain a vacuum is during the first hour while the epoxy sets. If the bag leaks, you won't get a glassy smooth finish on the wing.*

14 *After the wing has cured, cut open the end of the bag without the tube. Cut as close to the caulk as possible because the bag is reusable. Unclamp the spruce trailing-edge strips, and remove the wing from the bag. The bag won't stick to the epoxy, so it should release easily. You'll notice that the paper towel is saturated with epoxy and has adhered to the Mylar. Carefully tear the towel loose, but leave any stubborn parts for now.*

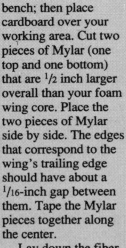

15 *Find the edge of the Mylar, and lift it until you can get a finger between it and the cured glass-cloth. Run your finger the length of the core, and the Mylar should begin to peel away. Once that side is done, peel off the other. Be careful along the trailing edge, as it's razor-sharp. Save the Mylar; it's reusable. You should now have a core that's as smooth as glass. Once you've trimmed the excess glass-cloth from the edges, you're ready to paint. If you decide to paint the wing (you can fly it as is), then lightly buff the surface with steel wool. I suggest red oxide auto primer as a base coat, followed by your favorite paint or enamel.*

this technique is relatively easy and produces stronger, better flying airplanes in nearly any category.

Here are the addresses of the companies mentioned in this article:

Composite Aircraft Engineering & Supply, P.O. Box 866, Lapeer, MI 48446.
Aerospace Composite Products, P.O. Box 16621, Irvine, CA 92714

■

16 *Top: main wing panel for Ligeti Stratos. I used 3-ounce cloth and no-fray tape, with a second layer of 3-ounce cloth on the top from the LE to the spar. No LE dowel was used. Weight: 4 ounces. Middle: canard panel for Ligeti Stratos after trimming, but before 60-degree sweep cut at wing root. Three-ounce cloth was used with a carbon-fiber tow spar on the bottom; ¹/₈-inch dowel LE, weight 2¹/₂ ounces. Core weight before bagging, 1 ¹/₄ ounces. Bottom: canard panel for Stratos with sweep cut. Six-ounce cloth used. Carbon-fiber tow, top and bottom; ¹/₈-inch dowel LE; weight 4 ounces.*

17 *Leaks sometimes occur in the plastic bag or the pump. If the bag leaks, you must replace it. If your pump leaks, it might be the pressure-relief cap. Simply remove the valve cap and re-glue it with thick CA; this usually seals any leaks.*

M A T E R I A L S

- MityVac vacuum pump or the Sucker Kit
- Vacuum bag material
- 3M Press-in-Place caulk
- Drafting Mylar
- 3- or 6-ounce glass-cloth
- 12 feet of carbon-fiber tow (no-fray tape is best)
- E-Z LAM epoxy or similar laminating epoxy
- Can of spray mold release
- Isopropyl alcohol (not rubbing)
- Bondo paddles
- Paper cups, paper towels and rolling pin
- Masking tape
- Large piece of cardboard (so you don't ruin your work-bench)

Build Lighter Foam Wings

and increase performance

by ROLLY SINGSON

The foam-cutting procedure described here removed over a pound of weight from this airplane. The improved performance makes it worth the effort!

IF YOU'RE BUILDING planes with foam wings, you can use this lightening technique to enhance your model's performance.

I used this procedure on one of two, identical 74-inch wings—wing area 950 square inches—for my 1.20-size sport/pattern airplane. The conventional, solid, foam-core wing weighed 8 ounces more than the one I lightened. If you also lighten other areas of the aircraft in addition to the wing, weight reduction could be up to a pound.

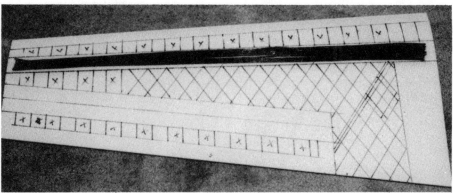

This is how your wing will look after you have marked off the "honeycomb" pattern.

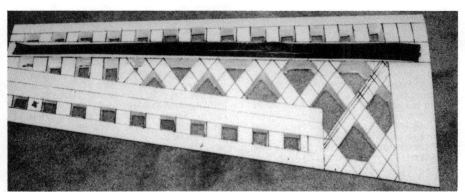

The honeycomb has been cut. Note the solid foam along the spar and hinge lines.

I'll concentrate on building the wing, although the methods presented here may be applied to the construction of any other part of the aircraft.

PREPARING THE CORE

Because foam melts when it's cut with a hot wire, a foam-core always has some "foam hair" clinging to it, and it may also have some bumps. Remove these by lightly sanding the wing surface with a block sander. (I recommend one that's at least 18 inches long with 120- to 180-grit sandpaper.) Then, brush or vacuum the surface to remove as much of the foam dust as possible.

Find the spar center line and, with a felt-tip pen, draw a line from the root to the tip about an inch on either side of the spar line. Use a straightedge for accuracy. Do this on both the top and bottom surfaces of the wing, and make sure that the ends of the lines align with each other at the root and tip. Do the same thing for the control-surface hinge lines (see photos).

Also, draw lines approximately 1 inch from the leading, trailing and tip edges. Next, draw a line, parallel with the root chord, 2 to 4 inches from the root edge, depending on the size of wing. As a rule of thumb, I draw a line 2 inches away from the root edge for a 60-inch wing, 3 inches for 72-inch wing, 4 inches for 84-inch wing.

Next, I'll focus on the areas between the leading-edge line and the front spar line, the aft spar line and the front hinge line, the aft hinge line and the trailing-edge line and the tip line and the root lines.

Draw diagonal and perpendicular lines, $1/2$- to $1 1/4$-inches apart, in these sections to create an "egg-crate" effect. Mark x's on the areas that need to be removed (see photos). If you're building a wing that will have landing-gear blocks or retracts installed, mark off these areas and be sure to leave enough foam in them to accommodate the mounting blocks and gear wells.

CARBON FIBER

Next, lay up graphite or carbon fiber on the top and bottom spar areas along the wing panel's entire length. (I used carbon-fiber tow, but carbon-fiber tape can also be used.) For added insurance on bigger wings, glue a $1/4$- to $1/2$-inch strip of carbon fiber on the forward hinge line. The fiber must run from root to tip.

(Continued on page 136)

USING CARBON

TIPS FOR BUILDING WINGS

by GREG POPPEL

CARBON FIBER isn't a "top secret" material that's only available to top fliers! In fact, everyone who owns a plane—from ¹/₂A to giant scale—should be using it. I've read a lot of articles, and the consensus seems to be, "Build light; light flies better." Hey, facts are facts!

This series will give sport fliers some tips on how to use carbon fiber to "build light" without sacrificing strength. In this part, I'll discuss how to strengthen wings.

Carbon fiber's high tensile strength makes it stronger than steel, yet as light as a feather. It's so light that many glider pilots and ¹/₂A-Texaco pilots have been using it for a long time. There are a few things you should remember about working with carbon fiber:

No big secret!

● Wear gloves when you work with it. The fiber tends to splinter, and pieces of it could lodge in your fingers.

● It's very difficult to cut, so you'll need a carbide-rod saw or a razor saw. (Although you could use an X-Acto knife,

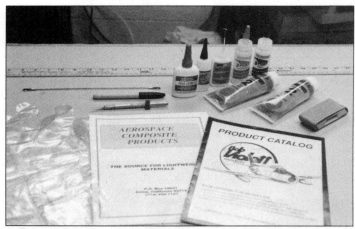

1. Here are the tools and adhesives you'll need to work with carbon fiber. Although many companies sell and distribute carbon fiber, few know as much about it as Aerospace Composite Products* and Bob Violett Models*.

2. It's easy to strengthen foam wings with carbon fiber. All you need is a ¹/₄-inch-wide strip of .007-mil-thick fiber that's cut to about 80 percent of the wing's length. Find the wing's highest point and make a cut in it that's as deep as the blade on a no. 11 X-Acto knife will permit.

3. Use a straightedge to cut a straight slit. Center and test-fit the piece of carbon fiber. In this example, we're adding the carbon-fiber strip to the wing's top surface to increase its ability to withstand negative Gs (the assumption is that the wing is already adequately stressed for positive Gs). Whether you add carbon fiber to the top surface, the bottom surface, or both, depends on what you want the wing to do.

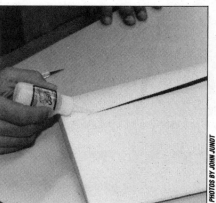

4. Insert the carbon fiber into the slit, and glue it into place. (The thick version of UFO* CA is safe to use with most types of foam.) If the wing is hollow you might want to put a similar piece of carbon fiber on the bottom surface, too. If the plane has retracts, put a 6-inch-long piece of .014-mil-thick carbon fiber along the trailing edge of the cutout (i.e., between the rear of the cutout and the wing's trailing edge).

PHOTOS BY JOHN JUNDT

FIBER

it would take forever, and the blade would become dull quickly.)

● You have to scuff the carbon fiber's surfaces with sandpaper before you apply CA or epoxy to them. Wear a filter mask when you sand.

● Many types of CA and epoxy work well with carbon fiber.

● To strengthen wings (foam and wooden), you should use .007-mil-thick fiber. To reinforce the area near retract cutouts, .014-mil-thick fiber is best.

In a future issue, I'll provide more useful information on using carbon fiber.

Here are the addresses of the companies mentioned in this article:
Aerospace Composite Products, *P.O. Box 16621, Irvine, CA 92714.*
Bob Violett Models, *1373 Citrus Rd., Winter Springs, FL 32708.*
UFO; *distributed by Satellite City, P.O. Box 836, Simi, CA 93062.* ■

5. For a wooden wing, use .007-mil-thick carbon fiber that's the same width as the main spar. Glue it to the top and bottom of the spar before you add the cap strip and the sheeting. This will strengthen the wing by 300 percent!

New High-Frequency Servo Technology

Did you know that, in most cases, a servo's maximum torque isn't reached until the servo has moved significantly away from center position? In fact, maximum torque may not be reached until the servo has travelled as much as 24 degrees away from center. Because of this, feedback from the plane's control surfaces, e.g., flaps, ailerons, rudder and elevator, can cause the servo's position to be deflected from where you want it to be.

> Control becomes more precise, and control surface "flutter" as a result of servo feedback is virtually eliminated.

Enter high-frequency servo technology. Normally, the servo's amplifier cycles power to the electric motor about 60 times per second, but with high frequency, this speeds up to about 2,200 times per second. The result is a significant increase in torque from center. In fact, maximum torque may be reached in as little as 1 degree from center. Control becomes more precise, and control surface "flutter" as a result of servo feedback is virtually eliminated. Unfortunately, high-frequency servos drain batteries more quickly than standard servos, but for many, the results are well worth it.

As of this writing, only JR Remote Control* offers high-frequency servos (models NES-4000 and NES-7000), although I suspect that other manufacturers will be addressing the need for increased torque from center position. Whether or not they resort to high-frequency technology has yet to be seen. ■

Making Wingtips WITH Rohacell Foam

by MICHAEL LACHOWSKI

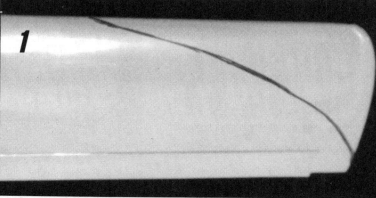

▲1. The Antares' original wing is basically square and made with a small balsa block. Draw the outline of the new wing tip design on the wing. The black line in the photo roughly shows the shape I wanted for the new wing tip.

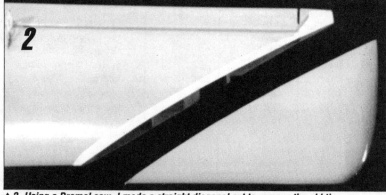

▲2. Using a Dremel saw, I made a straight diagonal cut to remove the old tip.

W HEN YOU SCRATCH-BUILD a model, you often need blocks of balsa for wing tips or fuselage parts. If you want lightness, you must search through hobby shops, and if you're lucky, you'll find some light pieces. (Diehard scratch-builders probably have a select piece of balsa stashed away from years ago.) Modern technology has now eliminated the need to search and has even produced a block that weighs less than one third the weight of balsa!

This wonder material is Rohacell*—a closed-cell foam. Not only is it light, but it's also available in a variety of densities. As well as Rohacell 31, which I use here, there are Rohacell 51 and Rohacell 71, which have densities of 3.1 and 4.4 pounds per cubic foot, respectively. The "crush strength" of Rohacell 71 far exceeds that of balsa. You won't have to modify your building techniques, because you

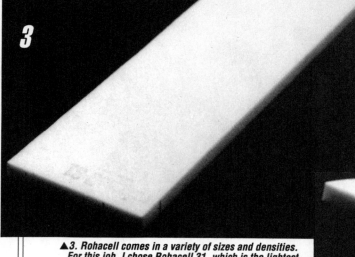

▲3. Rohacell comes in a variety of sizes and densities. For this job, I chose Rohacell 31, which is the lightest variety. It has a density of 1.9 pounds per cubic foot. (Balsa probably has a density of 6 pounds per cubic foot.) Rohacell's crush resistance is comparable to that of balsa, and it's much greater than that of any other lightweight foam you might have worked with.

▲4. Rohacell foam can be cut very easily with a saw.

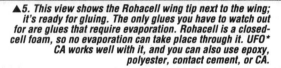

A strong, lightweight alternative to balsa block

▲5. This view shows the Rohacell wing tip next to the wing; it's ready for gluing. The only glues you have to watch out for are glues that require evaporation. Rohacell is a closed-cell foam, so no evaporation can take place through it. UFO* CA works well with it, and you can also use epoxy, polyester, contact cement, or CA.

▶6. The next step is to carve the wing tip. Rohacell doesn't have a grain, so it's easier to carve than balsa. As you can see, a razor plane works well, and you can also use a knife to shape the tip roughly. Don't hot-wire Rohacell because the vapors produced are dangerous.

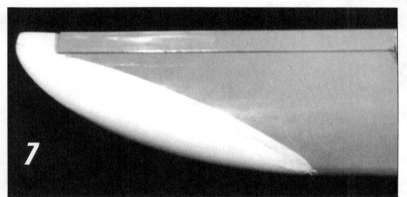

▲7. Sand the wing tip to the desired shape. If you're too aggressive with the sandpaper or have a gap between the block and the wing tip, use Carl Goldberg Models'* Model Magic filler where necessary. Strengthen the thinnest part of the Rohacell (near the trailing-edge wing tip) with carbon fiber. To reinforce the wing beyond the aileron, glue a strip of .007x³/₈-inch carbon fiber into a slot in the foam where it meets the balsa trailing edge. Cut the slot with a razor saw, and sand the foam so that the carbon fiber is flush with the underside of the wing. (To produce a sharp tip that holds up, you must do this with balsa, too.) Harden the leading edge of the Rohacell by smearing CA along the surface of the sanded leading edge. You can also use light fiberglass cloth to strengthen any thin parts.

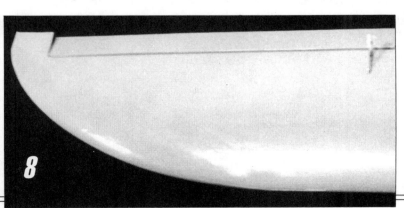

▲8. Finish the tip with Oracover*, which can be applied directly over the Rohacell without any further preparation of the surface.

can use Rohacell in the same way as you use balsa.

Rohacell can be used in many ways, but here, I describe my experience with it when I made a new wing-tip shape for my Antares. The photos show a simple way to build a tip like this: cut the wing, add a block of Rohacell, and carve it to the desired shape.

Of course, all this isn't free! Rohacell costs about three times as much as balsa, but if you have to make large parts, it's easier to find Rohacell than to find a decent balsa block. As for the wing shown in the photographs, I've noticed an improvement in the flying characteristics of my aircraft with the new wing tip.

I bought my Rohacell from Composite Structures Technology, which also offers a book on shell construction for those who like to experiment (Rohacell sandwiched between fiberglass to form a hollow wing "shell"). I now include Rohacell in my stock of building supplies, and you should try it, too.

*Here are the addresses of the companies mentioned in this article:
Rohacell; distributed by Composite Structures Technology, P.O. Box 4615, Lancaster, CA 93539. Tel: (805) 723-3783.
UFO; distributed by Satellite City, P.O. Box 836, Simi, CA 93062. Tel: (805) 322-0062.
Carl Goldberg Models, Inc., 4734 W. Chicago Ave., Chicago, IL. 60651
Oracover; distributed by Hobby Lobby International, 5614 Franklin Pike Cr., Brentwood, TN 37027. ■

QUICK-BUILD A
Fiberglass Cowl

This alternative to balsa is easier to make than you may think!

by BRUCE HALL

WHILE CONSTRUCTING my latest plane (an Ace 4-40 Bipe), I realized how much better it would look with some type of engine cowl. I read an article about building a balsa cowl, but I wanted something that was less likely to become soaked with fuel. I decided to use light, durable fiberglass cloth saturated with CA. I was so pleased with the results that I wanted to share the process with other modelers.

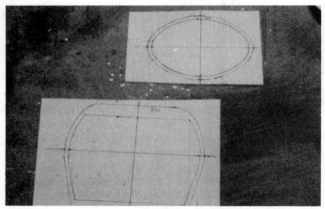

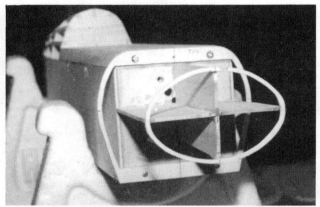

1. To start, decide which type of cowl would look good on your plane. Sketch the outline on the plans, allowing 1/16 inch between the front of the cowl and the back of the prop or spinner. If your plans show an engine, great!—if not, measure the distance from the rear of the engine mount to the rear of the prop and deduct 1/16 inch. This will be the length of your cowl.

You'll need front and rear formers. To make a pattern for the rear former, stand the fuse on its nose and trace around it on a piece of paper. Find the thrust line on the outline, and draw both a horizontal and a vertical line through it. This will help you to align everything later.

Next, draw the shape of the rear of the cowl on the outline. You'll have to cut out the inner part later, so draw a second line inside the first. Be sure to make the former wide enough to take the screws that secure it to the firewall. (My rear-former pattern is wider on the top and bottom, because that's where I installed the screws.)

To make a pattern for the front former, draw a horizontal and a vertical line on the paper. Where these lines intersect will determine where the thrust line is. Now draw the shape of the front former over these lines. (As you can see, I drew my former so that the thrust line was located in the center of the oval.) Cut out the patterns for the front and rear formers, and trace their outlines onto 1/8-inch plywood. Make sure that the thrust lines are transferred as well, and then cut out the wooden shapes.

2. Draw the thrust lines on the plane's firewall, and align them with those on the rear former. Drill holes, and mount the rear former to the firewall with socket-head screws.

To position the front former, make a crutch out of scrap balsa. Cut the balsa pieces to the correct length, allowing for the thickness of the front former and the 1/16-inch clearance. Use a triangle to keep the balsa pieces as square as possible, and "spot glue" them to the firewall on the thrust lines. Glue the front former onto the crutch, making sure the thrust-line marks on it align with those on the crutch and the rear former. To double-check the length of the balsa crutch, measure from the firewall to the front of the former.

3. To complete the next few steps, you'll need foam, Hot Stuff* UFO CA, 6-ounce fiberglass cloth and plastic wrap. Cut a block of foam to fit between the front and rear former in each of the four sections, and glue them to the crutch with UFO. (Any type of foam will work, but I use the kind that florists use in arrangements, because it's very porous and easy to shape.)

4. Using a knife, roughly cut the foam to the shape of your cowl. Finish it by sanding lengthwise with a 100-grit sanding block until you hit both formers. This will give you a smooth surface on which to glue the cloth.

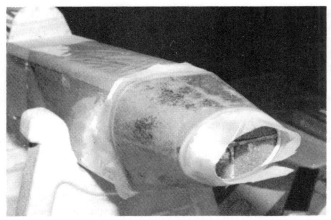

5. To prevent the fiberglass cloth from sticking to it, cover the fuse behind the rear former with plastic wrap. Spray one side of the cloth with 3M 77 glue, and wrap it around the cowl, making sure it's glued to both formers. When it's dry, saturate the cloth with UFO thin CA, just as you do when you reinforce the center of wings.

6. When this has cured, trim off the excess cloth and dig into the foam until you can reach the screws. Take the cowl off the fuse, and then start to remove the rest of the foam. Break out the crutch, and finish cleaning out the inside of the cowl. To reinforce it, coat the inside with another layer of cloth and either CA or epoxy.

Make cutouts to suit your engine, and finish and paint the cowl, or cover it with film. (I chose the latter method, as my paint didn't match the film I was using.) It's easy to add blisters or cheek fairings that have been carved out of balsa or built-up of foam, cloth and CA.

7. As you can see, a cowl can really spruce up a sport plane's looks. Try this method on your next project. I know you'll be pleased with the results—and when someone on the fight line asks where you got the cowl, you'll be able to say, "I made it!"

Here's the address of the company mentioned in this article: **Hot Stuff**, *Satellite City, P.O. Box 836, Simi, CA 93062.* ■

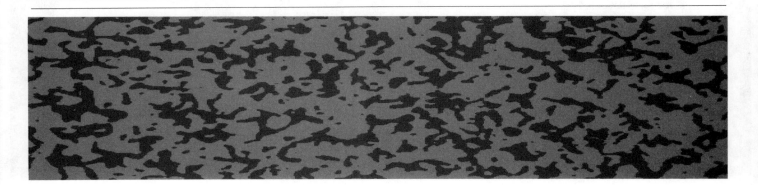

■ 1. *Make sure that the cores are straight, and sand the high spots.* ■ *2.Have a flat, clean table and your supplies ready. Sand and then vacuum the foam-cores. Keep solvents away from them!* ■ *3. Put a large piece of wax paper under the wing skin. Mix a small amount of Z-Poxy, and pour it onto the wing skin in small puddles.*

SHEETING
FOAM-CORE WING PANELS

by FRANK TIANO

A "Sporty Scale" Special Report

You might be surprised to learn that over 50 percent of the R/C modelers in the U.S. have never sheeted a foam-core wing with balsa wing skins. For many of us, sheeting (skinning) a foam-core is like going to the dentist! In the past few years, many of the people I've talked to have admitted that they'd like to enjoy the advantages of a foam wing, but they didn't have the nerve to tackle such a "high-tech" procedure. Well, I'm here to tell you that it *isn't* high tech, and it *is* easy! If you've ever wanted to trust someone about this procedure, trust me—it's a piece of cake!

In this article, I'll take you through the step-by-step process of sheeting a set of Aggressor II wings from a Bob Vi-olett Models* kit. I suggest that you grab a cup, bottle, or glass of your favorite beverage, relax in a quiet spot by yourself, and read what follows—read it twice if you have to, but read every word, and look at every picture. I promise that, in less than an hour, you'll be an expert, too!

PROPER PREPARATIONS

Before you begin sheeting, make certain that the foam-cores are absolutely straight and free of dents. To keep them neat and clean, always work on the cores while they're still in the bottom half of their foam-sleeve packaging. In photo no. 1, you'll see my friend Charlie Chambers checking to see whether the Aggie's cores were straight and true. They were!

To cut or relieve any area of a wing that requires it, fasten a sharp knife or a piece of music wire (bent into the shape of a box) to your soldering gun. It's quite a simple procedure, really. Just pull the trigger on the gun, wait for the wire to get hot, and slice through the foam—it can be cut as easily as warm butter! Use a long sanding block to smooth any ripples left from the hot wire used when making your set of wings. When you've completed the construction and sanding, you're ready to start sheeting.

To do a good job, you'll have to take care. Make sure that your work area is level, clean and uncluttered (you don't want an errant screwdriver to make nasty impressions in the delicate foam), and don't forget to scrape away all those hardened CA globules that are left over from previous projects! You don't want anything to mar the fragile foam-cores.

■ 7.*Use the bottom foam sleeve as a cradle, and place the wing skin onto it (glue side up), followed by the core. Press down evenly.* ■ *8.Apply a little epoxy to the wood-frame areas surrounding the retract and bellcrank bays. Notice that Charlie is working in the foam cradle (or sleeves).* ■ 9. *After you've applied the glue, press the top skin into place, and smooth the surface with your hands to ensure contact with every square inch.*

■ 4. To cover the entire skin, squeegee the epoxy spanwise with an old credit card or playing card. Work slowly and carefully—too much epoxy only adds weight! ■ 5. A layer of epoxy covers the entire skin. ■ 6. The wing skin is ready to be placed onto the foam-core. Put epoxy around the areas of the core that need reinforcement.

(Don't worry; in less than 15 minutes, they'll go from being as fragile as a piece of your favorite crystal to as strong as a builder's 2x6!)

SUPPLIES & SUCH...

OK, now you can gather the necessary supplies. You'll need mixing cups (small paper cups are fine); a squeegee (an old credit card, or a regular playing card will do the job); mixing sticks; rubbing alcohol and paper towels (to clean up); and some of your favorite epoxy. Use an equal-mix type that has a pot life of 20 to 30 minutes and a curing time of 4 hours, or so. We use Z-Poxy* Finishing Resin, but if you have another long-curing epoxy, go ahead and use it. *Please*, stay away from anything that doesn't offer an equal-mix formula, and *never* substitute a 30-minute epoxy. (Thirty-minute epoxies are designed for construction; good ones will be too heavy for sheeting wings and quite rubbery after they've cured. They aren't meant to be sanded like finishing resins!) Something else to remember: don't be in a hurry, and *never* add extra hardener when you mix the epoxy. (Unlike polyester resin, epoxies become "gummy" when you add extra hardener—*not* harder, or more crisp!)

PAINLESS PROCESS!

Sand the assembled wing skins with a large, flat sanding block, and then vacuum the skins and the cores. Next, prepare about 1 ounce of epoxy in a cup, and pour it onto the wing skin in small puddles. (Check out photo no. 3.) Now, squeegee the epoxy all over the wing skin so that a smooth, even film covers every inch of the surface. Notice Charlie's method shown in photos no. 4 and 5. Photo no. 6 shows the skin with all the epoxy spread evenly. You can pick up any excess finishing resin with your squeegee, return it to the cup, and use it on the foam-core in areas that require beefing up. You'll notice that, in photo no. 6, Charlie has added excess Z-Poxy to the areas that had been cut from the foam-core and to the Violett Supply carbon-fiber reinforcement strip that runs spanwise along the foam panel.

Once you've applied a smooth, even coat of epoxy to the skin, as well as extra epoxy to areas that should be strengthened, place the wing skin onto the foam-core. Lay the skin in its cradle (glue side up) and nestle the foam-core into it. Make sure that the skin is in the proper location, and then go on to the other wing skin. Charlie and I worked on the bottom skin first and then the top.

Once again, we mixed an ounce of Z-Poxy, squeegeed it over the skin, and put a little extra along the retract recesses and the carbon-fiber reinforcement strip. In photo no. 8, we're now working with the foam sleeves to maintain a straight structure.

Position the top wing skin and smooth the structure by repeatedly rubbing the surface with your hands. This ensures that the thin coat of epoxy contacts every inch of the foam-core! Photo no. 9 shows how it's done, and in no. 10, you see the finished product. Check out pics 11 and 12, and you'll see why these cores must be absolutely perfect.

Put a piece of scrap plywood, or some other material, onto the foam sleeves, which now encase the sheeted cores. Use as much weight as you can (e.g. boxes of books), and distribute it *evenly* over the surface of plywood. The weight will keep the wing skins in contact with the foam-cores while the epoxy cures. For optimum results, let the structures cure overnight. Repeat the procedure for the other wing panel, stack it on top of the first panel, and put weight on top of both. It doesn't make any difference whether you weight the wing panels one at a time or together,

(Continued on page 92)

■ 10. One wing panel is almost ready to be put away overnight. ■ 11. Put the sheeted core back into its corresponding sleeve. The trailing edges will stick out slightly, but that's OK. ■ 12. You must distribute the weight evenly. The foam sleeves compress the skins and keep them next to the cores while they cure.

What is a coreless motor?

Servos use two common types of electric motors: cored and coreless. Of the two, the cored servo motor is the more conventional design. It features a central, rotating armature. An armature, in this case, consists of steel plates "stacked" around the motor shaft. Conductive wire (copper) is wrapped around the segments of the stack. When current is applied to the wire, an electromagnetic field is generated, which either repels or attracts (depending upon the flow of electricity through the wire) the field of the permanent magnets of the surrounding motor can, causing the armature to spin.

A coreless motor is like an "inside out" cored motor, in that the armature actually surrounds the permanent magnets. The conductive windings of the coreless motor are formed into the shape of a hollow tube—no stacked plates. Resin is applied to maintain the shape of the windings, which are bonded to a circular plate that holds the center shaft. The hollow armature is placed in between the permanent magnets and the motor can. Similar to the cored motor, voltage applied to the windings causes an interaction between

> In general, coreless motors produce more torque in proximity to the desired position of the servo.

the electromagnetic field and the permanent field.

By design, a coreless motor will have more torque and accelerate more quickly than a cored motor. Because of its larger diameter, the cored motor's armature wields a larger "lever" on the motor shaft for increased torque over that of a similar cored motor. Quicker acceleration comes from the lower rotating mass of the coreless motor's armature—less to get moving! Less weight also means that the coreless motor will stop quicker for better servo response and less "overshoot."

In general, coreless motors produce more torque in proximity to the desired position of the servo. This allows for better position "hold" and an increased ability for the servo to center. The downside to servos with coreless motors is that they tend to be more expensive than cored servos. Although early coreless servos were more prone to damage caused by vibrations than cored servos (the windings would sometimes fall apart from heavy shocks or sustained vibration), newer materials and manufacturing techniques make coreless servos much more reliable. ■

FOAM-CORE WING PANELS

Charlie used some Zap-a-Gap to seal the trailing edges. Trim and sand the panels to prepare them for fiberglassing. (Covered in the next installment.)

but you *must* distribute the weight as evenly as possible!

The next morning, remove the weights, and slip the sheeted cores out of their sleeves. Run a bead of Zap-a-Gap* along the trailing edges of the balsa skins, and pinch them together as you go. The trailing edges must be glued this way, because they were outside the area of the sleeves that was under the weight. Before you add the leading edges and the wing tips, put the wing panels back into their respective sleeves, and sand or trim them. Finish-sand the wing panels with 320-grit paper, and put them aside for covering.

On a scale model, or very high-performance ducted-fan aircraft like the Aggressor, the wings should be finished with fiberglass cloth and resin for more integrity and durability.

ONE PART DONE— ONE TO GO!

That completes stage one: sheeting the foam-core wings. It was simple, wasn't it? Just think of how many designs you've avoided over the years, simply because you didn't think you could do this!

For those of you who are saying that sheeting wasn't so bad, but how, in the name of Stunning, do you apply fiberglass cloth? Who makes the cloth? Which glue do you use, and how much? How many coats, and when can you sand it? Do you have to use primer, or can you go right to paint? *Relax!* I cover these questions in "Fiberglassing Sheeted Wings." Stay tuned, and in the meantime, why not go out and check a few sixes!

*Here are the addresses of the companies mentioned in this article:
Bob Violett Models, 1373 Citrus Rd., Winter Springs, FL 32708.
Z-Poxy Finishing Resin, Pacer Technology, 9420 Santa Anita Ave., Rancho Cucamonga, CA 97130.
Zap-a-Gap, Frank Tiano Enterprises, 15300 Estancia Ln., W. Palm Beach, FL 33414. ■

FIBERGLASSING
SHEETED WINGS

A "Sporty Scale" Special, Part II

by FRANK TIANO

APPLYING FIBERGLASS cloth to a balsa structure is commonly called "glassing." Years ago, modelers applied many coats of model-airplane dope to balsa to create a more durable surface—one that could be readily painted and that would resist a certain degree of "hangar rash." Later, someone suggested adding a layer of tissue paper to the doped surface for an even better finish; and still later, for increased durability, we incorporated heavy silkspan on our large, heavy flying models.

The biggest breakthrough in protecting a model's very delicate balsa structure came in the mid '60s when someone suggested bonding a layer of very light fiberglass cloth to it. Because it increased a model's life, the new method provided just about everything an R/C pilot could hope for! The fiberglass-cloth-and-resin combination creates a tough "skin" that's easy to paint and is as resistant to "dings" as possible. As a bonus, the fiberglass cloth helps to prevent the balsa from splitting along its grain in the event of a hard landing.

This glassing procedure was confined to more serious modelers; competitors, if you will. A hot Formula I pilot or an expert pattern flier wouldn't be caught dead without a glassed airplane, and many of the up-and-coming scale pilots learned the same thing: if you wanted an airplane to last, iron-on coverings just weren't the way to go!

Today, with the introduction of a new ARF every other minute, fewer and fewer people enter our sport for the enjoyment of *building* model airplanes. Many of them have an entirely different interpretation of the word "dope"; they've never heard the word "silkspan"; and they'd certainly be mortified if their new kit actually involved more than a dozen steps from start to finish!

Every day, someone comes into my shop and asks how to do something that I find elementary. They just haven't been exposed to the art of model building. For them, model-aircraft *flying* is a hobby, but model-aircraft *building* is as far from their minds as it can be!

Because of all the wonderful ARFs available today, fewer and fewer modeling skills are being passed from one enthusiast to another. Glassing is one of these mysterious skills. Although it isn't quite as intimidating as skinning a foam wing, it probably ranks right up there with meeting your girlfriend's parents for the first time!

MATERIAL MENAGERIE

To fiberglass a fuselage, wing, or stab successfully, you must first get all your materials together. You'll need a smooth, clean work surface, a couple

1. Sand the structure very carefully. Glass-cloth is so fine that any little protrusions will snag it and cause it to run—just like a nylon stocking.

2. The cloth is cut slightly oversize and laid over the parts that will be covered. (Sharp scissors are a must!) You can use either polyester or epoxy resins and achieve good results.

3. Using a soft brush, work the resin through the cloth's weave and onto the balsa. Brush it out toward the edges.

All these parts were glassed on both sides in one day, and this includes the time spent waiting for the first side to cure!

of yards of light fiberglass cloth, epoxy resin or polyester resin, some throw-away brushes, a good 1-inch brush, a squeegee (a playing card, an old credit card, or one sold by Sig*), a very sharp pair of "shop" scissors, some single-edge razor blades, a few mixing cups and an 8x3-inch sanding block.

Fiberglass cloth is classified according to how much 1 square yard of it weighs (e.g., 2-ounce cloth means that a 36x36-inch piece weighs 2 ounces). We want a high-quality,

lightweight cloth with a close weave. K&B Manufacturing* offers such a product, and you can buy it in 1-yard packages at your favorite hobby store. I prefer the cloth sold by Dan "Pappy" Parsons* in Albuquerque, NM, and my reasons are simple and numerous. For one thing, most lightweight cloths claim to weigh $^{3}/_{4}$ ounce, but many actually approach $^{7}/_{8}$ ounce. (Not too bad though, unless you're building a very "weight-conscious" airplane.) For those of you who care, however,

Pappy's cloth weighs $^{3}/_{5}$ ounce per square yard, whether you buy it today or next July—whether you buy 1 yard or several! Second, I find the luxury of buying more than a single yard in a package really advantageous, especially when I'm glassing one half of a 90-inch wing that requires a piece of cloth that's at least 50 inches long if you include the overhang. Experience has played a part in my preference. I simply prefer the way Pappy's cloth

(Continued on page 136)

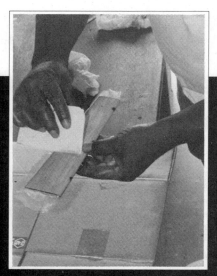

4. Charlie uses a squeegee to wipe away the excess resin. Don't leave any puddles.

5. Another way to remove excess resin is to use a paper towel. The surface should appear a little "wet," but it shouldn't have brush marks or streaks.

6. Here's a finished wing panel. After the resin cures for a few hours, the extra cloth is cut and sanded.

EASY SHELL CONSTRUCTION

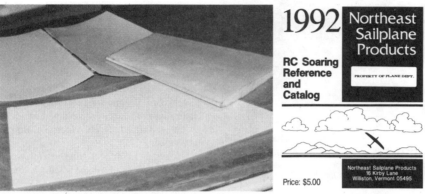

1992 Northeast Sailplane Products

RC Soaring Reference and Catalog

PROPERTY OF PLANE DEPT.

Northeast Sailplane Products
16 Kirby Lane
Williston, Vermont 05495

Price: $5.00

Left: the interior mold. Rohacell (foreground) has been cut to shape for the shell. Taped Mylar will be used to vacu-bag the exterior surface. Right: if you like sailplanes, you'll want this catalogue.

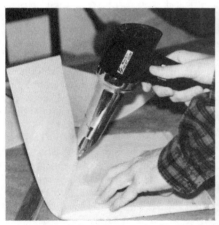

Left: form the Rohacell by warming it with a heat gun. Work carefully to prevent cracking and overheating. Right: after heat-forming the leading edge, trim the trailing edge so that the fin chord is correct along its length. Sand a taper along the interior surfaces of the Rohacell trailing edge so that the proper airfoil contour will result when the trailing edge is closed.

The mold, formed Rohacell and cut fiberglass are ready for bagging.

I HOPE you have your copy of Northeast Sailplanes'* 1992 catalogue. As usual, Sal and Stan have put together a great reference for anyone who is involved in R/C soaring, and it's only $5. More than a catalogue, it's filled with concise descriptions and measurements of more than 120 sailplane designs that range from slope to cross-country. Sprinkled throughout the catalogue are 32 articles on a variety of soaring topics, and most are new for 1992. If it had three-views and all the dimensions, NSP's catalogue could be called "All the World's Model Sailplanes."

"SANDWICH" SKIN SECRETS

Building composite sailplanes is now common, but hollow-shell construction is only for the truly dedicated. Shell construction uses a thin "sandwich," or laminate of fiberglass and foam that's shaped to the desired contours. The laminate is used to create the wing's top and bottom surfaces, which are vacu-bagged in or over a mold. The cured laminate retains the mold's shape, and the upper and lower surfaces are joined to form a hollow interior.

Typically, the shell is made with a negative mold to produce a very precise airfoil surface. Mold construction is time-consuming, and some builders actually "CNC-cut" the molds, i.e., they use computer numerical control! This is just too much work for the average builder.

I like the idea of using a shell for the fin, because it's easier to install and set up the elevator linkages or the bellcranks in the hollow interior. The question is how to build a shell quickly and with minimal work. With normal vacu-bagging techniques, you can make a shell by using a mold of the hollow interior. The pictures show the construction steps for the fin of my Aeolus 92.

The mold can be easily vacu-bagged once you determine the proper shape. The shape must account for the thickness of the shell, which can be created with any good airfoil plotting program, such as Chuck Anderson's Model Design Program* or Cygnet Software's* Foiled Again. I used

Left: apply an extra layer of fiberglass to the leading edge of the folded, heat-formed Rohacell. Some final sanding may be needed. Right: after you've wetted out the interior fiberglass layer on release film and wrap it around the mold, slip the Rohacell over this. Place this inside the outside layer of fiberglass and Mylar.

Top: the cured fin just out of the vacu-bag. Right: the Mylar is peeled off leaving a smooth finish. Next, remove the shell from the mold.

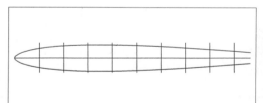

Left: this template for an interior foam mold is used to create a composite shell. To increase mold stiffness, the trailing edge is ¼ inch thick. To accommodate the shape of the mold, the SD8020 airfoil has been opened slightly at the rear to reflect the shape of the mold. This adds strength and separates the trailing edge so it's easier to remove the mold.

1.5mm Rohacell and layers of 1.4-ounce fiberglass (available from Aerospace Composite Products*, Composite Structures Technology* and Weston Aerodesign*). The mold, which consists of foam that has been cut to the modified airfoil shape, has a shaped, spruce, leading edge and a ¼x½-inch spruce trailing-edge extension. The illustration shows the airfoil and the shape of the foam and spruce. To finish the mold, vacu-bag a few layers of ¾-ounce fiberglass over the foam-core (with the Mylar taped together at the leading edge), and clean the surface after curing.

Rohacell foam is a good selection for the interior section of the shell wall. Cut the foam so that it's oversized, and wrap it around the mold's leading edge using a heat gun. Be careful not to crack the Rohacell, and don't overheat and blister the glassed mold. Trim the trailing edges equally on each side, and taper the Rohacell at the trailing edge with sandpaper. Now you're ready to vacu-bag the shell. Cut the fiberglass or Kevlar for both the interior and exterior surfaces, and cut an extra strip for the leading edge. Put the inner layer of cloth on some release film and the exterior cloth on the Mylar, and "wet out" the cloth with epoxy. Tack an extra strip on the Rohacell's leading edge and wet it out. Now wrap the release film around the mold (with cloth on the outside of the film), slip the Rohacell over the mold, and place all of this on the Mylar as you would with normal vacu-bagging. Fold the Mylar over, put the lay-up in the

(Continued on page 138)

The shell before trimming the edges and joining the trailing edge.

Glue vertical spars inside the shell before you cut the rudder. This fin is designed for a tape hinge.

The completed fin installed on my Aeolus.

6
CONSTRUCTION— BUILDING SECRETS

This section was printed and run, in its entirety, as a special supplement to one of our issues. We call these techniques "secrets" because they work quite well but aren't widely known. For example, did you know that a carpenter's contour gauge, a precision-scale plastic model and an overhead projector can be key tools for developing blueprints of a scale model? To find out more about this and other unusual techniques, read on.

BUILDING SECRETS

SPECIAL SECTION

Design and construction are key facets of our great hobby. Even diehard fliers of ARFs must repair an injured ship from time to time! And who can resist the occasional temptation to customize a model, build from a plan, or scratch-build a new design? To help you build better models, we want to bring useful building techniques to your attention—whatever your present level of skill. Do you have a building technique you'd like to share with our readers? If you do, we'd like to hear from you.

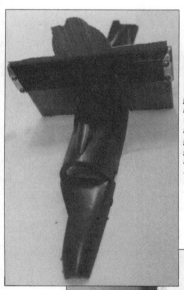

1 When you press a contour gauge onto an object, its many parallel sliding steel wires copy the object's shape precisely. Press the gauge onto the model, and gently push the ends of its steel wires so that they capture the model's contour accurately.

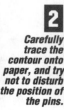

2 Carefully trace the contour onto paper, and try not to disturb the position of the pins.

SCALING UP WITH A CONTOUR GAUGE

by RUSS PRIBANIC

ONE WAY TO build an accurate scale version of an airplane is to use a precisely scaled plastic model. Revell, Inc.* is one of several companies noted for highly accurate scale plastic models. In this article, I'll show how I used Revell's 1/32-scale Harrier Jump Jet kit to scale up to a 1/8-scale, 56-inch-long ducted-fan version with a 48-inch wingspan. Although I also used other documentation (i.e., military color-scheme blueprints), the Revell model provided me with key information about the fuselage's compound curves.

You'll need a carpenter's contour gauge (available at most hardware or lumber stores) and an overhead projector. The photos tell the story.

CONTOUR GAUGE

3

Draw a 2-inch line next to the tracing. (Any length will do as long as it's measured accurately.) When you enlarge the tracing, use this line as a guide to help you capture scale proportions.

4

Transfer the tracing to a piece of the clear plastic film that's used on overhead projectors.

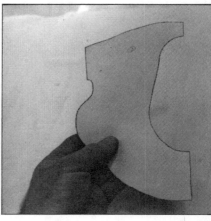

5

Hang some tracing paper on the wall where you plan to project the image. Adjust the projector so that the image isn't distorted. (One way to do this is to draw a square around the tracing on the plastic film; adjust the projector until the projection of the square is accurate.) Using the line next to the tracing as a guide, enlarge the tracing to the scale you want. (To create a 1/8-scale Harrier, I had to enlarge the 1/32-scale tracing four times, so I enlarged the image until the 2-inch line measured exactly 8 inches.) Again, check that the projection is accurate, and then trace the projected image.

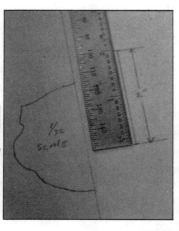

6

Here's a sample former template for the 1/8-scale Harrier that I created using this procedure.

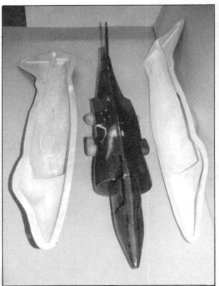

7

I used this plywood former to make a plug for the Harrier. I made a fuselage mold by laying fiberglass over the finished plug.

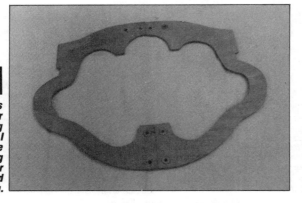

8

The joined fuselage halves are flanked by the molds.

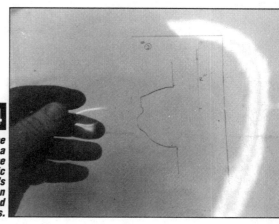

9

Here's the completed fuselage shell made of fiberglass cloth and epoxy.

Here's the address of the company that's mentioned in this article:
Revell, Inc., *Dept. FS1, 363 North 3rd St., Des Plaines, IL 60016.*

1

The foam scroll saw is easy to build.

2

First, cut the upright saw arm out of a 16-inch piece of 2x2-inch lumber. Then cut a ¹/₂-inch bevel in one end. This bevel allows the cross arm to swing, and it adjusts the tension on the cutting wire.

3

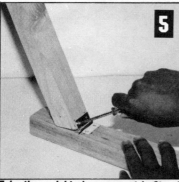

Next, cut a 16-inch cross-arm piece from another 2x2-inch piece of lumber. Draw a line about 4 inches from one end of the cross arm. Screw a hook into the same end, about 1 inch from the end of the piece.

4

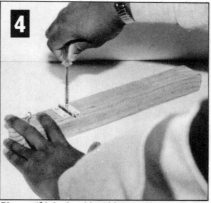

Place a 1¹/₂-inch cabinet hinge on the cross arm, centering on the mark you made earlier, and screw it into place.

5

Take the upright piece you cut in Step 2 and screw the other end of the hinge into place on the longest side of that piece (see beveled end in photo).

6

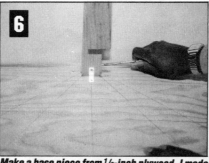

Make a base piece from ¹/₂-inch plywood. I made my base out of a piece of 18x30-inch scrap. Size isn't critical. Secure the upright to the base with angle brackets. The upright should be centered on the rear edge of the base.

7

► Install a hook on the rear of the upright, about 9 inches from the top.

Strip the insulation off ³/₈ inch of one end of a piece of a 10-foot lamp cord (lamp cord is recommended in the instructions with the hot-wire kit) and install Sermos* connectors in accordance with their instructions. Strip one inch off the other end of the lamp cord, and then part the wires for about 2 feet.

8

Attach one wire from the lamp cord to the front end of the cross piece. Sandwich the wire between two washers, and wrap it around the wood screw that holds the washers in place. Don't tighten the screw yet. Wrap a piece of .032-inch safety cutting wire or nichrome wire around the screw two or three times, and then tighten the screw.

9

PHOTOS BY BILL GRIGGS

BUILD A FOAM SCROLL CUTTER

by BILL GRIGGS

FOAM AND FIBERGLASS fuselages can be made more easily with the help of a simple, inexpensive tool called the "foam scroll cutter" (see photo 1). Many scale three-views show a variety of fuselage cross sections. You can make simple templates of these cross sections out of cardboard and then cut foam blocks to shape using the scroll saw. These blocks can then be stacked, epoxied together, and covered with fiberglass to form a fuselage. You have the option of making the foam fuselage partially hollow by cutting appropriate cores out of the sections, or dissolving the foam out entirely after you've applied fiberglass.

MATERIALS

- **Homebuilders Hot-wire Kit**
- **2 feet of stainless-steel safety wire**
- **2x2x32-inch piece of scrap lumber**
- **18x30x¹/₂-inch piece of scrap plywood**
- **1¹/₂-inch cabinet hinge and fastening screws**
- **2 eyelet or wood-screw hooks**
- **10-foot length of electric lamp cord**
- **2 wood screws and 4 metal washers**
- **5 rubber bands**

FOAM SCROLL CUTTER

10

Drill a hole in the base directly below the end of the cross arm (the wire will drop through this hole). Use a carpenter's square to precisely set the alignment. Pass the end of the safety wire through the hole.

11 ▶

Secure the safety wire to the bottom of the base—again with a wood screw and washers. Also connect the other end of the lamp cord to the screw. Attach approximately five rubber bands to the hooks on the back of the upright and cross arm. Adjust the length of the safety wire until it's taut, then tighten the screw. For neatness, tape the lamp cord to the cross arm and upright.

12

Aircraft Spruce & Specialty Co.* offers a Homebuilders Hot-wire Kit. It also sells stainless-steel safety wire by the foot or the roll. You can get the kit and all the safety wire you'll need for less than $25.

*Here are the addresses of the companies mentioned in this article:
Sermos Snap Connectors, Cedar Corners Stn., P.O. Box 16787, Stamford, CT 06905.
Aircraft Spruce & Specialty Co., Inc., P.O. Box 424, Fullerton, CA 92632.

13

14

Cut templates of light card stock and stick them to the foam blocks with double-sided tape. Just hook up the transformer and turn the power up until the foam melts easily, and you're ready to go. When all the formers have been cut, glue them together, and cover the fuselage with light fiberglass cloth.

LIGHTER TAIL FEATHERS

by RANDY RANDOLPH

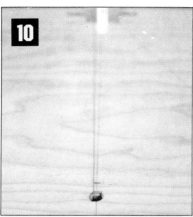

1

Here, over half the wood in a typical stab has been removed. Make sure that the leading and trailing edges of the stab and the elevator are about three times as wide as they are thick (e.g., if the wood is $1/8$ inch thick, the surface should be $3/8$ inch wide). The tips should be a little wider because of the wood's cross-grain. Next, notch the leading and trailing edges of both surfaces at the rib locations. As a rule, rib spacing of about half the average chord is usually right. The ribs should be square and of the same thickness as the surface. In some cases, you can strip them from the wood that you removed during the lightening process.

A SK ANY OLD-TIMER how to improve a model airplane's performance, and he'll say, "Add lightness." An oxymoron it is, but it can be done. The primary place to reduce a plane's weight is its tail. Most manufacturers make tail surfaces of solid-sheet balsa, because it's easy, it cuts production costs, and it reduces the kit's retail price. Air is still lighter than wood, however, so the tail surface is a good place to start a weight-reduction program. If you reduce a plane's weight in this area, you can also reduce weight in its nose and keep the balance point in the proper place. An ounce saved in the tail can sometimes enable you to reduce a finished plane's overall weight by $1/2$ pound.

2

◀ The lightening job isn't difficult, and the result is a surface that's as strong as the original but much lighter. This procedure can also be used on the fin and rudder.

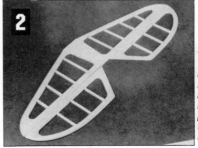

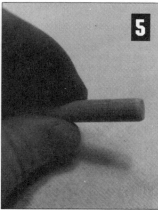

EASY, MULTIPURPOSE FIBERGLASS SHEETING

by RUSS PRIBANIC

[1]

Choose a pane of glass that's large enough to suit your project's needs. Clean the glass, apply mold release (e.g., Partall Mold Release offered by Wicks Aircraft Supply*), and wait 10 minutes for it to dry. Then cut out a piece of 3-ounce glasscloth (it weighs 3 ounces per square yard) that's 1 inch smaller than the perimeter of your glass pane. Lay the cloth on the glass.

LIGHTWEIGHT, DURABLE fiberglass and epoxy sheeting can easily be made to order. On one side, it has a glass-like finish, and on the other, it's textured so it bonds well to your model. This finished sheeting is ideal for covering wings or building structural members such as bulkheads, firewalls, hatches and the like. How light is this sheeting? Obechi wing sheeting that's .023 inches thick, with MonoKote*, weighs .92 ounce/square foot, or .22 ounce/square foot *more* than this much stronger fiberglass sheeting. Using a 3-ounce glasscloth, this sheeting weighs .7 ounce/square foot.

[2]

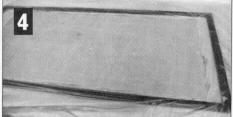

Mix approximately ½ ounce of Safe-T-Poxy* (a two-part resin epoxy) for each square foot of glasscloth, and pour the mixture over it. Use a plastic card to squeegee the epoxy evenly over the glasscloth.

[3]

[4]

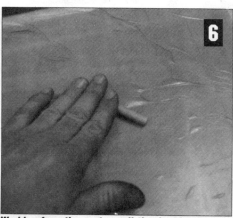

Cut a piece of plastic from a garbage bag. The piece should be larger than the pane of glass. Lay the plastic over the epoxy.

[5]

Bevel the ends of a 2-inch piece of ½-inch wooden dowel so that it won't rip or dig into the plastic.

[6]

Working from the center, roll the dowel across the plastic to smooth the epoxy, and push any excess past the edge of the glasscloth and onto the rim of the glass pane.

[7]

Leave the plastic on while the epoxy cures in a warm (80 to 90 degrees Fahrenheit) area for 24 hours, then remove the plastic.

FIBERGLASS SHEETING

Now peel the glasscloth off the glass pane. Notice the perfectly finished surface of this flexible, light, super-strong sheeting. Its upper surface retains a light texture from the weave of the cloth. It can be cut to any shape and glued (e.g, with spray-on adhesive or CA) or attached (with double-sided tape) to model surfaces, with its textured side facing down. It can also be used to create super-strong bulkhead formers (see my next article).

*Here are the addresses of the companies mentioned in this article:
Wicks Aircraft Supply, 410 Pine St., Highland, IL 62249.
Safe-T-Poxy; manufactured by Wicks Aircraft Supply.
MonoKote; distributed by Great Planes Model Distributors, 1608 Interstate Dr., P.O. Box 4021, Champaign, IL 61824.

EASY COMPOSITE FORMERS

by RUSS PRIBANIC

YOU CAN MAKE light, super-strong bulkheads and formers by gluing vertical-grain balsa between two pieces of fiberglass sheeting (see "Multipurpose Fiberglass Sheeting" in this section). Use epoxy to bond the fiberglass to the balsa. You can cut bulkheads or formers out of the composite-laminate blanks that you've made. This composite-laminate material weighs one-third as much as aircraft plywood of the same size and strength.

Put a piece of fiberglass sheeting (rough side up) on some plastic, and put the vertical-grain balsa on the fiberglass sheeting. Leave about $1/8$ to $1/4$ inch of its perimeter uncovered. If one piece isn't big enough, you can use several pieces of balsa to fill out the length or width of the former. Glue the balsa to the sheeting's rough side with the same epoxy that you used to make the fiberglass sheeting (e.g., Safe-T-Poxy).

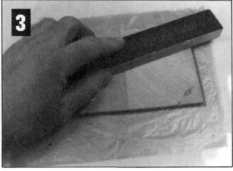

Use a sanding block or another flat tool to ensure that the balsa pieces are aligned properly, and allow the laminate to cure in a warm room for 24 hours. Then sand the top of the balsa until it's perfectly flat (don't worry about sanding it smooth; just make it true).

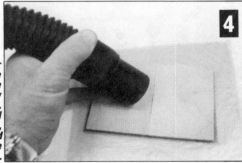

Vacuum the balsa's surface to remove any residual sawdust. Lay down the second sheet of fiberglass, rough side up, and epoxy the balsa side of the laminate to it.

Vertical-grain balsa strengthens the composite bulkheads or formers tremendously in much the same way as the shear webs strengthen a wing. Cut the balsa so that its grain is perpendicular to the fiberglass sheeting.

In this edge view of a finished laminate, you can see the balsa's vertical grain. Now you can cut a former or a bulkhead to the shape you need. This composite laminate can be used to build other structural components that have to be strong, yet light (i.e., spars, landing gear or belly-plate mounts, firewalls, hatches, etc.).

1

◀ Carbon-fiber mat. See how thin it is?—and it weighs almost nothing.

▶ Glider cradles on a Telemaster .40. Thanks to Jack Conelya for making the test cradles, which work well!

2

3

A carbon-fiber angle bracket from Bob Violett Models.

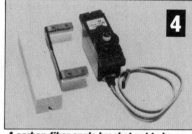

4

A carbon-fiber angle bracket cut to be used as a servo mount for the servo shown.

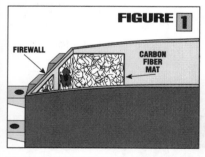

FIGURE 1

FIREWALL

CARBON FIBER MAT

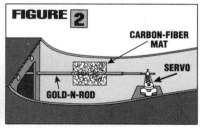

FIGURE 2

CARBON-FIBER MAT

SERVO

GOLD-N-ROD

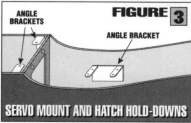

ANGLE BRACKETS

FIGURE 3

ANGLE BRACKET

SERVO MOUNT AND HATCH HOLD-DOWNS

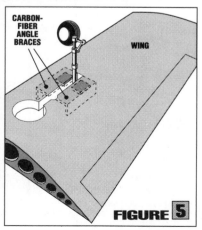

CARBON-FIBER ANGLE BRACES

WING

FIGURE 5

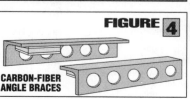

FIGURE 4

CARBON-FIBER ANGLE BRACES

USING CARBON FIBER MAT

by GREG POPPEL

IN THIS ARTICLE, I look at two useful carbon-fiber products—mat and angle brackets—which are available from Bob Violett Models* and several other suppliers of composite building materials.

CARBON-FIBER MAT'S MANY USES

This paper-thin mat is made of many thinly spread, small-diameter strands of carbon fiber, and it can be applied with thin CA, gap-filling CA, or any type of epoxy. Its potential uses are nearly endless: I use it in place of fiberglass to reinforce the firewall on my sport planes (see Figure 1), and I've also seen it used to reinforce wing center sections, where fiberglass cloth might otherwise be used.

Glider buffs who like the idea of towing their ships aloft might appreciate a cradle made of 1/8-inch medium-weight balsa that's sandwiched between carbon-fiber mat (see photo). The mat was covered with Satellite City's* UFO glue and then pressed with wax paper on each side. The paper allows a very smooth finish, and the completed cradle is stronger than plywood, but only half its weight. The cradle shown was mounted on Hobby Lobby's* Telemaster .40 and used as a carrier for gliders.

You can also use the mat to support the control rods in your airplane. If you use Sullivan* Golden-N-Rods for your rudder and elevator, you can minimize play in them by using the mat to bind the guide tubes to the fuselage sides. A local jet pilot uses it to support all the control rods in his fiberglass fuselage. He uses Flex Zap* CA and a strip of mat as shown in Figure 2.

L-ANGLE BRACKET

Another useful carbon-fiber product is the angle bracket shown in the photo. I use it as a

USING CARBON FIBER MAT

servo mount (see photo). I cut the angle stock to the overall length of the servo, and then I cut out a section of the same size as it. Next, I used thick CA to glue a piece of 1/8-inch plywood to the bottom of the tabs on which the servo is mounted. The plywood supports the servo-mounting screws. To make a good surface for bonding, use 220-grit sandpaper to roughen the side of the angle bracket that will be attached to the fuselage (Figure 3). Now you have a great servo bracket that's strong and light!

Again, following the same principle and using 200-grit sandpaper and 1/8-inch plywood, you can also use angle brackets to make hatch hold-downs (see Figure 3).

One of the best ways to use the angle bracket is as a brace for retractable landing-gear supports in foam wings (Figure 4). Use your hobby blade to make a slot in the foam that's the depth and the length of one side of the bracket. To ensure that the bracket sits flush with the wing's surface, you'll have to make a slight recess in the foam where the exposed part of the angle bracket will be attached to the bottom of the wing. Trial-fit all parts before you epoxy them. You'll be impressed with the strength of this light, reinforced, retract mount (Figure 5).

I haven't finished yet! Next month, I'll talk about carbon-fiber rods. Remember: fuel 'em, flip 'em and fly 'em. ∎

*Here are the addresses of the companies mentioned in this article:
Bob Violett Models, 1373 Citrus Rd., Winter Spring, FL 32708.
Satellite City, P.O. Box 836, Simi, CA 93062.
Hobby Lobby International, 5614 Franklin Pike Cr., Brentwood, TN 37027.
Sullivan Products, 1 North Haven St., Baltimore, MD 21224.
Flex Zap; distributed by Frank Tiano Enterprises, 15300 Estancia Ln. West Palm Beach, FL 33414.

This photo shows the finished arming switch with the auto fuse plugged into a set of Sermos connectors (left); the fuse after it has been modified (middle); and a standard auto fuse with two 1/16-inch-thick pieces of 3/16x1/4-inch brass stock that are used for the modification (right). To create a rounded outer surface on the fuse lugs, crimp these brass pieces slightly lengthwise.

Apply solder to the concave side of each brass piece and to the lug; then position the brass pieces and solder them into place.

After soldering, file the brass pieces until the lug is smooth and fits neatly into the Sermos connector. Although the rounded side "locks" into the connector easily, you can insert this type of fuse so that either the rounded, brass side or the original fuse lug touches the lead in the Sermos connector.

*Here's the address of the company featured in this article:
Sermos R/C Snap Connectors, Cedar Corner Stn., P.O. Box 16787, Stamford, CT 06905.

ELECTRIC-FLIGHT AUTO-FUSE ARMING SWITCH

by RUSS PRIBANIC

YOU CAN REDUCE your plane's weight, increase safety and minimize electrical resistance by using an arming switch made of an automotive fuse, some 1/16-inch brass stock and Sermos* Power Pole connectors. Always install an arming switch to safeguard against the motor spinning the prop between flights. To minimize power-robbing resistance, keep the wiring harness short. To arm your electric-flight power system, you simply slide the modified fuse into a jack made with Sermos connectors. The photos show how easy it is to make this fuse arming switch, and you can install it wherever you choose—under a hatch or a canopy, or through the outside of the fuselage wall. You can loop a small nylon cord or thread around the modified auto fuse to facilitate removal. ∎

7
TECHNIQUES

A modeling technique, for the purposes of this volume, is an approach, methodology or procedure that has been developed over time and has proven successful. This section contains the wisdom of experts on a number of key modeling subjects, from adjusting your carburetor to servo-output tricks. We think that these articles will add to your enjoyment of the hobby and your success at the flying field.

SIMPLE PROGRAMMING

DAVID C. BARON

SERVO OUTPUT TRICKS

BEFORE THE ERA of computer radios, limited mixing and servo-travel adjustments were set by switches, and the range of throw was set on potentiometers. Because servos left the factory set at their maximum throw settings, we were able to use these switches to compress servo travel. While these abilities were considered wonderful at the time, they've led many of us into a trap of which you may be unaware. Consider these questions:

• Have you ever used dual rates to tame an aircraft that was sensitive in the pitch, roll or yaw axis, and then not readjusted the linkage connections at your control horns or servo-output arms at the end of a flying session?

• Have you ever used your adjustable travel volumes to reduce control-surface travel in pitch, roll, or yaw?

• Has an aircraft of yours ever experienced flutter?

If you answered yes to either of the first two questions, you've been sacrificing servo power (and precision) for convenience. If you answered yes to the third question (and your pushrods and linkages aren't suffering from slop), then aerodynamic forces may be overpowering your servos.

With the advent of programmable radios, you can control servo-travel expansion as well as reduction, i.e., you can use all the potential power and efficiency of your servo's full range of travel. A servo that drives a control surface a total of 45 degrees while traveling through its full 120 degrees of motion will exert a more precise and powerful force on the control surface than a servo that's restricted to 60 degrees of motion to move the same surface the same 45 degrees. The gear drive of a servo that moves through 120 degrees, by comparison, spreads the load out across the servo's full range of travel.

Most servos have the mechanical ability to travel through 120 degrees of throw.

(The only exception that I am aware of is the Airtronics systems that are designed to allow only 90 degrees of motion.) Every time that we restrict (or compress) our servo's throw, we are giving up chunks of information that represent lost motion. Test your own setup by making a paper protractor that is graduated into 15 degree sections. Punch a hole in the center and mount it under the output

Figure 1

The little numbers on the output arms of your servos correspond to how many degrees of offset the arms will be from an arbitrary starting point on the output spline (see text). The spline is the notched shaft on which the servo wheel or multi-point arm is mounted. Manually adjust the output wheel/arm so that the arm to which the pushrod is attached is perpendicular to the length of the pushrod. This is better than changing the centering with your transmitter.

arm of your servo. Are you using the full 45 or 60 degrees available in each direction? If you aren't, the motion you are not using could be increasing power and precision on your control surface.

I'm not suggesting that all modelers are cutting down the throws that drastically, but did you know that two of the major manufacturers are keeping 33 percent of the servo's travel and power in reserve? You may not have noticed because of the way the information is presented in the manuals and on the transmitter's information screen! All this lost motion and power can be released from the transmitter.

SETTING UP

To use your servo throws to maximum advantage, you must install your airborne system with great care. Your servos may be moving a lot farther than they ever did before. The output arms of the servos must be carefully set so that they're perpendicular to the control rods. Remember that the numbers at the base of the arms on the "multiple-horn" servo-output arms correspond to degrees from zero.

Thus, if you rotate the servo wheel or multi-point output arm on the servo spline, i.e., by removing, rotating and reinstalling it, to find a position where one of the arms most closely approaches the desired position, you'll find that each servo arm will be positioned slightly differently with respect to your control rod. These differences are matters of a few degrees, and those degrees are specified by the numbers on the arms.

Use this mechanical method, instead of any electronic method, to arrive at a perfect perpendicular angle to your pushrod. This way, the radio is left at zero with an equal amount of electronic signal for each direction of servo throw. To take advantage of maximum servo travel, you'll also need to use the large control horns on your control surfaces, but this will only increase the precision and efficiency of your installation.

NEED TO RESET SERVO CENTERS?

Any programmed offset either side of a servo's center affects the total travel to either extreme when you are using all of the travel available. To guarantee your servos are centered, you may want to use the reset function whether you're modifying a previously used program or starting from scratch. It's also a good idea to use your transmitter to reset the servo centers to zero if you've used any of the following functions that affect servo centering:

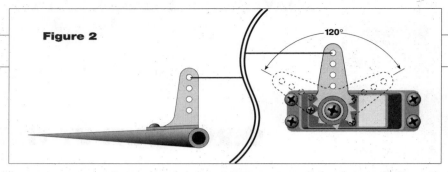

Figure 2

Full motion of the servo will drive the control surface with the greatest precision and power. The outermost hole on the control horn should be used to extract the smoothest control. If there's too much throw, move the pushrod to an inner hole on the servo's control arm to desensitize the linkage.

• "Trim memory" or "sub trims" (Futaba*)
• "Sub trim" or "Trim offset adjustment"(JR*)
• "Electronic surface centering" (Airtronics*)

HOW MUCH THROW?

Most of the manufacturers use travel-volume extremes that exceed 100 percent. This has always seemed a little odd to me because I don't expect that there could be a range beyond 100 percent. The manufacturers are really describing incremental points of travel throw as percentages. To my knowledge, only Airtronics uses 100 percent to represent maximum servo throw. This is in their Infinity and Vision series of radios using their "ATRCS" system. Here are some observations that may be of interest if you own one of these major brands of computerized radio.

ALL RADIO SYSTEMS

When manipulating servo travel, remember that each side of neutral must be adjusted separately. If you adjust one side, remember to change the other as well. This may not be of paramount importance on the elevator channel, but it could be critical with the ailerons!

FUTABA

Futaba radios vary depending on the model. They all have the feature ATV (adjustable travel volume), but they'll either have a range of 0 to 110 percent or 0 to 120 percent on either side of neutral. All of the Futaba radios start at 100 percent when new, or if reset. One of the additional features in the 9VAP radio is AFR (adjustable function rate). This feature is specifically designed for those of us who use heavily mixed radios, and it provides an additional margin of travel throw! (More on this in the future.)

JR

JR radios abbreviate endpoint adjustment in different ways. It's called ATV on the PCM-10, and on the X-347, it's called "T.ADJ." Both have a maximum of 150 percent throw to either side of neutral. This gives you very fine control over the extremes of servo travel.

AIRTRONICS

The default setting for the servo-throw extremes is 66 percent. (This applies to the Infinity 600 and Visions series radios.) While this is very realistic in terms of your flying needs, it allows a coarser adjustment than the other manufacturers offer. (Airtronics will be offering a finer adjustment system in the upcoming Infinity 660 and 1000 radios due out later this year.) One advantage of the Infinity 600 system is that when a transmitter says you have achieved 100% of servo throw, it means 100% and there is no more available.

ACE

Ace's* system for setting travel throws is unique. You use the appropriate transmitter stick to deflect the specified control surface while in the "Setting endpoints mode" (3.3a). This allows you maximum servo travel, and you choose throw by displacing the "stick" to the amount you want. When you depress the "Option" button, this amount of throw becomes the new limit of travel. As always, care must be taken to mechanically set up your servos to allow the appropriate control-surface travel before fine-tuning with the transmitter.

BENEFITS

By using these tricks, you may avoid the need to buy more powerful servos for a larger or faster plane you're planning, or you may even cure a flutter problem. You can be assured of more precise control. The only trade-off for power and precision is transit speed, yet a servo doing less work can also be a faster servo. Another point to remember is that in the manufacturers' servo specifications, speeds/times are sometimes recorded with 6V battery packs. Watch out for the fine print!

*Here are the addresses of the companies mentioned in this article:
Futaba Corp. of America, 4 Studebaker, Irvine, CA 92718.
JR; distributed by Hobby Dynamics Distributors, P.O. Box 3726, Champaign, IL 61826.
Airtronics Inc., 11 Autry, Irvine, CA 92718.
Ace R/C Inc., 116 W. 19th St., Box 511C, Higginsville, MO 64037. ∎

> *I invite you to send in any problems (or creative solutions) that you may have encountered as you've programmed your radios. Be sure to include the make and model of your radio, as well as a rough description of your aircraft's layout, e.g., let me know if you're using a separate servo for each aileron. Include a complete description of what you're trying to accomplish. Send inquiries to Simple Programming, Model Airplane News, 251 Danbury Rd., Wilton, CT 06897.*

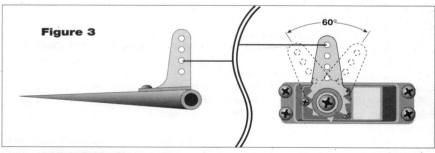

Figure 3

With reduced servo throw, you must use a hole that's closer to the inside on the control horn at the control surface. This gives the pushrod less leverage to overcome the burdens of weight and airflow as it moves the control surface.

Trim Sailplanes for Aerobatics

For more precise maneuvers

by JEF RASKIN

I T CAN BE difficult to trim a model sailplane for aerobatics. For example, if a plane never finishes a loop in the direction from which it started, this can be the result of bad aileron trim or rudder trim—assuming that you're flying the plane correctly. The two effects can look the same. This article explains how to tell what bugs have gotten into your plane, how to tell similar effects apart, and how to fix them. A lot of these techniques are the same or similar to those used to set up aerobatic power planes; in fact, we have a simpler task, since there's no torque from the spinning propeller and no spiraling slipstream to complicate the way our planes fly.

What we want to achieve is an ideal aerobatic sailplane. It should have the same response upside-down (inverted) and right-side up, which means that it can maneuver equally well and with the same control inputs in either orientation. A well-trimmed sailplane should track easily through inside and outside loops without rolling to right or left, and it should come out on the same heading as when it started. Applying rudder should yaw the plane sideways without causing to roll, climb, or dive.

To test your airplane, you'll have to be able to fly upright and inverted and do inside and outside loops. Rudder, elevator and aileron control are assumed, although some of these tests apply to 2-channel planes. The case where there are flaps (usually coupled to the elevator) is also considered.

BENCH TESTING

Trimming starts on the building board. The first thing to check is whether one wing is heavier than the other. How you test this depends on the plan: with some fuselages, you can put a pin in the tip of the nose and another in the end of the tail cone. Tie two threads to these pins and suspend the airplane from the threads. The heavier wing will, of course, rotate to the bottom. You can correct the condition by putting weights in the wing tip of the lighter wing.

Flight testing can distinguish incorrect aileron trim from either wing-heaviness or incorrect rudder trim, but it can't diagnose both at once. This is why we must correct any wing heaviness (which, unlike the other problems, can be detected in the shop) before we start flight testing.

It's essential that all control surfaces have no free play. They must

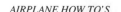

2.
Use a gauge to check centering and throw.

center to their neutral position precisely. Don't simply eyeball this, but check with a ruler or other guide to see that all surfaces return precisely to the center from both sides. If a surface has free play or doesn't return to center, then you can't flight test for proper trim, since the airplane is a different beast depending on what you last did! You can't fly precision aerobatics unless you have a model built with precision.

The balance point must be as described in the plans or as calculated by the usual formulas. When using a program (such as MaxSoar) that gives you a range of balance locations, you'll find that it's best to choose the rearmost point of the specified range, or even a bit behind it, since most computer programs are designed for non-aerobatic flight.

A fully aerobatic plane shouldn't have differential ailerons because the differential would work against

you in inverted flight or outside maneuvers. The ailerons should have no warps and move equal amounts up and down on both wings. Use a ruler or a homemade gauge. It's also important to seal the gaps between surface and control: unequal gaps can act like warped wings. The same goes for all controls. The control motion should never be more than 30 degrees each side of center.

• **Side view.** If the plane has a symmetrical airfoil, set the ailerons and elevator to neutral and check that the wing incidence and stabilizer incidence are both zero. I use an incidence gauge or measure from a flat surface. If your plane doesn't have a symmetrical airfoil, it's difficult to make it behave the same inverted as upright.

• **Top view.** Viewed from above, the wing and stabilizer must be perpendicular to the fuselage center line. In this regard, my planes are square within $1/32$ inch at the wing tips. I make sure the wing is centered and then check the distance from a corner of the wing tips (or some other easy-to-measure-from point) to the center of the fuselage at the rear. It takes a few tries to equalize these pairs of measurements, but it can be done. The fin should lie directly along the fuselage center line. Since there's no propeller, there's no reason for the fin to be angled as on some power planes.

3.
Measure the distance from the wing tips to the center of the aft end of the fuselage. The tips must be equidistant from that point.

• **Front view.** As seen from the front or rear, the wing and stabilizer should be parallel and horizontal. If there's any dihedral, it must be equal on both sides: most precision aerobatic sailplanes have no dihedral in the wing or stabilizer. The fin should be vertical and centered.

• **Control surfaces.** There must not be any free play; all gaps must be sealed; the surfaces must return perfectly to center from both sides, and they must have no more than 30 degrees of throw each side of neutral.

Summary. *If the plane isn't built right and tight, it won't do well in flight. All the rest of these*

1.
Test for lateral balance; the plane must hang with wings level.

tests will be useless if the plane isn't true and square.

TEST FLYING

The tests outlined here are given in a certain order. To detect the "culprit" in a plane that won't fly right, we have to examine our clues one at a time. Only after we've eliminated certain problems can we begin to diagnose others. Unfortunately, pilot error can mask some of the effects we're looking for (for example, you might be unknowingly adding a little aileron whenever you use the elevator), so do each test a number of times and, if you can, with more than one pilot.

THE HANDS-OFF TEST

To repeat: if, and only if, the plane has been built accurately will flight testing clearly reveal any further problems. The first test is to put the craft into straight and level flight. A good aerobatic plane is surprisingly stable and can fly for at least five seconds hands-off without any noticeable roll, pitch, or yaw in smooth air. If you can't trim it so that this is the case, then it was poorly designed, built crooked, has loose controls, or is tail-heavy.

DISTINGUISHING BETWEEN THE EFFECTS OF DIHEDRAL AND SWEEPBACK

Both excessive dihedral and excessive sweep will cause the plane to roll when you apply rudder. If your plane has no sweepback (as measured at the quarter-chord line, not at the leading edge) then you only have dihedral to worry about.

4.
Yaw-roll coupling can be caused by too much sweep or too much dihedral.

To avoid problems caused by excessive sweepback, I build my planes with less than 10 degrees of sweep to avoid any problems from this cause. Here's how you find out if you have a problem:

Fly upright straight and level. Apply rudder. The plane should yaw without dropping a wing. If the plane rolls right with right rudder, there's too much dihedral or sweepback; if it rolls left with right rudder, then more dihedral or

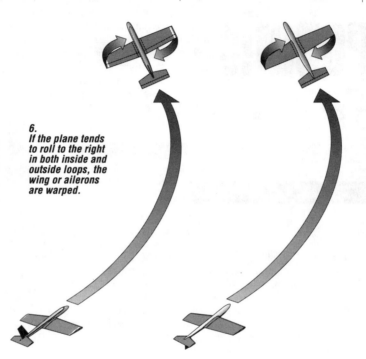

6.
If the plane tends to roll to the right in both inside and outside loops, the wing or ailerons are warped.

sweepback is needed. A high wing acts like dihedral.

To tell which is which, fly inverted straight and level. Apply right rudder. If the plane rolls right both upright and inverted the effect is due to too much dihedral. If it rolls right when upright and left when inverted, the effect is due to excessive sweep. It's a good idea to have no sweep (measured at the quarter-chord line) in an aerobatic plane.

If the plane pitches up or down when rudder is applied, then the fin and rudder are probably too large: shorten them. If the plane doesn't yaw, the rudder is probably too small. It's generally better to increase the chord of the rudder/fin assembly than its height, since if the fin and rudder are too tall, you'll get some yaw in your aileron-

only rolls. This is opposite the advice for thermal sailplanes where the efficiency of a higher aspect ratio surface is desirable.

Summary. *Design with no or little sweep. Then if right rudder rolls the plane right in upright flight, you'll know that there's too much dihedral; if right rudder rolls the plane left, there's too little dihedral.*

5.
Make sure that the plane yaws but doesn't roll with rudder input.

SEPARATING RUDDER AND AILERON EFFECTS

Both out-of-trim ailerons (or warped wings) and an out-of-trim rudder or fin can cause rolling when you apply the elevator. Here's how to tell them apart. From dead-level flight (perhaps after a dive to pick up speed) into the wind, do an inside loop upward. Do this a few times. It should loop without requiring aileron or rudder input. Note if it rolls one way or the other.

Say it rolls slightly to the right. This could be due to having one wing heavier than the other, to the ailerons being out of trim, or to the rudder or fin not being centered. The wing heaviness can be (and should have been) fixed on the bench. Technically, even if the wing is static balanced when you test it in the shop, an uneven distribution of the weight can still couple pitch to roll, but for any reasonably well-built wing, this effect will be too slight to notice.

If the plane rolls while you're

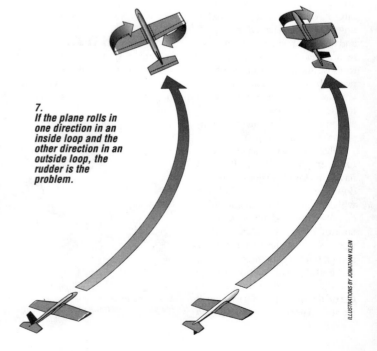

7.
If the plane rolls in one direction in an inside loop and the other direction in an outside loop, the rudder is the problem.

ILLUSTRATIONS BY JONATHAN KLEIN

Trim Sailplanes for Aerobatics

doing an inside loop, try flying the plane inverted and do an outside loop upward (just as you did the inside loop upward). If the plane still rolls to the right, then the problem is a warped wing or incorrect aileron trim. This effect can also signal a warped stabilizer.

If, however, the plane always rolls to the left in an outside loop and rolls to the right in an inside loop, there's some right trim to the rudder (assuming the wings are balanced).

Summary. *If inside and outside loops make a plane roll in opposite directions, the problem is rudder trim; if it rolls in the same direction, the problem is aileron trim.*

DISTINGUISHING WING WARP FROM AILERON TRIM

When flying at a constant speed, you can trim out the effects of wing warp with the ailerons. However, as your speed changes, the amount of aileron needed will also change, making the plane difficult to fly with precision. To test for this, trim the elevator for slow, hands-off flight; as slow as your plane can go without stalling. Then, using elevator only, gradually dive the airplane until it's pointed straight down. (I have a suspicion that it's best to start this test pretty high up.) If it rolls on the way down, you have a warped wing or, what's less likely, a warped stabilizer. A flexible plane can also cause problems—aerobatic mod-

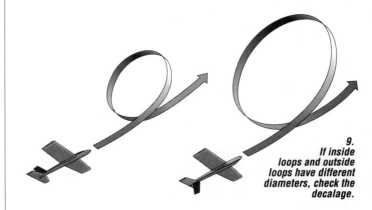

8.
If the plane snaps out of the bottom of a downward loop, the wing tips need more chord or a thicker airfoil. Too much sweep or a too-small or all-flying stab can also cause this.

els must be stiff! Misalignment of the fin or rudder can also cause a roll when diving, so you'll have to make sure that the fin and rudder pass their tests first.

ARE YOUR WING TIPS TOO THIN OR NARROW?

Some aerobatic models have the nasty habit of snapping out at the bottom of a downward loop. This can be caused by a stab that's too small, but inadvertent snapping is more often caused by tip stalling due to incorrect wing design, e.g., the wing tips may be too thin. Alternatively, the tips may have too little chord. The tip chord should not be less than half the root chord on an aerobatic model.

Excessive sweep is another cause of premature tip stalling, but if you have no roll with rudder as mentioned above, then the sweep probably isn't your problem. On some models, I've cured tip stalling by limiting elevator travel, but

a well-designed plane won't exhibit this problem under any conditions.

A last cause of inadvertent snaps is the use of an all-flying stabilizer. A conventional stabilizer with movable elevator is less prone to stalling. This is because it's a cambered surface and can achieve more force for a given area. It's generally best not to use all-flying surfaces in aerobatic models.

WHERE SHOULD THE PLANE BALANCE ?

This is a matter of taste, unlike, say, yaw-to-roll coupling which is always undesirable for aerobatics. If the plane won't fly hands-off unless you add some nose weight, then it's tail-heavy, as I mentioned above, but how can you tell if you've added too much weight? Trim for normal upright flight and then roll inverted. The plane should require only a tiny amount of down, well within the usual trim-control range, to fly level inverted. If it requires more than this, it's too nose-heavy. My best planes will fly either upright or inverted without trim change; none requires more than one or two clicks of the trim lever.

DECALAGE

If the wing has more or less angle of attack than the stabilizer, then inside and outside loops won't be the same diameter, and one will require more control input than

the other. A more precise test, however, is to fly the plane upright and inverted in slow passes in front of you. Observe the elevator deflection; it should be in the same amount but in opposite directions on the two passes. If there's too much angle of attack, there will be more elevator deflection when flying inverted; if there's too little, there will be more elevator deflection when flying upright. There's too much to think about when flying aerobatics to have to worry about different amounts of elevator input just because you're inverted.

FLAPS

It's getting more common to couple flaps or flap-ailerons (flaperons)

9.
If inside loops and outside loops have different diameters, check the decalage.

to the elevator (as with many control-line stunters). The flaps go in the opposite direction from the elevator, although they don't move through nearly as large an angle. This makes loops tighter, makes the plane more efficient, and allows the use of thinner airfoils. If you can uncouple the flaps from the elevator, first make sure that the plane is trimmed correctly without them. Then run the same tests with the flaps operational. Any problems introduced will then be due to the flaps, and you can diagnose them as aileron or decalage errors.

SUMMARY

Following this outline will help get you a sailplane that can do precision aerobatics. Flying the maneuvers is now up to you. ■

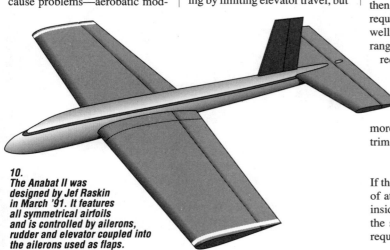

10.
The Anabat II was designed by Jef Raskin in March '91. It features all symmetrical airfoils and is controlled by ailerons, rudder and elevator coupled into the ailerons used as flaps.

How To Compute the Mean Aerodynamic Chord

Graphic solutions for straight, swept and tapered wings

by JAMES McCLURE

JUST ABOUT THE one most important factor in flying your model safely and successfully is balancing the model to place its center of gravity (CG) in the proper location. The generally accepted location of the CG is at a point that's at 25 percent of chord of the mean aerodynamic chord (MAC) from the leading edge of the MAC. This article shows you how to locate the MAC so that you have the proper reference for your preferred CG location, be it at the 20 percent or 25 percent or wherever.

First, let's define the MAC. In *Peery's Aircraft Structures,* by David J. Peery (McGraw-Hill Book Co. Inc., 1950), we find: "For a rectangular wing planform, the value of the MAC is equal to the wing chord, and for a trapezoidal planform of the semi wing the value of the MAC is equal to the chord at the centroid of the trapezoid." Note that it is *not* the average chord.

The following method for finding the MAC is from *Elements of Practical Aerodynamics,* by Bradley Jones (John Wiley and Sons, 1942).

1. Draw the wing full-scale, or to scale on graph paper, if it's a large wing. These dimensions are required:
a=length of root chord
b=length of tip chord
s=sweepback of leading edge of tip chord
y=perpendicular distance, root chord to tip chord

2. Construct the following lines:
25-percent chord line (between 25 percent points on root and tip chords)
50-percent chord line
Extend root chord "a" aftward by length "b"
Extend tip chord "b" forward by length "a"
Draw a line from 1 to 2 as shown on the illustration.

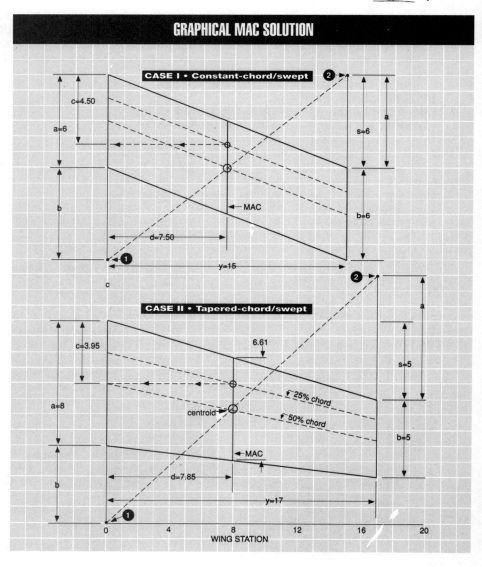

GRAPHICAL MAC SOLUTION

CASE I • Constant-chord/swept
c=4.50   a=6   b   d=7.50   y=15   s=6   a   b=6   MAC

CASE II • Tapered-chord/swept
c=3.95   a=8   b   6.61   s=5   a   b=5   25% chord   50% chord   centroid   MAC   d=7.85   y=17

WING STATION

3. Where line 1-2 intersects the 50-percent chord line is the centroid of the half wing, and a chord drawn through the centroid is the MAC. Draw in this MAC, and the intercept of the MAC with the 25-percent chord line is the 25 percent MAC that we're looking for. Project this point perpendicularly to the root chord. This gives us dimension "c." as shown on the illustration. Now we have the answer, using only graphical methods. Locate and mark this position on your fuselage.

4. If you're handy with math, or wish to check the precision of your graphical solution, you can calculate dimension "c" directly, as follows:

$$c = \frac{s(a+2b)}{3(a+b)} + \frac{1}{6}\left(a+b-\frac{ab}{a+b}\right) \quad (25\% \text{ MAC only})$$

Case I is a typical, constant-chord swept wing. Since it's constant chord, the MAC is at mid-span, and dimension "c" can be found by drawing the mid span chord, locating the 25-percent point on the chord, and projecting this point to the root chord. Case II is a tapered/swept wing, which requires the full solution. Now let's do Case II by the geometry equation:

$$c = \frac{5(8+(2 \times 5))}{3(8+5)} + \frac{1}{6}\left(8+5-\frac{8\times5}{8+5}\right) = 3.9615$$

(You can compare this answer to 3.95.) This method is applicable only when both leading and trailing edges are straight. Remember that the leading and trailing edges must be drawn so that they continue to the center of the fuselage, even though you might not be able to see the wing inside the body.

It's that simple, and it sure beats the "eyeballing" method when you're scratch-building a tapered-wing plane. ∎

Make realistic pilot figures

You can do several things to make inexpensive pilot figures look more realistic. A shiny, bug-eyed pilot looks better than no pilot at all, but not very lifelike.

FEATURES

When painting a pilot figure, the biggest mistake most modelers make is to make the eyes too big. With one quick look in the mirror, you'll see that you don't have big round eyes—unless you're some relation to Eddie Cantor.

PAINT

I frequently see entire figures painted with glossy paint. A pilot with shiny hair looks like a rock star from the '50s; and whoever heard of high-gloss skin? Flat paint should be used for hair, skin, clothing and just about everything except the things that are naturally shiny, such as eyes, seat-belt buckles, etc. You probably won't find this paint at your favorite R/C shop; it's sold in hobby shops that sell plastic models, trains, dollhouses, etc., comes in small bottles and is inexpensive. There's only one drawback: it isn't fuelproof, so if you have an open cockpit, you'll have to put a clear coat of flat, fuelproof paint on the figure.

INSIGNIAS

While you're at the hobby shop, look at the decal sheets. Miniature decals make excellent insignias or squadron emblems. You can add details to helmets and clothing that will really set your pilot apart from the crowd of plastic dummies.

POSITIONING

Real pilots rarely sit straight up and stare straight ahead, but most pilot busts do. Many pilot figures allow the head to be positioned. Moving it a little left or right and down and forward will make a major improvement to your pilot's looks. If you have a pilot figure with an attached head, simply cut the head off at the neck where it joins the collar, reposition it, and glue it back into place.

CHARACTER

If you don't like the "Ken doll" look of most pilot figures, it's easy to change. You can shape Sig Epoxolite two-part putty with a wet finger or tool, and carve or sand it when it's hard. It sticks well to plastic, and it's easy to paint. Use it to make hair, sideburns, or beards, or to change any of the pilot's features.

Why not put yourself in the pilot's seat for your next project?

—*Faye Stilley*
∎

> Miniature decals make excellent insignias or squadron emblems. You can add details to helmets and clothing that will really set your pilot apart...

The author's first R/C model.

PLOTTING AIRFOILS

by AL CULVER

It's easy when you understand the basics; this should help!

With a hot 40, it runs with the Q 500s.

Generating airfoil sections has always been a problem for novice model-airplane designers. Many have addressed the issue, but they make it so technical that most "non-engineers" are left in the dark. Airfoils do amazing feats of lifting and transporting my creations around the sky. I've never flown a kit airplane that came close to providing the excitement of flying my own design, and I won't waste my time on ARFs. If that sounds like a real ego trip, all I can say is, "Try it; you might like it!" Model building can be as much fun as model flying.

To keep the technical stuff to a minimum, let's define some of the terms. I assume you know what leading edge, trailing edge, span and chord are. If not, please ask one of your flying friends.

• **A chord line** is the line drawn from the leading edge to the trailing edge, and it passes through the center of both.

• **The chord plane** is the plane formed by all the chord lines in the wing. Note that washout, or wash-in, or using more than one airfoil in a wing, cause the chord plane to bend, and it will no longer be a flat plane.

• **Airfoil thickness** is expressed as a percentage of the chord.

• **Aspect ratio** is the ratio of chord to span.

• **Mean aerodynamic chord** (MAC) is simply the wing's average chord. MAC is vitally important to the designer.

Since this article is geared toward beginning designers, I'll write in generalities. What I say won't be true for every case but it will be for most, and as you gain experience, you'll develop your own rules.

Twelve-percent airfoils (thickness-to-chord ratio) are close to optimum for our use. If you *increase* the thickness of the airfoil, the lift and drag increase.

The author's third .40-size F2G and his second wooden fuselage.

LEARN MORE ABOUT AIRFOILS

Want to know more about airfoils and aerodynamics? Read the book! "Model Aircraft Aerodynamics," one of the best sources on this subject, is a practical guide to standard aerodynamic theory as it applies to model planes. It discusses the factors that affect lift and drag; basic performance problems; trim and stability; camber and drag; and turbulent-flow and laminar-flow airfoils. Complemented by many charts, graphs and illustrations, the information is presented in an easy-to-read format. The author, Martin Simons, is a professor at the University of Adelaide in Australia, and the book is available from Motorbooks International in Osceola, WI.

Because drag usually increases faster than lift, the airplane will have a slower top speed and a slightly slower stall speed. If you *decrease* the thickness of the section, the lift and drag will decrease. In this case, lift decreases faster than drag, so the airplane will have a narrower speed range, i.e., a slightly higher top speed and a higher stall speed. Racers are willing to trade the broad speed range for all-out top speed, whereas many sport and scale airplanes trade the broad speed range for the soft, gentle handling qualities of the 16- to 18-percent airfoils.

If you had only one airfoil to work with, the above statements would be specific; when you've determined what characteristics and speed range you're after, however, you can optimize performance by choosing the right airfoil.

CHOOSING AN AIRFOIL

• **Symmetrical wing sections,** i.e., those with the same curve above and below the chord line, on a wing with a large area-to-weight ratio will make the plane aerobatic and provide good overall flying characteristics.

• **Flat-bottom wings** produce high-lift, stable, slow-flying airplanes and, as a result, show up on trainers and many scale models whose airfoils duplicate those used on the full-scale original. Most airfoils fall between these types, combining the best qualities of each.

The airfoils of model airplanes are *functionally* similar, but not identical, to the airfoils used in full-size airplanes, because air molecules refuse to cooperate by shrinking at the same ratio. Usually, the best and worst characteristics in any airfoil degenerate as its size is reduced until, at about 3 inches of chord, a flat plate would be just as good at producing lift.

I collect old wing ribs and label them according to type of airplane they came from and whether I liked the way they flew. If I build something similar, I have a starting place for the airfoil. Most model airfoils are made with a French, or ship's, curve and use the "pleasing-to-the-eye" design criteria. Once again, this is possible because of the short chords we use.

Not all wings are constant chord and constant thickness, and many don't even use the same airfoil at the tip and root. Given these possibilities, how do you draw the individual ribs? I hear you saying, "Build a foam wing." That's a solution, but it isn't the only one. Considerations such as control-linkage routing, equipment mounting, flying- or landing-load distribution may make a built-up wing more desirable, so let's look at some ways to draw sections of different sizes.

The first step is to determine the airfoil coordinates. These are the points that, if connected by a line, would describe the airfoil. If you use an airfoil shown in a book or some other ref-

erence source, this is how it's described. Until you do it yourself once or twice, it may not be easy to understand, so let's try it:

Draw the airfoil on a piece of paper (the sharper the pencil, the better). Next, draw a chord line through the airfoil section. Lines drawn perpendicular to the chord line at the leading edge and trailing edge will give you the 0-percent and 100-percent points of the chord line. Divide the chord line into 10-percent intervals and label each line.

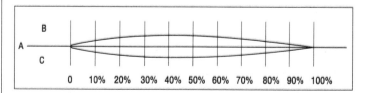

At this point, a good vernier caliper is the best tool for the job, but you can use a set of dividers and a good scale. Set up a table like this to record your findings:

	10%	20%	30%	40%	50%	60%	70%	80%	90%
AB	.333								
AC	-.333								

Measure A to B and divide by the chord length. I'll use a chord length of 12 inches, AB equals .333; .333 divided by 12 equals .02777, which equals 2.78 percent (expressed as a percentage of the chord), so you enter:

	10%	20%	30%	40%	50%	60%	70%	80%	90%
AB	2.78								
AC	-2.78								

If the wing is symmetrical, AC will be the same, and it's entered as -2.78 percent. Find all the other percentage stations in the same way, and enter them. Measurements above the chord line are positive; those below are negative. (With a reflex trailing edge, it's possible to have a -AB, and an undercambered section could have a +AC.)

To develop a different-size rib, merely determine the new chord length and multiply them back. For example: with a 9-inch chord, .0278 multiplied by 9 equals .250 (or ¼ inch). Note that this time, your table is in inches, not percentages, because you have defined the new chord length as 9 inches.

	10%	20%	30%	40%	50%	60%	70%	80%	90%
AB	.250								
AC	-.250								

This means that, for the same airfoil, on the beginning 12-inch section, 1.2 inches from the leading edge the airfoil is .333 inches above and below the chord line. On the 9-inch chord, .9 inch from the leading edge, the thickness is .250 inch above and below the chord line. Both spots are at the 10-percent chord line. Obviously, the more divisions you make on the airfoil, the more accurate your reproduction will be.

This is the easiest way I know to get all the ribs for an elliptical wing that uses the *same* airfoil all the way to the tip. If you want to change the airfoil from the root to the tip on one of these elliptical-planform wings, you're already past the scope of this article.

How about non-elliptical wings that change airfoils from the root to the tip? As long as the leading and trailing edges are unbroken (straight root to tip), the following method works well and is accurate. Draw the two airfoils, complete with chord line and percentage stations.

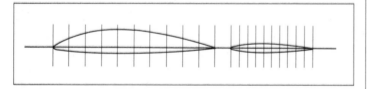

The math gets a little tricky, so I'll do this one mechanically. Measure each airfoil as before, but make a front-view drawing of each station that's the thickness of the rib. Lay out the length of half the span. We'll measure the points on the root and tip ribs.

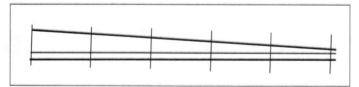

Measure the distance at each rib location to get the individual rib coordinates for that percentage point. (The diagram above shows the points of maximum rib thickness from root to tp.) Ten of these drawings will give you all the rib coordinates. The more percentage points you use, the more accurate your drawing will be.

I don't want to talk about center of gravity and center of lift too much because, in the model field, small chords seem to distort some of the facts that apply to full-scale airfoils. I will say that the further forward the maximum thickness is on a model airfoil, the more critical the center of gravity (CG) will be. Most of my airfoils have a maximum thickness at about 40 percent; on Quicky 500s, I've flown wings with maximum thickness points as far aft as 60 percent.

Aft CGs and critical CGs (not always the same) often mani-

This 93-inch P38 isn't contest material, but they love it at fun flys.

fest themselves first in poor takeoff behavior and degenerate from there; the worst case is an uncontrollable airplane that stalls and snaps into the ground on takeoff.

The only airplane that's too nose-heavy is one without enough elevator power to flare it on landing. Start with the CG well forward and work it back until the ship flies the way you want. Make the CG changes gradually; when it snaps out of a loop or a stall, you've gone too far!

Initially, I locate the CG at 25 percent of the MAC. I've never gone behind 35-percent MAC on conventional planforms. The trap we fall into is accurately locating 25-percent MAC. Several of my friends have flown kit-built CAP 21s; because the plans showed the CG at 30 percent of the *root* chord (what's known as an aft CG), they were plagued with "snappers."

Look down on the wing and imagine a line drawn through the 25-percent chord ordinates. If the wing has a straight leading edge or is swept back toward the trailing edge, that line will not be straight from tip to tip. Obviously, only constant-chord, rectangular-planform wings will allow the 25-percent point to remain fixed across the span.

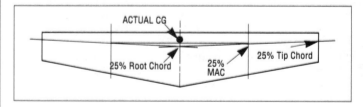

As I've already said, the MAC is the average of the tip and root chords. A line drawn from the 25-percent MAC on each wing will pass through the proper CG location and fall forward of the 25-percent *root* point. This is often enough to cause a critical CG, and the difference between CG points can make a dramatic difference in stability.

I hope I've kept this article understandable and helped some of you along the way to expanding your hat size. Nothing will make you more "big-headed" than to hear someone say, "That flies great! I want to build one! Where do I get it?" If you're tired of flying belly-button planes (everybody has one), and you're ready to try something new, *then do it yourself!* ■

To land successfully, the airplane must fly through the key position, which is located about 10 to 15 feet above the end of the runway. Here, the plane has flown through the key position and is approaching touchdown.

Flying through the key point

THE GILBERT APPROACH TO LANDING

by BOB GILBERT

MANY R/C pilots fly all the time; they make a lot of landings and wreck a lot of planes. They typically make only one landing in each flight, and it's performed only as a necessity. Although they may be accomplished, high-time pilots, they haven't mastered landings. These pilots usually get the plane back to the field in one piece and, in doing so, often run off the side or the end of the runway.

Taking off is infinitely easier than landing, especially with the overpowered aircraft seen at the field, and many people feel that if they know how to take off, then they automatically know how to land. If any of this describes you, please read on.

These steps are designed to help you become proficient in the execution of landings. To master landings, there are two things you must do:
● find a technique that works for you and your airplane;
● practice and then practice some more.

The technique that I describe is borrowed from Roger Maves who taught me to fly a full-size Piper Cub way back in 1954. I've applied it to R/C and practiced it a lot. Now, on occasion, I do more than 60 touch-and-go's in one flight, and it's a lot of fun. So here goes. Read it a few times, set up your aircraft properly, and then bring this article to the field and read the important parts again before you fly. Happy landings!

EIGHT STEPS

● **Aircraft selection.** I strongly suggest that you use a 3-channel trainer. If you're using a 4-channel aircraft, and you really know how to control the rudder, then go ahead and use it. Be honest with yourself. If you don't know how to keep the aircraft straight ahead on takeoffs and landings, go back to that good old 3-channel rig.

● **The pattern.** Refer to the pictorial provided, and learn the basic parts of the pattern. Memorize the position of the *key point*. This point is the most important ingredient for successful landings.

Go to your local airport, and watch the full-size aircraft fly the pattern. Notice that it's rectangular and that it's normally flown with four distinct turns. (The turn from downwind to final is often flown as one sweeping 180-degree turn, but I don't recommend this. See the diagram.)

● **Preparation.** Set up your airplane so that it idles without stalling and its throttle response is good. The size of the wheels should suit the runway conditions. I don't care how small the plane is or what the kit calls for. On grass, the wheels should be no less than 2¾ inch in diameter, and you should also remove the wheel pants.

Now it's time to fly. Be sure to operate in accordance with the rules of the field. Try to pick a time when there aren't many others there so that your operations won't interfere with theirs.

● **Throttle and stalls.** Take off and climb to altitude out of the pattern. At this point, you must learn and practice how to use the throttle correctly and how to perform straight-ahead stalls. To start, slowly reduce the throttle while

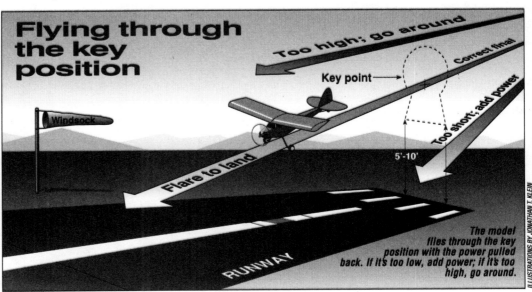

Flying through the key position

Too high; go around

Key point

Correct final

Too short; add power

Windsock

5'-10'

Flare to land

RUNWAY

The model flies through the key position with the power pulled back. If it's too low, add power; if it's too high, go around.

ILLUSTRATIONS BY JONATHAN T. KLEIN

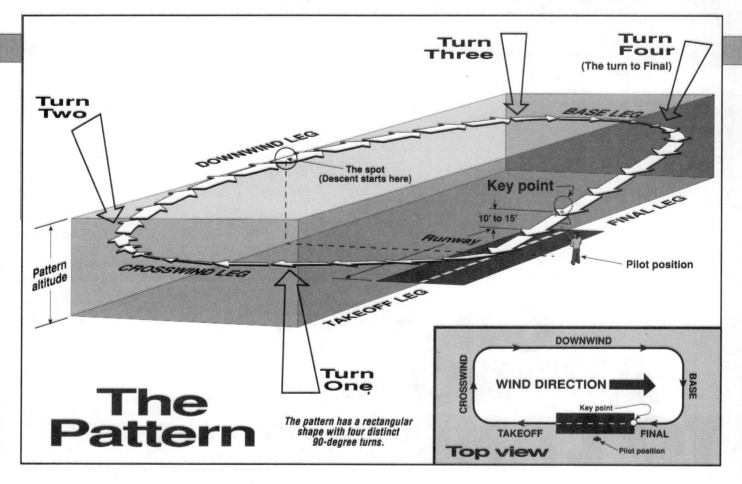

Turn Two

Turn Three

Turn Four (The turn to Final)

DOWNWIND LEG

BASE LEG

The spot (Descent starts here)

Key point

10' to 15'

FINAL LEG

Runway

Pattern altitude

CROSSWIND LEG

Pilot position

TAKEOFF LEG

Turn One

The Pattern

The pattern has a rectangular shape with four distinct 90-degree turns.

DOWNWIND

CROSSWIND

WIND DIRECTION

BASE

Key point

TAKEOFF

FINAL

Pilot position

Top view

you hold the aircraft straight ahead and at a constant altitude. Reduce the throttle until the plane reaches idle, and feed in up-elevator until the aircraft stalls. A trainer-type plane (low wing loading) may stall straight ahead. A plane with a higher wing loading may drop one of its wings and then its nose. To recover, add some power and up-elevator. Full throttle isn't necessary.

Practice this stall and recovery until you recognize the speed at which the aircraft stalls. This will also enable you to practice with the throttle—something that you must learn to operate to make good landings.

● **Fly the pattern.** Return the plane to the pattern area. Keep it at a constant altitude, and fly the rectangular pattern until you're comfortable with it (especially the four 90-degree turns). Fly at a moderate speed—certainly at less than full throttle. When you feel that you know how to fly the pattern, move on to the next step.

● **Go-arounds.** Look at the runway, and find the key point. It's about 10 or 15 feet above the approach end of the runway. To make a good landing, you must fly through the key point. To learn this, make a series of go-arounds. Every landing approach need not be followed by a landing. If the approach is poor, the landing will be poor. A good approach will generally

produce a good landing. You should make a go-around whenever it's apparent that the approach isn't good.

The assumption at this time is that the wind is light to nonexistent. Don't attempt these exercises in high wind until you've gained some experience. The landing approach starts when the aircraft is on the downwind leg opposite you. When it's in that position, reduce the throttle. Most trainers glide well enough to allow you to close the throttle completely. Start the descent. Control the speed by changing the pitch attitude—nose-up or down. Make a nice, gradual turn to base and continue to descend. Keep the aircraft speed slow, but stay well above the stall speed. If you descend below the desired glide path with insufficient speed to pull the plane's nose up without stalling, add a

little power. Keep the key point in mind and turn to final, with the nose heading right through the key point. When the plane is just above the end of the runway, going through the key point, apply some (not full) throttle to go around. (Using less than full throttle reduces the engine's torque output, so less rudder correction is required to keep the aircraft straight.) Climb to the normal pattern altitude, and repeat the procedure.

Determine the altitude at which you want to fly and precisely where you should cut the throttle. Find the spot in the sky that allows you to close the throttle completely and come through the key point at close to stall speed, without ever opening the throttle. The plane should glide from the midpoint of the down-

(Continued on page 138)

What makes a landing perfect? When the plane stalls just as its wheels touch the ground.

ENGINES ALOFT

BOB GILBERT

IT'S ALIVE! – AVOIDING DEAD-STICKS

WHEN I END a letter, I often precede my signature with "Keep 'em flying!" Flying R/C is something that I love to do; I do it regularly; and I love watching others do it.

Often, when I'm at the field, however, I find would-be fliers who are having trouble keeping them flying. In an effort to help those of you who may not have that friendly engine expert standing by, I've generated a list of items that I've seen cause my planes and the planes of others to experience engine failure. Following each common problem, you'll find the most likely cause and its cure.

ENGINE FAILURE JUST AFTER TAKEOFF

Cause I. High-speed needle is set too lean. (I see this almost every time I go to the field, and it's avoidable 99 percent of the time.)
Cure. Open the needle valve a bit, then be sure to test by holding the nose straight up with full throttle. The engine must *not* sag when this is done. Especially with a new engine, or on any first flight, be sure the needle valve is set a little on the rich side.
Cause II. The fuel-tank clunk is in the front of the tank. This often happens on the flight following a hard landing or crash.
Cure. Grip the aircraft firmly, and thrust it forward. If the clunk wasn't audible before this movement, but it *is* now, it has probably repositioned itself correctly. Test by

running the engine for a few minutes at full throttle with the nose up.
Cause III. The fuel-tank line came off in the tank, and the tank was only half full at takeoff.
Cure. Remove the tank and install a new line. (See the first tip under "Helpful Hints.")

ENGINE LEANS OUT AND QUITS

Cause I. The high-speed needle valve is too lean.
Cure. Open the needle valve and test by holding the nose straight up with full throttle.
Cause II. The muffler pressure line came off.
Cure. Replace with a new line.
Cause III. The fuel filter has opened up (the halves are loose).
Cure. Tighten the halves firmly. Test-run the engine on the ground.
Cause IV. There's a split in the fuel line—usually at the fuel tank.
Cure. Remove the line and replace it with a new one. (See the first tip under "Helpful Hints.")
Cause V. The fuel tank is foaming, causing air bubbles in the fuel line.
Cure. Balance the prop and wrap the tank in foam.

Be sure to test the high-speed needle valve by holding the nose straight up with full throttle.

ENGINE THROWS PROP WHEN STARTING

Cause I. The engine is badly flooded.
Cure. Remove the glow plug, and spin the engine. Caution! Keep your eyes clear of the plug opening as raw fuel will spurt out, and it could harm your eyes. Test the plug and replace it.
Cause II. The prop nut is loose.
Cure. Tighten the prop nut. Remember that the nuts for wooden props, in particular, should be tightened before each flying session.
Cause III. The glow plug is the wrong one.
Cure. Try a "colder" plug (for "later" ignition timing).

ENGINE LOSES RPM WITHOUT THE GLOW BATTERY

Cause I. The glow plug is defective.
Cure. Replace the glow plug.

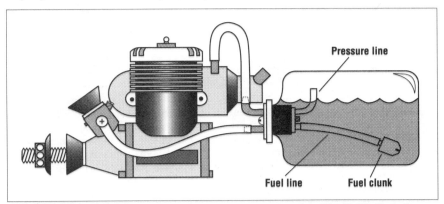

If the fuel clunk gets jammed forward during a hard landing, your engine will probably die during your next flight. Make sure it's correctly positioned, as shown here.

Pressure line

Fuel line   Fuel clunk

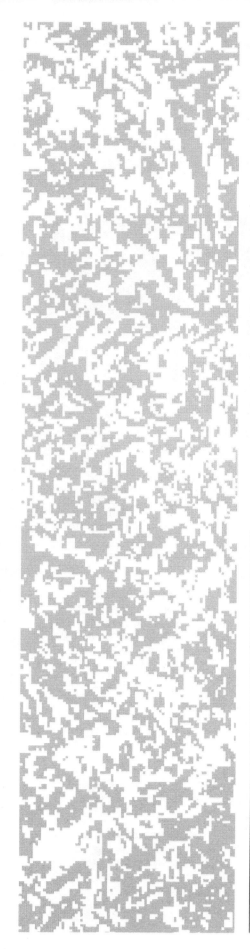

Cause II. The needle-valve setting is much too rich.

Cure. Turn the needle valve in a little at a time until the engine speeds up, then re-move battery.

ENGINE FAILS IN FLIGHT, BUT ISN'T OUT OF FUEL

Cause I. The fuel tank is too low.

Cure 1. Raise the tank until its center line is approximately on the same level as the carburetor.

Cure 2. If Cure 1 isn't possible, add an external pump to the engine.

Cure 3. See also "Engine Failure Just After Takeoff."

Cause II. The engine overheats.

Cure 1. The engine is new and requires some additional break-in. Try running through a few more tanks of fuel on the ground with the carburetor set on the rich side.

Cure 2 The prop is too large. Try one with a smaller diameter or a lower pitch.

If you wrap your fuel tank in protective foam, you'll minimize the chance of leaning-out because of fuel foaming. (Shown here: Model Aviation Products Secur Rap.)

Cause III. The back cover has loosened. This will also make it difficult to start.

Cure. Tighten the back cover. The gasket may have to be replaced, or the use of silicone gasket maker may be in order.

Cause IV. The glow plug has loosened.

Cure. Tighten the glow plug.

Cause V. The muffler has loosened.

Cure. If you're lucky, you'll start to hear more noise, at which time you should immediately throttle back and land. If you do, you may save the screws and can then tighten them. If the muffler has fallen off, don't throttle back all the way, as the engine will die. Wait until you have the field made, then close the throttle and shut off the engine.

HELPFUL HINTS

• If possible, use a new fuel line rather than just trimming back the old one. The new line will stay on better because it hasn't stretched, and its "flex life" is just starting.

The next hints are for beginners—just to try to help you get airborne faster and more often.

• If possible, make your fuel-tank lines visible. Put a fuel filter somewhere on your fuel can to filter the fuel going into the tank, but *do not* put one in your fuel line.

• Round off the leading and trailing edges of those props, and then balance them.

• Stay away from those .60 engines and pattern planes until you've had quite some time at the sticks. I also strongly suggest that you *do not* start with an engine that's smaller than a .20, and be sure it's a 2-stroke.

• Don't put a cowl around the engine—at least, not for the first few flights.

• Use a glow-battery system that has a meter or some other means of alerting you to a dead glow plug.

• This has nothing to do with engines, but if you fly off a grass field, *do not* attempt to do so with wheels any smaller than $2^{1}/2$ inches in diameter.

Well, that does it for this month. I welcome your comments, so please drop me a line in care of *Model Airplane News*. Please help me to write a column that will really help others keep 'em flying. ∎

HOP-UP THE ZENOAH G-23
EASY BOLT-ON POWER
by NEIL DAVIS

The Zenoah G-23 as it comes out of the box. The hop-up parts can be easily bolted on.

I RECENTLY read an announcement in my Peninsula Channel Commanders Club newsletter about a local R/C zealot who's producing high-power after-market components (hop-up parts!) for the Zenoah G-23 engine. This is the engine I use and love in my 1/4-scale model of the J-3 Piper Cub, built from a Sig kit. For those of you who aren't familiar with this kit, this is a 105-inch wingspan, 14 pound airplane—a big, easy-to-fly and "fun" model. The newsletter article claimed an increase to as much as *double* the stock horsepower. The newsletter also said, however, that this hopped-up G-23 is used for high-speed R/C boats. OK; no problem. If the engine can produce big power in a boat, why not the same in an aircraft?

Fifteen minutes after a friendly phone call, I had the privilege of meeting Bruce

the higher-performance cylinder along with the larger carb and a solid-state ignition system.

After that, I could hardly wait to bolt on the goodies and fly.

AVAILABLE HOP-UP PARTS

New cylinder with necessary gaskets—$62.50. This cylinder isn't a re-work of the stock item. To achieve the sufficiently large fuel-transfer ports and the larger intake and exhaust ports, the cylinder must be manufactured specifically as a high-performance replacement. The new cylinder also in-

SPECIFICATIONS	
Displacement	22.5cc
Fuel	Super unleaded 40:1 oil mix (Echo Premium chain-saw oil)
Prop	Dynathrust 16x8
rpm before mod.	7,400 with Tatone Pitts-style manifold
rpm after mod.	9,000 with Tatone Pitts-style manifold
hp before mod.	1.8
hp after mod.	2.8
dB level	104 on hard clay with floats attached; 98 on level grass with wheel landing gear

Note: use of the Hanson muffler produced 8,300rpm and 94dB.

The Sig 1/4-scale J-3 Cub and the Zenoah G-23 are an excellent combination. With the extra hop-up power, the model climbs and flies with authority.

The newly modified engine installed on author's 1/4-scale Cub.

the piston 180 degrees. This will ensure that the rings don't catch on the edge of the transfer ports. If your engine is getting tired, this would be a good time to also replace the piston and rings (available from Hanson at $35). You now have a "top overhaul" and should be able to look forward to many more operating hours. This engine is rated as a 1,000-hour engine, and Bruce tells me that the original lower end is so strong and the new parts of such high quality that the hop-up won't shorten engine life.

The high-performance carburetor kit, including a new manifold and

Hanson, owner of B.H. Hanson Co.—Model Marine Products*. Bruce is an engineer and former Air Force jet pilot. This guy is no stranger to R/C aircraft. Bruce currently owns and often flies model airplanes, and in 1975, he competed in the Tournament of Champions. His principal interest is in producing and selling variations of the 22.5cc Zenoah G-23 engine as well as high-performance, bolt-on components for it.

The good news out of all of this was, yes, I could purchase an air-cooled version of

cludes a redesigned squish band that results in a slightly higher compression ratio. This could be a favorable replacement alternative if you damage your cylinder in a re-kitting maneuver. Laugh not; one of my flying buddies did just that.

Part of your hop-up will include turning

gaskets—$62.50. This is basically a larger carb that allows you to take maximum advantage of the enlarged cylinder intake port and will supply a sufficient amount of mixture for the new, internal-cylinder, fuel-transfer ports. Bruce explained that you don't get more power just by installing a

HOP-UP THE ZENOAH G-23

A combination hop-up kit for fliers. This includes the cylinder kit, new piston rings, the carb kit and the ignition module.

The original cylinder on the right and the high-performance cylinder on the left. Notice the larger exhaust port and the heavier casting in the cooling-fin area.

The high-performance cylinder on the left shows the larger intake area, and the mounting base is compatible with the larger carb.

larger carb on a standard cylinder. For a larger carb to give you any appreciable increase in power, the engine cylinder must be modified so that it will pull a greater volume of mixture "through the hole"! This is the reason for modifying the cylinder. The larger fuel-transfer ports and the larger intake and exhaust ports allow more of the fuel mixture to pass through the carb, into the combustion chamber and out through the exhaust. More fuel burned equals more power. Now that's kind of a simplistic explanation that could annoy some of the more scientific types. But let's face it folks: I'm a simple kind of a guy—one who likes to see his Piper Cub go way up and keep going up until it's just a little dot way up in the sky, then put it into a spin and see how many times it spins before I chicken out!

The solid-state ignition module—$17.50. This eliminates the magneto points (located in front of the flywheel) and provides 5 degrees of ignition advance as rpm increase; easier starting; smoother idling; better transition from idle to mid range; and an additional top-end power output.

Bruce tells me he'll also offer a combination hop-up kit for fliers. This will include the cylinder kit, new piston rings, the carb kit and the ignition module, all for $129.50.

Let's not forget the dreaded noise problem! Bruce offers a direct, bolt-on muffler that will provide a maximum noise level of 94dB. Complete with bolts and gasket, this little jewel sells for only $19. The Pitts-style manifold that I've been using on my engine was measured at 104dB. I tried the new muffler, and it's considerably quieter (see specification box). I wasn't able to use it on my engine as it didn't fit under the cowl of the Cub. The rpm readings in this article were taken using my Pitts-style manifold.

IN THE AIR

How the Cub flew before and after the engine modifications: this airplane has always been a great flier! The original engine was a Super Tiger .90 that provided more than enough power for realistic scale performance. This was the lightest engine installed so the plane could fly *veeerrry* slowly. The original engine was later re-

placed by a stock Zenoah G-23. This gave me faster takeoffs, better climb rates and better power for zoom-up-style maneuvers. After installing the Hanson cylinder, carb and ignition module, the flying just got better! Now it goes straight up a lot farther and climbs to spinning altitude faster. I pull larger loops and have greater authority during aerobatics. Maneuvers that require a lot of up-front-pull, like a respectable outside loop and good knife-edge flight, look good now; they weren't possible before. But the *real* plus is that my Cub is now a whole bunch more fun to fly!

*Here's the address of the company featured in this article:
B.H. Hanson Co.—Model Marine Products, 2228 S. El Camino Real, Ste. 123, San Mateo, CA 94403-1853; (415) 345-5592.

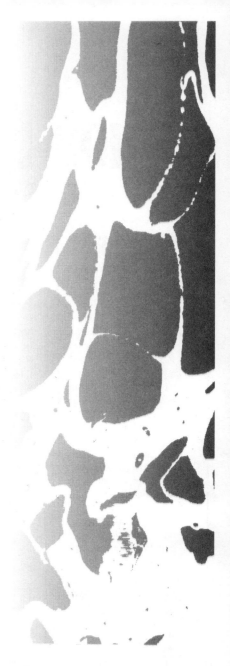

The larger carb on the left includes a pump (clear flexible bowl on the top) that's used to draw fuel manually from the tank to the carb.

Hooked on towing

by DAVE HERBERT

PHOTOS BY BOB BRUCKER & DAVE HERBERT

Know how to tow

A front view of the Telemaster towing a sailplane.

I F YOU'VE read any of my past articles, then you know that the Capistrano Aero-Dumpmaster Special Effects Team—led by yours truly—doesn't follow the norm. If someone says that something can't be done, we usually take on the challenge. We fly as a team, and as senior pilot, I must thank my ground crew. They work in harmony, and because of this, we pull off some amazing stuff. I could tell you some interesting tales....

Our latest summer venture is using R/C gas-powered planes to tow R/C sailplanes. One of our senior members, Lyle Maxey, is a world-class pilot of full-size sailplanes. (He won the 1956 National Soaring Championships.) When he suggested that we try an R/C

towline setup, we all looked at each other and smiled—the challenge began. We had never seen this done or even read about it. I thought about whether I had a plane in my arsenal that would make a good tow-plane, and my old, trusty, Lou Andrews Aeromaster biplane seemed to fit the bill. Dave Raubinger provided a sailplane, and he installed a servo with a towline release in its nose.

IMPORTANT TIPS

Lyle said that the most important thing the pilot of a full-size tow-plane has to keep in mind is that, "the tow-plane must maintain a constant air speed." This isn't as easy as it sounds. A tow-plane speeds up when it reaches a thermal, and when the sailplane hits the same thermal, it speeds up, too. Trying to keep the towline taut is difficult. When the line slackens and then tightens abruptly, the situation can get really hairy. (The slack is difficult to see when you're standing on the ground!) Lyle also told us that the sailplane must maintain the same altitude as the tow-plane, or fly just below its wash. (This is also difficult to see from the ground.)

Full-size towlines are usually between 200 and 300 feet long, and their braided construction allows them to stretch and absorb slack. A full-size sailplane pilot's worst fear is that the towline will be released during takeoff, before he has enough altitude to turn around and get back safely to the field.

MODEL MISHAPS

For the towline, we settled on a 75-foot length of braided-nylon cord. To increase elasticity, we attached a 2-foot-long heavy rubber band to the cord, close to the tow-plane. Then

Hooked on towing

we mounted the towline to the tail wheel (as is done on the full-size versions), and we were ready for the first attempt.

A major difference between our R/C setup and a full-size setup became apparent during the takeoff run. Solving the problem was a frantic "yelling" experience. The sailplane lifted off almost immediately, and it was 5 feet higher than the Aeromaster. I finally got the bipe off the ground, but it had difficulties climbing, and when I thought the tough part was over, my bipe began to fly downward—full-up didn't help! Just before the bipe was in danger of crashing, Dave detached the towline from the sailplane, and I recovered the tow-plane. We had learned our first lesson: the towline *must* be attached to the top of the tow-plane's fuselage, close to its center of gravity. This way, if the sailplane flies above the tow-plane, it doesn't force the tow-plane into a dive by pulling its tail up. I attached the line to the Aeromaster's left rubber-band dowel, and this solved the problem.

The second takeoff was uneventful, and all seemed well until the first left-hand turn. This is when we discovered that it's best for the sailplane to follow the outside of a turn, just below the tow-plane. I made a left turn that was too sharp, and this caused the line to slacken. When it tightened, Dave's sailplane did three snap rolls while still attached to the tow-plane. We both hung on, and it was quite a thrill!

It's important not to make any sudden moves. The tow-plane pilot must pull steadily. To make turns that are similar to those made by the full-size planes, I used most of my bipe's rudder. I also had to be careful not to

Here, the release mechanism is held in place with the wing hold-down rubber bands. It works every time!

Dave Raubinger (left) with his scratch-built sailplane and Dave Herbert (right) with the Telemaster they use for towing.

snap-roll the tow-plane (Aeromasters snap easily). This can happen while towing, because you use so much rudder and elevator.

When the planes reached an altitude where I could no

(Continued on page 138)

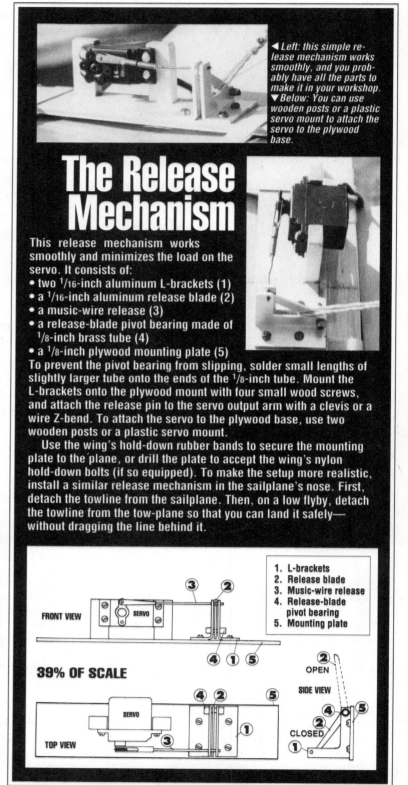

◄ *Left: this simple release mechanism works smoothly, and you probably have all the parts to make it in your workshop.* ▼ *Below: You can use wooden posts or a plastic servo mount to attach the servo to the plywood base.*

The Release Mechanism

This release mechanism works smoothly and minimizes the load on the servo. It consists of:
- two $^1/_{16}$-inch aluminum L-brackets (1)
- a $^1/_{16}$-inch aluminum release blade (2)
- a music-wire release (3)
- a release-blade pivot bearing made of $^1/_8$-inch brass tube (4)
- a $^1/_8$-inch plywood mounting plate (5)

To prevent the pivot bearing from slipping, solder small lengths of slightly larger tube onto the ends of the $^1/_8$-inch tube. Mount the L-brackets onto the plywood mount with four small wood screws, and attach the release pin to the servo output arm with a clevis or a wire Z-bend. To attach the servo to the plywood base, use two wooden posts or a plastic servo mount.

Use the wing's hold-down rubber bands to secure the mounting plate to the plane, or drill the plate to accept the wing's nylon hold-down bolts (if so equipped). To make the setup more realistic, install a similar release mechanism in the sailplane's nose. First, detach the towline from the sailplane. Then, on a low flyby, detach the towline from the tow-plane so that you can land it safely—without dragging the line behind it.

1. L-brackets
2. Release blade
3. Music-wire release
4. Release-blade pivot bearing
5. Mounting plate

FRONT VIEW   SERVO

39% OF SCALE

TOP VIEW   SERVO

OPEN

SIDE VIEW

CLOSED

INCREASE THE VERSATILITY
OF THE ACE DIGIPACE

by BILL HAYWOOD

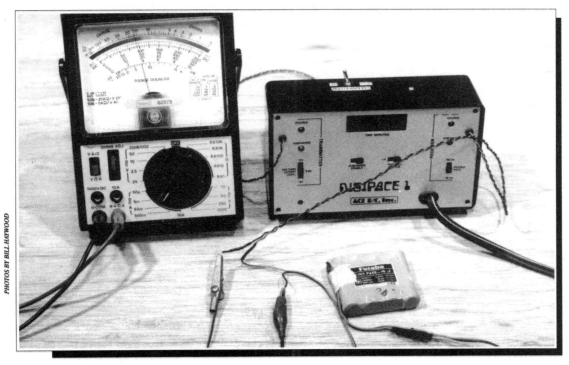

PHOTOS BY BILL HAYWOOD

[Editor's note: this modification applies only to the original Digipace—not to the Digipace II that's currently sold by Ace.]

Here, the ammeter shows a reading of approximately 20mA. The front panel switch is in the down position, and the newly installed switch is set to the 20mA charge rate.

THE DIGIPACE by Ace R/C* is limited to servicing two sizes of receiver battery packs. The 50mA rate for a 500mA pack is usually provided as standard, and you can choose one other receiver charge rate—either 20mA or 120mA. The Digipace provides three charge rates for the transmitter. The ability to switch to three receiver charge rates is very desirable, especially for those who fly 1/4 scale and the .049 variety of R/C aircraft.

The Digipace is designed so that changing the value and wattage of one resistor on the circuit board will change the receiver battery charge rate. To switch quickly from a 20mA to a 120mA charge rate, it's only necessary to provide the ability to switch from one

of the resistors to the other. This is an easy process, and the parts should cost no more than $10.

MOD PROCEDURES

First, study the instructions that come with the Digipace. Remove the four screws from the front corners of the instrument, and remove the circuit board from the plastic cabinet. (Set the cabinet aside.) One screw remains on the metal faceplate to secure it to the circuit board. It's on the bottom left side, directly below the transmitter selector switch. Remove this screw and nut, and slide the rubber grommets in the faceplate over the AC power cord and the two charging wires. Don't disconnect the wires or

remove the faceplate from the cord.

Remove resistor R14 from the circuit board (R14 is located on top of the circuit board near the right end). It can be found on the right of and parallel to receiver charge-selector switch S2. Carefully remove the resistor lead near transistor Q5. This lead is soldered onto both the top and bottom of the circuit board. Insert the ends of two 6-inch lengths of no. 22 stranded hook-up wire into the circuit board where the resistor leads were removed, and then solder them. The wire near Q5 must be soldered on both sides of the board, front and back. The other wire is soldered onto the back only. Connect the opposite end of one of the two wires to a center pin of the new double-pole/double-throw switch, and

Left: The 6-inch no. 22 black and white stranded wires run from the circuit board to the two center terminals of the switch. The five-lug tie post has been mounted inside the black case. Extra-long wires allow all soldering to be completed before the components are fastened inside the case.

then solder. Connect the second wire to the switch's other center pin and solder it. This leaves the four end pins on the switch without wires.

Solder the larger, 68-ohm, 2W resistor (blue, gray, black) to the two outer lugs on the five-lug tie post. Solder the 820-ohm, 1/2W resistor (gray, red, brown) to the two inner lugs, and leave the center lug unused. Cut four, 6-inch lengths of no. 22 wire. Solder one piece to each of the four lugs where the resistor leads were just soldered. Solder the two leads from the 820-ohm resistor to the two pins on one end of the DPDT switch. Solder the remaining two leads from the other resistor to the last two pins on the opposite end of the switch. This completes the wiring.

Drill two holes in the plastic cabinet top for mounting the switch and tie post. Choose a location that will clear the back of the cabinet and the back of the circuit board. Mount the switch and the five-lug tie post. Inspect all solder joints and all wiring for errors. Check the switch for good solder joints and for shorts between pins. With an ohmmeter, check the circuit board, top and bottom, for good connections. Slide the faceplate along the wires to its original position, close to the circuit board. Carefully replace the small screw and nut, and secure the faceplate to the circuit board. Reinstall the circuit board and faceplate in the case, and insert and tighten the four bolts that secure the faceplate to the case. This completes the conversion.

CHECKING CHARGE RATES

To identify switch-position charge rates, check the modified Digipace's operation with an ammeter. To check charge rates, cut one lead of the Digipace receiver charging wires, and remove the insula-

No.	Item	Radio Shack No.
1	DP DT sub-miniature toggle switch	275-614
1	5-lug tie post	274-688
1	3-color no. 22 stranded hook-up wire. (3 spools)	271-130
1	Available at most electronics specialty stores: 820-ohm, 1/2W resistor	
1	68-ohm, 2W resistor	

tion from the ends. Connect a standard 500mA receiver battery to the Digipace. Place the ammeter leads in series with the Digipace charging wire, which was cut for this test. Before connecting to AC power, be sure to set your meter to the 500mA scale, and slide the Digipace receiver switch up to the 50mA position. This will prevent a meter burnout if a mistake has been made in the wiring.

At this point, the Digipace can be plugged into the 115V AC wall outlet.

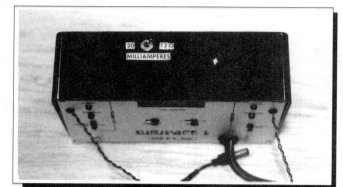

Labels identify charge-rate switch positions. This switch is inoperative when the Digipace receiver charge-rate switch is in the 50mA position. Slide that switch down, and the new switch shown here is used to select the two remaining charge rates.

Make sure that the meter doesn't swing off scale. If it does, disconnect the AC power immediately! Switch the meter or the leads, as necessary, and reconnect to

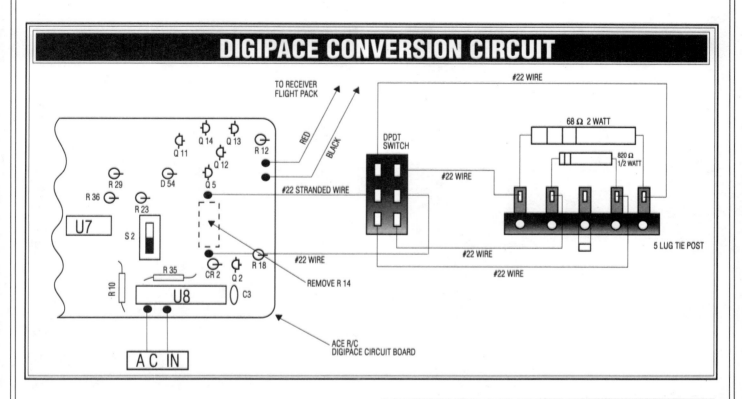

DIGIPACE CONVERSION CIRCUIT

Labels within diagram:
TO RECEIVER FLIGHT PACK
#22 WIRE
RED
BLACK
68 Ω 2 WATT
820 Ω 1/2 WATT
DPDT SWITCH
#22 WIRE
#22 STRANDED WIRE
#22 WIRE
#22 WIRE
#22 WIRE
5 LUG TIE POST
Q 14   Q 13
Q 11
Q 12
R 12
R 29
R 36
D 54
Q 5
R 23
U7
S 2
R 35
R 10
CR 2   Q 2
R 18
U8
C3
REMOVE R 14
A C IN
ACE R/C DIGIPACE CIRCUIT BOARD

the AC power. The charge rate should read 50mA. If the operation is correct, push down the receiver-selector switch on the face of the Digipace. In the down position, this switch automatically transfers control of the charge rate to the new two-way switch. One switch position will be for 20mA, and the other will switch in the 120mA current flow. (Your meter will tell you which position it's in.) Label the positions on the new rate switch, which is on top of the Digipace.

To check the discharge rate of your Digipace, be certain to disconnect the AC power and reverse the ammeter leads. (The current will change direction during the discharge cycle.) Now, connect the Digipace to AC power, and push the discharge-enable switch. Ace R/C gives a discharge rate of 300mA, plus or minus 5mA. The meter used in the original modification measured 285mA, which is close enough. Don't be surprised if you get the same reading in all switch positions; the discharge rate is always the same. Disconnect the test setup and reconnect the wire you previously cut for testing.

If you have problems, go back and check all solder joints, especially the

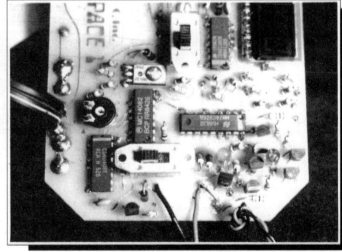

Right: Receiver charge-selector switch (near the bottom of the photo) is just above the black and white wires that have been soldered into two holes left when the R14 resistor was removed. The twisted wires at bottom right are Digipace receiver battery wires.

wire near Q5, where both the front and back of the board must be soldered. Also, check the switch pins to be sure there are no solder bridges between them.

If you don't have all the parts for this modification (see materials list), Radio Shack stocks most of what you'll need (except the 68-ohm, 2W and the 820-ohm, 1/2W resistors, which can be obtained from your local electronics specialty store). The modified Digipace

has been used many times. It has proven so reliable that if I buy another, I'll convert it. With a minimum of effort, the Digipace receiver cycling capability has been increased a giant 33 percent!

Here's the address of the company featured in this article:
Ace R/C, Inc., 116 W. 19 St., Box 511C, Higginsville, MO 64037. ∎

HOT WINGS

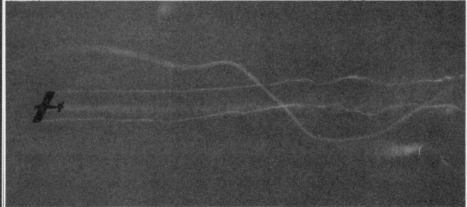

Getting your wings to smoke isn't teaching bad habits!

WING-TIP SMOKE from a full-size plane is really eye-catching; you can see it on Lasers, biplanes, or jets at any air show. Once, at the Sussex County Air Show, I saw it on Leo's Laser, and it looked so good that I simply had to try it on a model.

by DAN SANTICH

The first plane I modified was the Knight Twister, which was featured in the October '85 issue of *MAN*. Because of its smoke, the Twister received a lot of attention at fly-ins; in fact, *MAN* Senior Editor Chris Chianelli remembered it so well that he asked me to write about my experiences.

This article won't teach you how to set up your engine to run a smoke system. It will, however,

WINGS

▶ *Here's the Big Hots producing smoke at full throttle.*

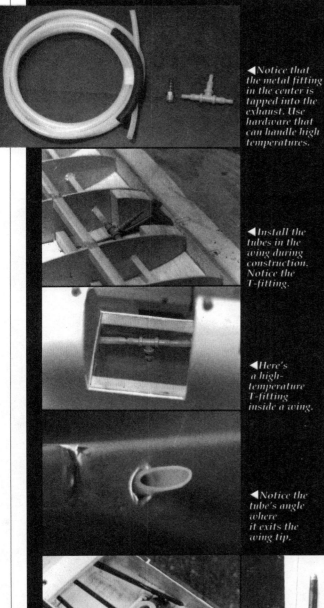

◀ *Notice that the metal fitting in the center is tapped into the exhaust. Use hardware that can handle high temperatures.*

◀ *Install the tubes in the wing during construction. Notice the T-fitting.*

◀ *Here's a high-temperature T-fitting inside a wing.*

◀ *Notice the tube's angle where it exits the wing tip.*

▲ *The tube in the fuselage receives the fitting in the wing.*

▶ *The high-temperature hose is supported by a wire clamp that's between the gear.*

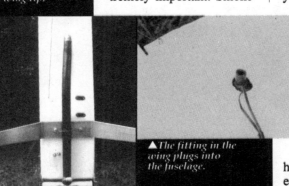

▲ *The fitting in the wing plugs into the fuselage.*

show you a variety of engine/smoke-system setups and explain how the smoke is piped to the wings.

ENGINE SMOKE

Wing-tip smoke is created in the engine's exhaust system and then piped to the tips of the wings through plastic tubing. To produce the smoke, a special "smoke" fluid is pumped from a separate holding tank (any commercial fuel tank will work) and injected into the engine's exhaust chamber where it's heated. For smoke fluid, I've had good results with a 50:50 mixture of kerosene and diesel fuel. There are commercial smoke fluids available such as those sold by B&B* Specialties, which also sells highly efficient smoke pumps for gas engines. (I use one in the Big Hots for this article.)

The amount of smoke that a model engine can create is proportional to the amount of heat it can produce, and the method used to inject smoke fluid into an exhaust chamber is extremely important. Smoke-fluid pumps (electric or engine driven) usually work best. I don't recommend that you use direct engine pressure from the crankcase to pressurize your smoke-fluid tank, because it's inadequate.

Some folks think it's tough to get a 4-stroke glow engine to produce smoke, but that isn't true. With a 4-stroke glow engine, you have to preheat the smoke fluid just before you inject it into the engine exhaust. To do this, I wrap a piece of 1/8-inch brass tubing (through which the fluid will pass) around the exhaust tubes four or five times before it enters the muffler. To get the smoke fluid into the exhaust chamber, I use an electric fuel pump that's compatible with the fluid mixture.

WING-TIP SMOKE

Producing wing-tip smoke isn't very difficult. The most important thing to remember is that exhaust fumes are hot, and plastic tubing will melt if you run it too close to the exhaust. It's also important to make sure that all the tubing connections are tight, or your airplane will be saturated by diesel fuel and kerosene!

I tapped into my muffler and installed a third exhaust outlet (my Hots uses a Slimline* muffler that has two exhaust outlets). Make sure that you don't restrict the usual exhaust passages, because the engine might be damaged by the overheating this would cause. The tap you install on the muffler should have a diameter similar to that of a regular exhaust outlet. A $1/2$- or $3/8$-inch threaded brass coupler (available at any hardware store) can be used. I clamped a piece of $3/4$-inch, high-temperature hose onto this outlet, and I ran it along the bottom of the fuselage to the middle of the wing. Here, I attached a brass tube with a 90-degree bend; it enters the fuselage between the rear servos. I covered the tube with two pieces of silicone and a rubber adapter, which stay in place. As you can see, when the wing is installed, the wing fitting plugs into the tube.

It's better to install the tubes in the wing as you build it. Make sure that the "T-fittings" and tubes that run inside the wings to their tips are made of high-temperature nylon (available at most plumbing-supply outlets). Remember, the larger the tube's diameter, the more smoke you'll get from it. (The photos clearly show the tubing's layout.)

There you have it. Getting your wings to smoke is fun and easy.

*Here's a list of companies that supply smoke-system products:
B&B Specialties Inc., 14234 Cleveland Rd., Granger, IN 46530.
Slimline Mfg., P.O. Box 3295, Scottsdale, AZ 85257 (mufflers).
J'Tec, 164 School St., Daly City, CA 94014 (mufflers, valves).
CB/Tatone Products Corp., 21658 Cloud Way, Hayward, CA 94545 (mufflers, valves).
Du-Bro Products, 480 Bonner Rd., Wauconda, IL 60084 (fuel tanks, smoke valves).
Varsane Products, 546 S. Pacific St., Ste. C-101, San Marcos, CA 92069 (pumps).
Robart Mfg., 310 N. 5th St., St. Charles, IL 60174 (valves).
Sonic-Tronics. 7865 Mill Rd., Elkins Park, PA 19117 (pumps).■

SETTING UP A
Smoke System

You only need two elements to set up a smoke system in your model:
• a combustible fluid that's injected into your engine's exhaust
• an exhaust temperature that's high enough to cause a partial combustion of the fluid.

Injecting fluid into the exhaust can be accomplished in several ways.

Illustration 1—Use a separate fuel pump that's powered by its own batteries. Wire a microswitch, which is mechanically activated by a separate servo on an auxiliary channel, to the pump. When you activate the pump, it draws the smoke fluid from a separate fuel tank and injects it into the engine exhaust.

Illustration 2—Use the engine to pressurize the smoke-fluid tank and force the fluid into the exhaust. A servo-controlled shutoff valve starts and stops the fluid's flow and regulates the pressure. A passive check valve keeps the pressure and the fluid from backing up into the engine.

Illustration 3—Use a diaphragm pump that's driven by a pressure/vacuum source that's tapped off the engine crankcase. Because this type of pump uses an integral reverse-flow series of valves, a check valve isn't necessary. All that's needed is a servo-actuated shutoff valve.

Any type of commercial fuel tank can serve as a smoke-fluid tank, but the fuel line must *not* be of a silicone material (use neoprene or heat-resistant rubber). A 50:50 mixture of diesel fuel and kerosene makes a good smoke fluid, or you can buy ready-mixed smoke fluid.

In the November '84 issue of *MAN*, Charlie Kenny had a detailed article on how to set up and operate smoke systems. If you don't have this issue, write to *MAN*.

ILLUSTRATION #1
MUFFLER   VENT LINE   BATTERY
OUT   IN
VENTED SMOKE TANK   SMOKE FLUID PUMP   MICRO SWITCH   LINKAGE   SERVO

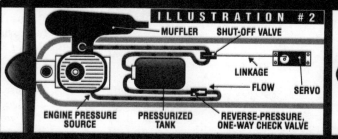

ILLUSTRATION #2
MUFFLER   SHUT-OFF VALVE
LINKAGE
FLOW   SERVO
ENGINE PRESSURE SOURCE   PRESSURIZED TANK   REVERSE-PRESSURE, ONE-WAY CHECK VALVE

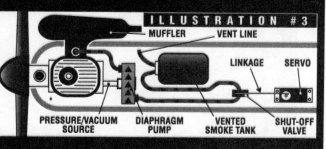

ILLUSTRATION #3
MUFFLER   VENT LINE
LINKAGE   SERVO
PRESSURE/VACUUM SOURCE   DIAPHRAGM PUMP   VENTED SMOKE TANK   SHUT-OFF VALVE

Supersonic Props?

by TOM ATWOOD

ON OCCASION, in the mail that's sent to the "Airwaves" column in *Model Airplane News,* we find an inquiry about prop-tip speeds. Typically, the question is whether a model airplane's prop-tip speed is likely to approach the speed of sound. One reader asked why we haven't seen the development of model gear drives that would slow down the tip speed of props and, by analogy with drive systems that power full-scale aircraft, increase prop efficiency. The answer is that model prop-tip speeds have yet to go supersonic, so there hasn't been a need for such model gear drives. But, at some point, there could be a need for them on some types of racing plane.

An example from Andy Lennon shows how to calculate the speed of a propeller at the tips of its blades:

If we assume a 10-inch diameter prop, then the circumference the prop tip circumscribes in a single revolution is: 10 inches (the diameter) times 3.1416 (pi) = 31.4 inches. If that prop is spinning at 10,000rpm, the tip travels a distance of 314,000 inches in 1 minute. Dividing that number by 12 shows that the tip travels 26,166.66 feet per minute. Multiplying that number by 60 tells us that, in an hour, the tip would travel 1,570,000 feet. Dividing by 5,280 feet to see what this is in mph indicates a prop-tip speed of 297.35mph. Using the same analysis, an Enya .49 spinning a 10x6 prop at 16,000rpm would result in a tip speed of 476mph. The speed of sound, of course, is approximately 700mph under standard atmospheric conditions at sea level.

The formula noted above doesn't include the forward speed of the aircraft. As the spinning prop moves forward through the air, each blade tip "draws" a line on the inside of an imaginary cylinder. Imagine taking a length of that cylinder that equates to one full revolution of the prop, and cutting a straight seam along the side from where the prop starts to where it completes a revolution. If you then uncurl and flatten out the cylinder section, you'll have a flat "piece of paper." You'll find that the "arc" cut by the prop tip is a straight line.

The path traveled by the prop tip is the

How to track your prop's in-flight tip velocity

Estimating in-flight propeller tip speed is surprisingly easy if you envision a cylinder that represents propeller travel, cut the cylinder open and uncurl it as if it were a piece of paper.

$$A^2 + B^2 = C^2$$

hypotenuse of a right triangle. As we know from geometry, the square of the hypotenuse is equal to the sum of the squares of the other two sides. By solving for the length of the hypotenuse and using it as the distance traveled in a single revolution, you can estimate the actual prop-tip speed during flight. Nonetheless, the simplified approach noted earlier, which assumes the engine and prop are mounted on a test stand, gives one a good picture of what's going on.

Larger props are now being used on the 100-inch unlimited racers. Will they be bumping up against the sound barrier? At the unlimited race in Tucson, Klaus Nowak of Aerrow, Inc. showed an A200S gas-powered opposed twin that could spin a 28x26 prop at 7,000rpm, static. Using the simplified formula, this equates to a tip speed of 583.1mph. When a plane flies through the air, the relative wind felt by the prop airfoil changes as it increases speed, and this results in a net reduction in the prop blades' angle of attack. This, in turn, reduces the drag on the prop, which consequently "unloads" and spins faster. This suggests that the designers of the most powerful of the new breed of racing planes may indeed have to concern themselves with supersonic tip speeds. ■

Carburetor Basics

by BOB GILBERT

Set-Up and Operation

I'M AN OLD-TIMER in the hobby, and my motto is "Keep 'em flying." Toward that end, I'll try to help you keep those engines purring!

As simply as possible, this article will enable you to properly set up 90 percent of the carburetors available today. I'll address 2-stroke sport-type engines of up to .65 displacement that don't have tuned pipes, pumps, or three-needle valve carbs.

THROTTLE? CHECK! FUEL? CHECK!...

• To start, set the throttle linkage. If your throttle servo doesn't have an adjustable arm, get one. It will help you immensely when you make these adjustments. (This won't be necessary with newer radios that have servo-travel adjustments built in.) With the linkage disconnected, hold the throttle arm so that you can rotate the barrel toward the closed position. Rotate the idle-speed stop screw so that the barrel closes fully, then rotate it half a turn more. Don't back the screw out any farther, because on some engines this screw also holds the throttle barrel in place. If there's a locknut on the screw, tighten it.

Now connect the throttle linkage to the servo, and adjust it so that the barrel is completely closed with the stick down and the trim fully down and

Idle-mixture screw
Air-adjustment screw:
Leaner (CCW)
Richer (CW)

Idle-speed stop screw

NOTE: mid-range adjustment found on some Enya carbs.

Air-bleed hole

High-speed needle valve:
Leaner (CW)
Richer (CCW)

ENYA CARB (air-bleed type)

100 percent open with the stick fully up. For idle, set the trim at the position that will open the throttle barrel $1/32$ inch (about the size of a round toothpick at its thickest point) when the stick is fully down.

• Next, check the fuel system. The spraybar/needle-valve assembly should be lined up no less than a third of the way down the tank, but no more than halfway. The fuel tank will be pressurized with muffler pressure. Inspect all fuel lines, metal and otherwise, for kinks and splits. Look inside the tank, unless it's brand new. Fuel filters can be a source of air leakage, so remove them for the initial setting.

• Always install a new glow plug. The object here is to be as sure as possible that other sys-

---

GENTLEMEN, START YOUR ENGINES
For a quick, sure cold start, just follow these step-by-step instructions.

1. Turn on your transmitter and receiver; observe the field rules for transmitter operation.

2. Open the throttle fully.

3. Watch for fuel in the line, and cover the throttle opening with your finger. Grip the propeller firmly, and rotate it until the fuel is just up to the carb. Don't flip it! Now turn the prop over—twice if it's warmer than 50 degrees Fahrenheit; three times if it's colder—to prime the engine.

4. With the glow plug disconnected, flip the engine over six to eight times.

5. Close the throttle and move the trim fully up. This should open the throttle barrel a little. Move the throttle stick up slightly to open the throttle barrel a little more. The throttle should be about a quarter open.

6. Grab the prop firmly, and rotate the engine until it passes through the compression part of the stroke. You should feel the engine "kick." If it does, it will now start on the first or second flip. Always use a "chicken stick" or electric starter for starting. If the engine doesn't start, flip the prop a few times with the glow plug disconnected, and try again. If it doesn't kick now, choke it one more time with the throttle fully open, flip the prop a few more times, reposition the throttle, light the glow plug and try again.

7. If, when your engine starts, it just revs up and quits, turn the high-speed needle valve $1/2$ turn counterclockwise to open it and try again. Repeat this if necessary.

8. If the engine starts, slows down and quits, and if there's a lot of smoke coming out of the exhaust, turn the high-speed needle valve clockwise to make the mixture leaner, a quarter of a turn at a time. Restart the engine.

9. When the engine has started, hold the throttle partially open, and let the engine warm up for at least 1 minute before making the final adjustments.

10. Most engines are harder to start when they're hot. To start a hot engine, draw the fuel up to the carb, but don't choke or prime it. Open the throttle to one quarter. Flip the prop *hard.* Use an electric starter if you have one available.

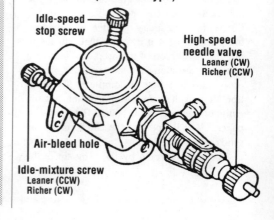

O.S. CARB (air-bleed type)

Idle-speed stop screw

High-speed needle valve
Leaner (CW)
Richer (CCW)

Air-bleed hole

Idle-mixture screw
Leaner (CCW)
Richer (CW)

tems won't interfere with the carburetor when you're setting it up.

• By this point, you should have run the engine a little and found that the carb settings are good enough to start the engine. Refer now to the sketches of the carburetors, and identify the one that looks like yours. You only need to identify the idle-mixture screw; the high-speed needle valve is always the longest and most prominent of the adjustment screws.

TECH TALK

CCW—counterclockwise
CW—clockwise

High-speed needle valve—sets the flow of fuel to the engine at high speeds (also called the "high-speed mixture valve"). It's always located on the side of the engine opposite the muffler. It's the most prominent needle valve.

Idle-speed stop screw—limits the motion of the throttle barrel toward the closed position. It's also called the "idle stop screw," the "throttle stop screw" and the "rotor setscrew."

Idle-mixture screw—sets the flow of fuel to the engine at low speeds. It's also called the "air-bleed screw," the "mixture control screw" (on some O.S. engines) and the "low-speed mixture setting screw". It's usually opposite the high-speed needle valve.

CARB ADJUSTMENTS

If you can, have a helper hold the transmitter. Tell your assistant to open the throttle fully when you point your finger upward, and to close it fully when you point your finger downward.

1. Start the engine and, using the throttle trim, set the idle speed. Typically 2,500 to 3,500rpm is correct. Then test to see whether, with the throttle stick fully down, moving the trim to the full-down position will shut off the

engine as an emergency cut-off. Adjust it as required.

2. Open the throttle fully. If the engine speeds up momentarily and then dies, open the high-speed needle valve one turn and restart. Once the engine is running smoothly, slowly turn the high-speed needle valve clockwise until the engine runs to maximum rpm. If you turn the needle valve in too far, the engine will die. Open it half a turn and restart. (Note: always restart at ¼ throttle or less. It makes starts easier and safer.) By now, you should have a feel for maximum rpm, so run the engine up to the maximum rpm point and turn the high-speed needle valve counter-clockwise just until you detect a slight slowing of the engine. This will put the setting a little on the rich side.

3. Now set the idle-mixture screw. For safety, stop the engine when you do this. Refer to the sketches, and find the carb style that matches that on your engine. From the sketch, you can determine where to make the idle-mixture adjustment and the direction in which to turn the needle for a rich or lean mixture. For example, on a two-needle carb such as a Webra, you'd turn the needle counterclock-wise to richen the mixture, because the fuel is being metered. With an air bleed, such as that found on many Enya engines, you'd turn the screw clockwise to richen the mixture because air is being metered.

Slowly pull the throttle stick on your transmitter down, and have the throttle trim full up. If the engine quits right away, richen the mixture a little and restart. Repeat this if necessary. If the engine slows down after a little while and then quits, make the mixture leaner.

When the engine idles at a reasonably slow speed (3,000rpm or so), you can fine-tune the idle mixture. To do this, idle the engine for 30 seconds, then quickly open the throttle fully. If it bogs down, and/or eventually quits, the mixture is too rich; if the engine quits abruptly, it's too lean. Make the suitable adjustments. Once it has been set, the idle mixture rarely, if ever, has to be adjusted.

4. Now you can make the final adjustment on the high-speed needle valve. Hold the plane level, open the throttle fully and

adjust it as you did before for just-below-maximum rpm. Now point the plane's nose straight up. If the engine stalls, open the needle valve slightly and try it again. Sometimes it's best to make the maximum rpm setting with the nose already up. The engine must run at maximum rpm with the nose up if you want to prevent your engine from stalling just after takeoff.

5. This is very important! *Don't* change the adjustment you've just made. *Don't* close the needle valves at the end of a flying session. Leave the settings where they are. The next time you go to the field, just fill up the tank, open the high-speed needle valve half a turn and start up the engine. When the engine is warm, open the throttle fully and point the plane's nose up. Repeat the final adjustment described in the previous paragraph.

TROUBLESHOOTING

The only types of needle valve that I've ever had trouble with are those that don't have a spring riding on the straight knurl of the needle body. These are often seen on old K&Bs and on old Super Tigres. It's difficult to set their friction locknuts to allow the needles to turn and yet not vibrate loose when the engine runs. I once locked an engine tight on the rich side and flew it all summer without changing it because of just that problem!

If you start to notice problems, look elsewhere before you start twisting the needle valves, e.g., check glow plugs, tubing, dirt in the fuel system.

That's all there is to it! Make your settings; don't change them, and keep 'em flying! ■

K&B SPORTSTER CARB

Idle-mixture screw:
Leaner (CCW)
Richer (CW)

Idle-speed stop screw

High-speed needle valve:
Leaner (CW)
Richer (CCW)

WEBRA CARB (two-needle type)

Idle speed stop screw

Low-speed needle valve:
Leaner (CW)
Richer (CCW)

High-speed needle valve:
Leaner(CW)
Richer (CCW)

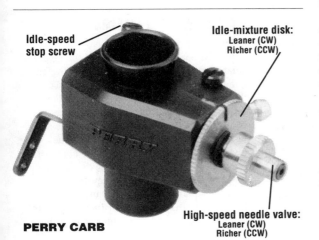

Idle-speed stop screw

Idle-mixture disk:
Leaner (CW)
Richer (CCW)

High-speed needle valve:
Leaner (CW)
Richer (CCW)

PERRY CARB

FORM CANOPIES

(continued from page 11)

screws and large washers. For extra insurance, screw another $1/4$-inch- to $1/2$-inch-thick forming support on top of the plastic into the main forming supports. This would prevent the plastic from tearing away from the screws as you stretch it. (This usually occurs when the plastic isn't hot enough and too much force is used to stretch it.)

The plastic will obtain a static charge as you work on it. To eliminate the charge and remove all the scrap particles that will accumulate on both sides of the plastic, wipe it with a cleaning solution such as Windex.

STRETCHING PROCESS

Place the plastic sheet and the forming supports on top of the metal support rods in the oven box, close the lid and turn on the heat gun. In 5 to 8 minutes, when the plastic sheet softens and sags noticeably below the support rods, remove the plastic from the oven box. The time may vary, so just watch for the plastic to sag.

Put on oven mitts—it's hot!—grab the support frames, quickly remove the plastic from the oven box and stretch the plastic over the mold. The plastic cools quickly, so keep the mold handy. Stretch the plastic just enough to let it form properly over the mold. If the plastic feels like a rubber sheet and you *can't* stretch it, then it isn't hot enough.

You might want to keep the forming supports level so they match the contour of the canopy base. You won't need to use too much force if the plastic is hot enough. Hold the forming supports against the side of the mold for a minute or so, until the plastic cools.

If something goes wrong as you stretch the plastic, don't worry. You can put the plastic back into the oven and reheat it. No matter how screwed up it is, you can still salvage it. It has a 100-percent memory; it will return to its original, flat condition when you reheat it. Mold at least three canopies: one in case of a trimming mistake, the other as a spare in case you need to repair the aircraft.

CUTTING THE CANOPY

Place the uncut canopy back on the mold. With an ink marker, mark the edges of the canopy as shown under the fiberglass covering. If you use vinyl, you can remove the ink with acetone later.

Use large scissors or tin snips to cut off the excess plastic. Cut it larger than necessary to allow for trimming the fuselage or canopy frame later. ∎

FUNCTIONAL CANOPY

(continued from page 14)

assist in the trimming operation.

Attach the canopy to the front canopy bow with no. $0\text{x}1/8$-inch or $3/16$-inch sheet-metal screws. Space the screws symmetrically around the canopy bow about 1 inch apart.

Next, attach the hinge assembly to the canopy and frame with a no. 1 flat-head sheet-metal screw about $3/8$ inch from each end of the hinge assembly. Experiment with the correct size drill bit for use with the no. 1 sheet-metal screw prior to drilling. A trim strip of aluminum will be placed over the canopy and the two screws later.

Fabricate two $1/4$-inch to $1/32$ inch-wide aluminum trim strips that will be used to cover the hinge on one side and provide a trim strip on the other side. These trim strips will continue to the rear of the canopy. Use no. 1 sheet-metal screws about $3/16$ inch long spaced about 1 inch apart. The screws will go through the aluminum trim strip, the canopy, the hinge (on one side) and into the $3/16$-inch aluminum tube.

The rear canopy section isn't attached to the trim strips at this time. The trim strips will be removed and painted later. After they've been painted, they're screwed back into place and glued to the rear canopy section.

Some sort of suitable canopy latch is required. The latch shown in the photos works quite well. The latch itself is made of $1/32$-inch-thick 4130 steel sheet. The bearing is a piece of nylon from an old nylon propeller. It's attached with no. 1 or no. 2 screws or $1/16$-inch rivets. The shaft for the latch is a 2-56 cap screw. The airfoil-shape handle is made of a piece of $1/32$-inch-thick brass. The screw head is on the outside of the handle, and the nut is on the inside. A large amount of solder is flowed around the handle to form a nice, streamlined shape. Two nuts are placed on each side of the latch and soldered to it. A small spring holds the latch closed.

The latch engages a no. 1 sheet-metal screw that's screwed into the aluminum frame. The nylon bearing block is attached after the latch has been positioned on the engaging screw on the frame, then attached to the fuselage. The latch looks realistic and is quite reliable. The canopy can be removed from the fuselage at any time simply by removing the hinge pin.

The canopy is dismantled for painting. After painting, attach the canopy to the frame. Use a large canopy molding strip (this material is similar to split tubing and is widely available) to seal the canopy to the windshield. Use slow-cure CA to bond the molding to the rear canopy section, but don't glue it to the front windshield! A medium-size molding strip is used for the rear of the canopy. This will hide any errors and keep the canopy from scratching the paint on the fuselage. The molding strips can be painted ahead of time or masked off and painted after they've been attached to the canopy.

I use a $1/16$-inch-diameter nylon cord to retain the opened canopy in the correct position. The cord is placed into a $3/16$-inch-long piece of thin aluminum tube, wrapped around the rear canopy bow and inserted back into the aluminum tube and glued in place. The other end is glued into a small solder lug that's free to rotate on a screw.

The canopy opening feature is necessary on the AL-1. All the switches and charging jacks are on the instrument panel. They're easily accessible by opening the canopy. Also, the canopy has to be opened to install the wing panels and to provide access to the R/C equipment and the gas tank.

The method used in my AL-1 aircraft canopy can be used for other similar canopy designs. Modify or redesign parts so that they meet your needs. I think you'll agree that this type of construction will greatly enhance any large model.

The following summarizes the materials and sources mentioned in this article:
• *Aluminum tubing, $1^1/16$ piano hinge, 2024 T-3 aluminum sheeting and 4130 $1/32$-inch steel sheeting are all available from Wick's Aircraft Supply, 410 Pine St. Highland, IL 62249; (618) 654-7447. Note: they offer an excellent catalogue with many items suitable for model use.*
• *No. 0 and no. 1 sheet-metal screws are available from industrial fastener supply houses or Sig Mfg. at most hobby shops.*
• *Cockpit molding strips are available at most hobby shops or from Fourmost Products, 4040 24th Ave., Forest Grove, OR 97116; (503) 357-2732.*
• *Zap and Goo are available from Pacer Technology at most hobby shops.*
• *K&B Mfg. polyester resin is available at most hobby shops.*
• *Vinyl is available at most plastic-supply houses. (See your "Yellow Pages" under "plastic.")* ∎

ELECTRIC TWINS

(continued from page 22)

drain, the peak wattage available can be calculated. After selecting a power loading and wing loading, the required area and size of the aircraft can be estimated. A check is necessary to be sure that the airframe can be constructed to meet the weight estimate. The prop selection technique is still the same.

Enough reading! Get out your abacus or pocket calculator and start designing your dream project. I'm sorry to say that I don't have any plans available for my airplanes, but I hope this article will inspire you to design your own. I'd be interested to hear about your results. My address is: 2756 Elmwood, Ann Arbor, MI 48104.

*Here are the addresses of the companies mentioned in this article:
Sanyo Electric, Battery Division, 200 Riser Rd., Little Ferry, NJ 07643.
Jomar Products, 2028 Knightsbridge Dr., Cincinnati, OH 45244.
AstroFlight, 13311 Beach Ave., Marina Del Rey, CA 90292.
Sermos R/C Snap Connectors, Cedar Corners Station, P.O. Box 16787, Stamford, CT 06905.
Leisure Electronics, 22971 B Triton Way, Laguna Hills, CA 92653.
Cox Hobbies, 1350 Rincon St., Corona, CA 91720.
Micafilm; distributed by Coverite, 420 Babylon Rd., Horsham, PA 19044.
Perfect Paints, distributed by Cheveron Hobby Products, P.O. Box 2480, Sandusky, OH 44870.
Rhom-Air Products, 924 65th St., Brooklyn, NY 11219.
MonoKote; distributed by Great Planes Model Distributors, P.O. Box 4021, Champaign, IL 61824.
Floquil-Polly S Color Corp., Route 30 North, Amsterdam, NY 12010.
Rev-Up; distributed by Progress Mfg. Co., P.O. Box 1306, Manhattan, KS 66502.
Top Flite Models, 2635 S. Wabash Ave., Chicago, Il 60616. ■

STATIC THRUST TESTER

(continued from page 27)

The other lead from the ammeter will connect to the positive pole of the motor.

TESTING

Mount the Thrust Tester in a Black & Decker Workmate or in any vise. Mount the motor between the wedge-blocks, and clamp it to the Thrust Tester by turning the wing nuts on the $1/4$-inch threaded rod. Make sure that everything is tight and in place. As you run the motor, read the thrust off the electronic scale, the amps from the ammeter and the rpm from the tach. Record the data that various combinations of propeller diameter and pitch produce to determine the best combination!

Good luck and happy landings!

*Here's the address of the company mentioned in this article:
Normark, 1710 East 78 St., Minneapolis, MN 55423. ■

IN-LINE RETRACTS

(continued from page 40)

center guide plate, flush with its sides. The hard-point block nests against the center guide plate and the front face of the down-lock cross brace. (See photo 10, where this block is partially obscured.) The gear-down hard spots serve as a fulcrum to splay the gear legs from parallel alignment into their fully extended position. The swing-arm plate-mount axle rests on this block when the gear is extended. The angles that should be cut are roughly diagrammed in the illus-

tration but, for these to serve as a fulcrum, you must customize them during assembly, which is fairly easy to do.

• **Gear-up hard points.** The $1/16$-inch-air-craft-ply gear-up hard points are the most difficult part of this project to describe. Although they look like flanges, they serve as a fulcrum to guide the main-gear legs into parallel at the beginning of the retraction arc. (See photo 10 and illustration.)

ACTUATION

• **Interconnecting the main gear and nose gear.** The nose-gear swing-arm plate is connected to the main-gear swing-arm plate by a push/pull rod. I recommend .0625-inch-diameter piano wire for the push/pull rod, because it's strong enough to operate the nose gear, but weak enough to bend if any parts should jam. Mount a horn on the main-gear swing-arm plate as shown. Bend the front end of the push/pull rod into an eye that fits over a perpendicular piece of the same diameter wire that's affixed to the nose-gear swing-arm plate. This should be customized: the idea is to create a pivoting, slop-free connection that can absorb some shock during landings.

After you've finished the main gear, glue in the bottom mount brace for the steering idler shaft. Mount the top of the idler shaft to the cabin floor.

Connect the double-armed horn on the nose strut to the double-armed horn on the idler shaft with pull/pull steering cables made of 30-pound-test shark leader. After you've completed these steps, install the rudder and elevator servos behind the trailing-edge bulkhead, and then install a nose-steering push/pull rod (use .0625-inch-diameter piano wire) from the idler arm to the rudder servo. (See photo 12.)

If you want to simplify the mechanism, you can mount a Cannon* servo directly onto the nose swing-arm plate for steering, and connect the rudder servo to it and the rudder servo with a Y-harness (not shown). This eliminates the idler arm, its axle and the rudder-servo-to-steering-arm linkage. Your retracts will weigh .7 ounce less, and the assembly will be slightly more durable.

• **Retract Actuation Servo.** To actuate the main-gear swing-arm plate, use a Futaba* sail-winch servo (or the equivalent). This 2.5-ounce servo is about one third as fast as the average servo, and its 129-ounce/inch torque adequately handles the job. Place the winch servo well aft of the trailing edge, elevator and rudder servos. This provides space in the cabin for aileron and gear linkage and for motor flight packs. Connect the winch servo to the main-gear swing-arm with a push-pull rod (use .0625-inch-diameter

piano wire.) It will be the second rod that's attached to the main-gear swing-arm horn. (See illustration.)

From this point, construction of the Aerostar is straightforward. (I also modified my Aerostar by using the NACA 0012 airfoil and by eliminating dihedral so that the plane would fly better inverted). Make sure that the aileron linkage clears the main-gear swing-arm throughout its up/down travel.

TRIM AND ADJUSTMENT

I quickly found that spraying the hard spots with silicone greatly improved the gear actuation, perhaps halving the torque required from the winch servo. I spray this area with silicone before each flight day, and do a test retraction cycle before each flight.

FLIGHT TEST

During my first flight, everything worked correctly, and the touchdown was smooth. Two things were noteworthy:

• There was a perceptible forward CG shift as all three gears folded forward and up to retract. This wasn't excessive—just noticeable.

• The airplane definitely accelerates when the gear is retracted, and it also glides much flatter.

It sure was a great feeling to see that gear go up after four months of work—even better to see it come down!

The second flight was just as smooth until touchdown, when I didn't correct quickly enough for a wind gust, and it landed very hard—nose wheel first. This broke the nose strut off its swing-arm plate, but with $1.75 worth of nylon landing-gear straps and an hour of labor, the Aerostar RG was ready to go. I hope you'll have as much fun with this retract design as I have!

*Here are the addresses of the companies mentioned in this article:
Midwest Products Co., Inc., 400 S. Indiana St., Hobart, IN 46342.
Hobby Lobby International, 5614 Franklin Pike Circle, Brentwood, TN 37027.
Cannon R/C Systems, 2828 Cochran St., Simi Valley, CA 93065.
Futaba Corp. of America, 4 Studebaker, Irvine, CA 92718.
Top Flite Models, 2635 S. Wabash Ave., Chicago, IL 60616. ■

FIBERGLASSING FLOATS

(continued from page 79)

midline, I had to apply the top glass with spray adhesive to make sure it would adhere to the sides (when wet), all the way around to the bottom shear. With an extra pair of hands, only a little lifting and repositioning was required; the cloth was positioned smoothly and conformed very well.

Rough-sanding the Kevlar was a nightmare, however! Kevlar fibers are so tough that it's possible to sand the cured epoxy resin out of the matrix and leave billions of tiny Kevlar hairs sticking above the surface! A subsequent coat of epoxy resin left the surface looking like 20-grit sandpaper!

My salvation was a small, hand-held Surform® planing tool. Its hundreds of razor-sharp edges allowed me to shear off the Kevlar fibers at the same rate as I removed the cured resin. After several hours of light shaving with the Surform®, I had a surface that could be primed and wet-sanded without raising the fuzz again. Kevlar cloth is best used as a base in a typical "layup" to keep it away from the surface that has to be sanded.

BACK TO THE PROJECT

Let's return to our sport-float glassing project and apply the final filler coat. In the past, I've used microballoons and epoxy in a 50:50 mix. This works well, but the microscopic glass spheres quickly wear out the sandpaper, and it's unwise to have microballoon dust floating around your work area. (Always use a cartridge filter mask when you work with these materials.) I recently discovered West Microlite Filler, which I think is far superior. Microlite is tan and has a consistency like that of talcum powder. It's twice as absorbent as microballoons, and it can be mixed with resin at such a high ratio that it's possible to feather-sand a cured layer that's adjacent to bare foam!

Whichever filler you use, apply a coat that's the consistency of thick batter and isn't "brushable"; the resin/filler mixture shouldn't run when applied to a vertical surface. Once again, it's best to apply the filler coat to the float tops first; do the bottoms after the top has cured. A spatula or squeegee is the best tool for applying the filler coat. Work the resin/filler mix around, pressing it into the glass, and strike off as much excess as possible. Remember: this final coat adds little strength to the float, so if you put it on thickly, you're only adding weight.

FINAL SANDING

When the filler coat has cured, you can begin the final sanding. Start with 100-grit paper wrapped around a sanding block, progress to 120-grit, hand-held, and finish with 220-grit (or more). Epoxy resin can be sanded beautifully, and it shears off in a white powder that won't build up on the sandpaper. *Caution:* always work in a well-ventilated area when using epoxy. It has almost no odor, so it's impossible to tell if

you're getting a dose that might prove harmful. Play it safe.

When you can see the weave of the glass-cloth in the float's surface, but not feel it (or any other irregularities), the final sanding is complete. Before you mount the floats, just apply a primer coat or two, finish-sand, and add a fuel-proof color coat. You can start a pair of floats on a Monday, have them painted by Friday, mount them on Saturday and fly on Sunday!

Because of their ease of construction, minimal covering time, durability, complete lack of voids and comparable weight, glassed foam-core floats are superior to any other type that's available. Some effort and expense is involved, but the product makes all the sweat and time worthwhile!

Here are the addresses of the companies mentioned in this article:
Sig Manufacturing Co., 401 S. Front St., Montezuma, IA 50171.
K&B Manufacturing, 2100 College Dr., Lake Havasu City, AZ 86403.
PEC's Hobby Supplies, 947 Stierlin Rd., Mountain View, CA 94043.
West System Epoxy, distributed by Weston Aerodesign, 944 Placid Ct., Arnold, MD 21012.
Spray & Stick, distributed by Swenson Specialties, P.O. Box 663, 2895 Estates Ave., Pinole, CA 94564. ■

LIGHTER FOAM WINGS

(continued from page 83)

REMOVING EXCESS FOAM

There are several ways to remove "unwanted" foam from the wing.
• **Piano wire**. A .020-diameter piano wire used with a variable transformer will give you the best cutting results since wire temperature is easy to regulate.
• **Hacksaw blade**. A hacksaw blade with one tip pointed (to ease the initial piercing) also removes foam. Keep your strokes as perpendicular to the surface as possible.
• **Soldering gun**. You can also use a soldering gun with a modified, homemade tip. I use a solid copper wire that's shaped like the original soldering tip, but long enough to extend at least 2 inches beyond the wing's thickest part. Depending on the gun's wattage and the wire's thickness and length, you may need to turn the gun on and off several times while using it so that it doesn't get too hot.

WING SKINS

Prepare your wing skins as you normally do. Here are a few pointers that may help:
• **Weigh the sheets**. If possible, weigh each sheet before joining so that you can evenly distribute the weight between both wing panels.
• **Sand joints**. On a clean, flat surface (I put

a full-length mirror on my workbench), sand the skin joints and surfaces to an almost ready-to-cover finish. This saves a lot of time in the finishing stage, and helps avoid uneven sanding when the skin is attached to the foam wing. Remove all sanding dust from the skins.

WING SKIN INSTALLATION

I use slow-cure epoxy (five parts resin to one part hardener). This gives me time to position the sheeting on the foam before I weigh it down, and it eliminates the possibility of building a warped wing (so long as the cradle sits on a flat surface). Slow-cure epoxy also generates less heat during the curing process, which can cause sheeting to de-bond from the foam. Once cured, the wing panels are ready for final assembly and finishing.

The benefits of this foam-wing lightening procedure are reaped on the flying field. When you want outstanding vertical capability from your aerobatic model, or a few extra ounces of detail on that "full-house" scale warbird, removing excess weight is the way to go. ■

FIBERGLASSING SHEETED WINGS

(continued from page 94)

accepts both polyester and epoxy resin, and how it stays put on the surface. (The fact that I really like and admire the rebellious old son-of-a-gun has absolutely nothing to do with it!)

Gathering the rest of the necessary materials is easy. You can buy throwaway brushes (sometimes called "acid brushes") and the single-edge razor blades at your hobby store. Wax-paper cups are good for mixing resin or holding acetone for cleaning up afterwards. You should buy an inexpensive pair of scissors at an office-supply store, and use them only to cut fiberglass cloth. Cutting other materials such as carbon fiber, plywood and music wire will dull them and remove the fine edge that's necessary to make clean, snag-free cuts in the cloth.

REASONS FOR RESINS

Choose the type of resin with which you'll be most comfortable working. Polyester resin cures rapidly and has a crisp surface that's easy to sand. Its primary drawback is its very offensive, harmful vapors. On the other hand, equal-mix epoxy resins offer almost the same benefits as polyester resins, but have no harmful odor. Epoxy resins do, however, have drawbacks. They take between 4 and 8 hours to cure, and they really shouldn't be sanded until they've cured for 12 hours. Another drawback of epoxy resins is that they aren't compatible with most polyester resins, i.e., they won't cure over 99 percent of them. (Yes, the reverse is possible; epoxy resins *will* cure over polyesters.) Why is this important? Simply because if you need to make a repair, it's faster to use a polyester resin (sometimes mixed with light filler) than to wait overnight for an epoxy to cure.

For this demonstration, I let my helper, Charlie Chambers, use the product with which he was the most familiar: K&B polyester resin. I chose Z-Poxy* finishing resin (my personal favorite) for three reasons: it cures quickly, its equal-mix formula is odorless, and it's the only epoxy finishing resin (that I know of) that's compatible with polyester resin. The choice is yours—both products provide a smooth, crisp finish. OK, with the educational background and preliminaries out of the way, let's get glassing!

GLASSING

These procedures outline how to glass a wing panel, but they're exactly the same for any balsa structure. First, Charlie makes sure that the sanding block's surfaces and edges are straight and free of glue globs or any other unwanted obtrusions. Remember that this surface is the foundation of an outstanding finish and, like when building a house, it must be perfect. (See Charlie working in photo 1.) When all the block's surfaces are smooth, wipe or vacuum them, and go get your glass-cloth!

Cut a piece of cloth to fit the shape of the part you'll be glassing, but cut it approximately 2 inches larger around the entire part. Now, you can use one of two methods:

• Lay the cloth on the wing panel and gently blow on it to remove any wrinkles. Using a smooth brush, literally brush out any stubborn wrinkles. Next, mix a 1-ounce batch of either the polyester or the epoxy resin and pour little puddles of it directly onto the cloth, or brush it on. Work from the part's center toward its edges. If you pour the resin, the squeegee will spread it fabulously so that the entire surface is covered with a thin film. If you brush it on, work it out to the edges so that the cloth remains wrinkle-free. To remove excess polyester resin, squeegee it off the panel and discard it, or blot the panel's surface and gently wipe it with a strong paper towel.

If you use epoxy resin, you can pick up the excess using the squeegee and return it to the mixing cup. In both cases, leave just enough resin on the panel so that there's a slight sheen when the part is held up to a light. You don't want to see heavy brush marks or ripples or ridges—just a smooth, even layer of resin over a wrinkle-free piece of fiberglass cloth. (Both methods of smoothing the cloth and removing the excess resin are shown in photos 4 and 5.)

• As an alternative to pouring the resin directly onto fiberglass cloth that's draped over the wing panel, you can brush a light coat of resin directly onto the wood, and then lay the glass-cloth onto the wet surface. Then, brush or squeegee the wrinkles away (again, start at the part's center and work outward).

There aren't any advantages or disadvantages to either method—both work well. The important thing is to get enough resin through the weave of the cloth to hold it securely in place, but not so much resin that sanding is difficult later.

Some modelers wait until this coat of resin has cured enough to permit handling before they remove the border of excess cloth; others wait for a partial cure and then glass the other side. Charlie chose the latter. He glassed one side of all the flying surfaces of the two Bob Violett* Aggressors in about 90 minutes, and he put them outside in the sun to cure. When they had cured enough to handle, he glassed the other side of each surface and put them back outside. After a couple of hours, he trimmed off the excess cloth with an *old* pair of scissors and gently sanded the edges with a long sanding block and 220-grit wet/dry sandpaper.

After both sides of a panel have been glassed and trimmed, you might need to apply a second, light coat of resin. Take a good look at the part and see whether the glass-cloth's weave is easy to see. If it is, you probably need another coat. If you used the polyester resin, lightly sand the first coat with 320-grit sandpaper, just scuffing the surface gently. Then, brush on a second coat of resin with a good-quality soft brush, using just enough to fill the weave. (You don't want any brush strokes cured into the surface.)

If you use the epoxy resin, you won't have to sand the first coat before applying the second. (Again, however, apply a *very thin* coat of resin.) In either case, the finished structure will be a lot easier to sand if you let the resin cure for a while.

SURE SANDING

Resins continue to shrink for many days, and they acquire a crisper finish with time. So, if your schedule permits, wait at least 24 to 48 hours, and then sand the resin's glossy finish using the sanding block and, initially, about an 80-grit sandpaper. (Use this grit to break through the glossy surface; when the gloss has been cut, replace the 80-grit sandpaper with some 180-grit stuff, and sand the surface until it's smooth.) If you were neat, careful and avoided making heavy brush marks earlier, your sanding chore will be much easier. If, however, you were sloppy, i.e., you didn't squeegee or blot up the excess resin, and there are ridges cured into the surface, you're probably cursing your head off and blaming me for a lousy procedure!

You'll find that both types of resin are easy to sand. The polyester type has a surface glaze that's a little tougher to break, and it occasionally develops little pinholes. A little elbow grease and some good sanding blocks make all the difference in the world!

For those who like to hand- or palm-sand (hold a folded piece of sandpaper in their hand), *forget it!* For good results, you *must* use a sanding block! This is one of the secrets of successful glassing. If you don't block-sand, you'll find many little shiny spots all over your work. These are low areas, and you'll make them if you hand-hold the sandpaper. If this happens, you'll have to put on still *another* coat of resin and start sanding all over again! So please, use the sanding block!

FILL-IN THE GAPS

When all the parts have been sanded, wipe them down with some denatured alcohol. Check for any building imperfections, and fill the dents, gouges, or tears with a mixture of resin and compatible light filler of your choice made into a thick paste. Squeegee the mixture over the imperfections and allow it to cure. After this mixture has cured, block-sand it smooth until it matches and flows with the contour of the surrounding area.

That's it! You've finished! You now have perfectly glassed parts that are protected from minor hangar rash, general bashing around and more than an occasional rough landing. You now have sealed surfaces that are impervious to oil and dirt and that won't crack under slight vibrations. Best of all, you now have the best foundation for paint that anyone could ask for. If you've done the work properly, you've only added a few ounces to a normal 60- or 70-inch airplane. If you still need reassurance, try to push your fingernail gently into the new, glassed surface. You'll be happy to see that you can't. Now try it on an airframe covered with a *plastic* film! That alone is the greatest reason for glassing an airplane!

PICK YOUR PROCEDURE

There are many articles on how to do this and how to do that. Please remember that no method is better than another if the results are the same. Pick a method that suits your building style, and run with it—perfect it. If you like the way a product works, stay with it. Results are all we're interested in.

*Here are the addresses of the companies mentioned in this article:
Sig Manufacturing Co., 401 S. Front St., Montezuma, IA 50171.
K&B Manufacturing, 2100 College Dr., Lake Havasu City, AZ 86403.
Dan Parsons Products, 11809 Fulmer Dr., NE, Albuquerque, NM 87111.
Z-Poxy; distributed by Pacer Technology & Research, 9420 Santa Anita Ave., Rancho Cucamonga, CA 91730.
Bob Violett Models, 1373 Citrus Rd., Winter Springs, FL 32708. ■

EASY SHELL CONSTRUCTION

(continued from page 96)

vacu-bag, and wait for it to cure.

Remove the cured lay-up from the vacu-bag and peel off the Mylar. Slide out the interior mold, and release the film, which leaves the shell. Trim the edges, and join the shell at the trailing edge. You now have a completed shell.

If you intend to paint the surface, I recommend that you paint the Mylar. This minimizes pinholes when you bag over the Rohacell, and the paint transfers nicely. You can cut out any control surfaces and finish the edges using your favorite methods.

*Here are the addresses of the companies mentioned in this article:
Northeast Sailplane Products, 16 Kirby Ln., Williston, VT 05495.
Model Design Program, Chuck Anderson, P.O. Box 305, Tullahoma, TN 37388.
Cygnet Software, 3525 Del Mar Heights, #237, San Diego, CA 92130.
Aerospace Composite Products, P.O. Box 16621, Irvine, CA 92714.
Composite Structures Technology, P.O. Box 4615, Lancaster, CA 93539.
Weston Aerodesign, 944 Placid Court, Arnold, MD 21012. ■

GILBERT APPROACH

(continued from page 118)

wind leg all the way to the runway. You're trying to achieve a full stall just inches above the runway. If the plane passes through the key point too rapidly, it will overshoot the runway, in which case, you should perform a go-around. If the plane is below the key point, it will crash; as soon as you see that you have insufficient altitude, throttle up and go around.

When you've mastered going through the key point with the throttle closed and at just above stall speed, you're ready to move on to the next step.

• **Landing…at last.** If you've really prac-

ticed the approaches and go-arounds, you'll have no trouble with landings. Just continue through the key point with throttle off, and feed in a little more "up" to cause the aircraft to stall when it touches the runway, i.e., flare. That's all there is to it! If the aircraft starts to veer off to either side and there's sufficient runway, apply some throttle and correct the rudder. Again, applying less than full throttle will help to keep the plane on the ground.

Touch-and-go's are easier to manage if you feed in some throttle a few inches before touchdown. This keeps the prop turning through the grass—and possibly the dirt—and gives you much better rudder control when the plane leaves the runway.

• **Handling the wind.** When landing in a substantial head wind, the base leg will be in a little closer, and the final approach leg will be steeper. Don't be afraid to point the nose downward to keep the speed up. It may also help to maintain a little power until the plane is about a foot above the runway.

I hope these steps are helpful. Remember: no crashes allowed; keep 'em flying. ■

HOOKED ON TOWING

(continued from page 124)

longer see my bipe, Dave detached the towline from the sailplane's nose. After that, I landed the Aeromaster and watched Dave fly his sailplane for 22 minutes. When he landed, we cheered and then began to digest what we had learned and to discuss improvements.

LESSONS LEARNED
• Make sure that you'll be able to see your planes from a distance. A big bull's-eye, a stripe, or your AMA numbers on the right wing will keep you oriented when the planes are up so high that you can hardly see what they're doing. (If you can't see it, you can't fly it.) Also, we could see the sailplane, but my tow-plane was a mere speck. I recommend that you use a tow-plane with a wingspan that's as large as or larger than that of the sailplane. If you really want some altitude, this is a must.

Jose Tellez solved this problem for us by letting me use his Senior Telemaster as the tow-plane. It's the best tow-plane we've tried so far, and it's large enough to see. In addition, Jose designed a towline release for it that's controlled by the fifth channel on his radio. This setup increases the realism and safety.
• Make sure the sailplane's battery pack can handle the expected flight times. Recently, several people took turns flying Dave's

sailplane. After more than an hour (the plane had never flown for that long before!), they lost it over a hill when its battery pack died. (Bud "Jungle Man" Parriott found the plane intact.)
• Don't let the tow-plane run out of gas. If it does, begin a dive immediately to maintain control and release the towline.

STUPENDOUS STUNTS
On several occasions, we've been able to trim the tow-plane and the sailplane to fly "hands off," while we relaxed on the runway. We've towed at night, too. There aren't any thermals, but the sight is awesome! Making the tow-plane drop the towline in front of us during a low-altitude flyby is also a real thrill. The only stunt I *don't* recommend is towing the sailplane with a helicopter. (We've tried this, too—need I say more?)

If you're as successful with R/C towing as we've been, you'll finally get the power guys and the sailplanes nuts together...at the same field! Happy flying, and remember: it isn't *how* you do it, it's whether or not you *can* do it! ■

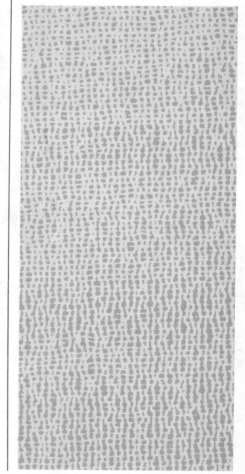